HAITI IN THE NEW WORLD ORDER

Haiti in the New World Order

The Limits of the Democratic Revolution

Alex Dupuy

WestviewPress

A Division of HarperCollins*Publishers*

Copyright © 1997 by Westview Press, A Division of HarperCollins Publishers, Inc.

Published in 1997 in the United States of America by Westview Press, 5500 Central Avenue, Boulder, Colorado 80301-2877, and in the United Kingdom by Westview Press, 12 Hid's Copse Road, Cumnor Hill, Oxford OX2 9JJ

This book was typeset by Letra Libre, 1705 14th Street, Suite 391, Boulder, Colorado 80302.

Library of Congress Cataloging-in-Publication Data
Dupuy, Alex.
   Haiti in the new world order : the limits of the democratic
revolution / Alex Dupuy.
      p.   cm.
   Includes bibliographical references (p.) and index.
   ISBN 0-8133-2113-1 (hardcover). — ISBN 0-8133-2114-X
   (pbk.)
   1. Haiti—Politics and government—1986–   2. Liberalism—Haiti—
History.   3. Social change—Haiti—History.   4. Haiti—Relations—
United States.   5. United States—Relations—Haiti.   I. Title.
F1928.2.D86   1996
320.97294—dc20   96-36190
                                                                            CIP

The paper used in this publication meets the requirements of the American National Standard for Permanence of Paper for Printed Library Materials Z39.48-1984.

10   9   8   7   6   5   4   3   2   1

To the memory of my parents
André "Aguy" Dupuy and Lisa Bellande Dupuy

Contents

ACKNOWLEDGMENTS

I would like to thank Anthony Catanese, Leslie Desmangles, Robert Fatton, Franck Laraque, and Gilbert Skillman for their valuable comments and suggestions on the chapters of this book. I am especially grateful to my wife, Wanda Dupuy, for thoroughly editing the manuscript. Thanks also to Westview Press Senior Production Editor Libby Barstow and Copy Editor Joan W. Sherman.

Unless otherwise indicated, all translations from French and Haitian Creole are my own.

Alex Dupuy

Acronyms

ANDP	Alliance Nationale pour la Démocratie et le Progrès (National Alliance for Democracy and Progress)
APB	Association Professionelle des Banques (Bankers' Professional Association)
ASDEC	Association des Exportateurs de Café (Association of Coffee Exporters)
BIP	Bloc Inyon Patriotik (Patriotic Unity Bloc)
CARICOM	Caribbean Common Market
CASEC	Conseils d'Administration de la Section Communale (Administrative Councils of Communal Sections)
CATH	Centrale Autonome des Travailleurs Haitiens (Autonomous Union of Haitian Workers)
CBI	Caribbean Basin Initiative
CDB	Caribbean Development Bank
CE	Conseil Electoral (Electoral Council)
CED	Comité d'Entente Démocratique (Democratic Agreement Committee)
CEP	Conseil Electoral Permanent (Permanent Electoral Council)
CHADEL	Centre Haitien de Défense des Libertés Publiques (Haitian Center for the Defense of Public Liberties)
CIA	Central Intelligence Agency (US)
CNG	Conseil National de Gouvernement (National Council of Government)
DEA	Drug Enforcement Administration (US)
DIA	Defense Intelligence Agency (US)
EAI	Enterprise for the Americas Initiative (US)
FADH	Forces Armées d'Haiti (Armed Forces of Haiti, or Haitian Army)
FBI	Federal Bureau of Investigation (US)

FMLN	Farabundo Marti para la Liberación Nacional (Farabundo Marti National Liberation Front)
FNC	Front National de Concertation (National United Front)
FNCD	Front National pour le Changement et la Démocratie (National Front for Democracy and Change)
FRAPH	Front pour l'Avancement et le Progrès d'Haiti (Front for the Advancement and Progress of Haiti)
GDP	gross domestic product
GNP	gross national product
GSPR	Groupement de Sécurité du Président (Presidential Security Group)
HPAE	high-performing Asian economy
ICITAP	International Criminal Investigations Training and Assistance Program (US)
IDA	International Development Association
IDB	Inter-American Development Bank
IMF	International Monetary Fund
INRA	Institut National de la Réforme Agraire (National Institute of Agrarian Reform)
KID	Komité Inité Démokratik (Democratic Unity Committee)
KONAKOM	Komité Nasyonal Kongrès Oganizasyons Démokratik (National Committee of the Congress of Democratic Organizations)
MIDH	Mouvement pour l'Instauration de la Démocratie en Haiti (Movement for the Establishment of Democracy in Haiti)
MNP—28	Mouvement National Patriotique—28 Novembre (National Patriotic Movement—28 November)
MOP	Mouvement pour l'Organisation du Pays (Movement for the Organization of the Country)
MPP	Mouvman Péyizan Papaye (Papaye Peasant Movement)
NAFTA	North American Free Trade Agreement
NIC	newly industrialized country
NGO	nongovernmental organization
NTAE	nontraditional agro-export
OAS	Organization of American States
OECS	Organization of Eastern Caribbean States
OL	Opération Lavalas (Operation Lavalas)

OPL	Organisation Politique Lavalas (Lavalas Political Organization)
PANPRA	Parti Nationaliste Progressiste Révolutionnaire Haitien (Progressive Revolutionary Nationalist Haitian Party)
PDCH	Parti Démocrate Chrétien d'Haiti (Christian Democratic Party of Haiti)
PMDN	Parti de la Mobilisation pour le Développement National (Mobilization for National Development Party)
PPL	Platforme Politique Lavalas (Lavalas Political Platform)
SAJ	Solidarité ant Jèn (Solidarity Among Youths)
SIN	Service d'Intelligence National (National Intelligence Service)
SSP	Service de Sécurité du Président (Security Service of the President)
TKL	Ti Kominotés Légliz, or Ti Légliz (literally, the "little church")
TNC	transnational corporation
UN	United Nations
UNICEF	United Nations International Children's Emergency Fund
UNDHA	United Nations Department of Humanitarian Affairs
UNDP	United Nations Development Program
URN	Union pour la Réconciliation Nationale (Union for National Reconciliation)
USAID	United States Agency for International Development
VSN	Volontaires de la Sécurité Nationale (Volunteers of National Security)

1

Meanings of the New World Order

Elected by a landslide in 1990 and taking office in February 1991 as Haiti's forty-fourth president, Father Jean-Bertrand Aristide would be overthrown seven months later by the military. That was the twenty-eighth coup d'état since Haiti gained its independence in 1804 and the fifth since the emerging popular movement impelled the military to overthrow the hereditary Duvalier dictatorship in 1986. But if the overthrow of President Aristide was in keeping with tradition for the Haitian military and surprised no one, the reaction of the United States was unexpected and astounding. In a clear break with its Cold War behavior, Washington declared its opposition to the coup, demanded the reinstatement of the deposed president, and urged the Organization of American States (OAS) and later the United Nations (UN) to adopt a series of sanctions—trade, financial, arms, and travel embargoes—against the military junta to compel the coup leaders to comply with the OAS and UN resolutions. When those measures failed to dislodge the putschists, U.S. President Bill Clinton, with prior UN Security Council approval, ordered U.S. troops into Haiti on September 19, 1994—three years after the coup—to remove the putschists from power and reinstate President Aristide.

In this book, I will argue that the United States could not justify the coup d'état on Cold War geopolitical grounds despite its dislike for Aristide, whom the U.S. Embassy in Port-au-Prince once labeled a "radical firebrand." Support for the coup leaders in Haiti could invite coups elsewhere in the hemisphere and undermine Washington's post–Cold War neoliberal agenda for that region. Nonetheless, the Bush administration, more responsive to the right wing in the U.S. Congress and more supportive of the Haitian military and business elite, undermined Aristide's return while maintaining a public stance against the coup.

This chapter is a revised version of a previously published article: "The New World Order and Social Change in the Americas: Ten Theses," *Radical America* 25, no. 4 (July 1995). It is reprinted with the permission of *Radical America*.

It took the Clinton administration to realize that the severe politico-economic crisis into which the coup leaders had plunged Haiti could only be resolved if Aristide was returned to power. Clinton's administration also recognized the challenges this presented for U.S. policy toward Haitian refugees in particular and toward the Caribbean region in general.

President Aristide was returned to office only after he agreed to make concessions to his domestic enemies and the United States and after the Haitian military was allowed sufficient time to crack down on the popular movement that had opposed the neo-Duvalierist military governments and supported Aristide. The primary reason for the military occupation of Haiti, then, was to ensure stability in Haiti and the implementation of Washington's neoliberal agenda.

I contend that the U.S. intervention and the return to constitutional government represented a defeat for the antidemocratic forces because those events led to the exile of the coup leaders and, most important, to the dismantling of the Forces Armées d'Haiti (FADH, Armed Forces of Haiti, or Haitian Army). This marked the end of the army's role as a power broker. The dissolution of the army and the resumption of the democratic process also made possible the strengthening of civil society and the reemergence of the popular movement for a participatory, democratic, equal, and just Haiti—despite the constraints imposed on that movement by the hegemony of the United States and of global capitalism in the post–Cold War "new world order."

The New World Order Doctrine

In his September 1990 address on the Persian Gulf crisis before a joint session of Congress, President George Bush declared:

> Out of these troubled times . . . a new world order can emerge: a new era—freer from the threat of terror, stronger in the pursuit of justice, and more secure in the quest for peace. An era in which the nations of the world, East and West, North and South, can prosper and live in harmony. . . .
> Today that new world order is struggling to be born, a world quite different from the one we've known. A world where the rule of law supplants the rule of the jungle. A world in which nations recognize the shared responsibility for freedom and justice. A world where the strong respect the rights of the weak (Bush, 1990:1359).

In January 1991, four months after Bush's speech, the United States and its allies unleashed a massive military assault to expel Iraq from Kuwait. Washington had rejected all diplomatic initiatives to compel Iraq to withdraw from Kuwait because the decision to pursue a military solution to Iraq's invasion of its neighbor had been made as early as October 1990, very soon after President Bush's September speech (Hitchens, 1991:99–100). The military offensive resulted in 62,000 to 99,000 Iraqi civilian deaths and 100,000 to 200,000 military deaths, according to recent estimates. Thousands of Iraqi soldiers were simply buried alive in their desert trenches by U.S. tanks mounted with plows, and tens of thousands of others were killed by U.S. and allied warplanes as they were retreating from the Kuwaiti border; U.S. pilots described their mission as "shooting fish in a barrel" (Sklar, 1992:15). President Bush's new world order was born in a bloodbath, not through the shuttle diplomacy alluded to in his speech.

Since Bush's speech, the foreign policy intelligentsia has been debating the policies that the United States should pursue in this new world order.[1] The debate starts from the triumphant premise that the demise of the Soviet bloc and the end of the Cold War represent a clear victory for the West and its liberal capitalist system over socialism in general and the Soviet communist system in particular. Some, like Francis Fukuyama, have gone so far as to argue that "what we may be witnessing is not just the end of the Cold War, or the passing of a particular period of postwar history, but the end of history as such: that is, the end point of mankind's ideological evolution and the universalization of Western liberal democracy as the final form of human government" (Fukuyama, 1989:4).

A consensus exists within the foreign policy establishment that, given its superpower status, the United States must remain actively engaged in the global arena and cannot afford to turn isolationist as some conservatives, such as Patrick Buchanan, advocate. Four arguments, taken together, constitute the ideological underpinning of post–Cold War U.S. foreign policy, in what I will call the new world order doctrine. My central argument is that U.S. foreign policy in the new world order continues to be oriented toward creating what the famous National Security Council strategic document of the Cold War known as NSC-68 referred to as "a world environment in which the American system can survive and flourish" (cited in Layne and Schwartz, 1993:5). I will interpret the new world order doctrine in that framework and address the implications of the post–Cold War world order for the prospects for social change in Haiti in the chapters that follow.

The first argument of the foreign policy intelligentsia posits that rather than becoming more stable with the demise of the Cold War and the East-West confrontation, the world will likely become more fragmented and unstable and increasingly resemble the pre-1939 world, characterized by regional power politics and national and ethnic conflicts (Schlesinger, 1991–1992:4). Reversing a long-held tenet of the Cold War, some analysts now contend that most conflicts in the Third World and in Eastern Europe were rooted in contradictions and antagonisms within and between these countries. The absence of the superpower checks, therefore, will likely intensify rather than abate them (Nye, 1992:95; Mearsheimer, 1992:233–234).

A second argument suggests that, as the world fragments and becomes more disordered, new regional powers will emerge to challenge the existing balance of power, which is favorable to the United States, and pull "the international system toward decentralization and anarchy" (Coll, 1992:48). The danger here is that with the rise of these new regional powers comes the spread of weapons of mass destruction, especially nuclear and biological weapons, in the hands of Third World states that could use them to dominate their regions.

A corollary to this argument suggests that many of the Third World countries that attempted to make the transition from authoritarian to democratic regimes during the 1980s suffered prolonged and severe economic crises that caused more widespread poverty and aggravated already explosive social cleavages. As these Third World countries faced mounting economic, demographic, and political problems that they could not resolve, the democratic process broke down and they became ungovernable, unstable, and more explosive. Haiti, along with several other Third World countries in Africa and Latin America, is said to fall in this category (Lipset, 1994:17).

All these actual or potential situations may pose unwelcome difficulties for the United States in its efforts to create a new and more stable world order. Although not all Third World states carry the same significance for U.S. foreign policy, the possible collapse of some of those states could create power vacuums that could be replaced by would-be hegemons inimical to Washington. Likewise, turmoil in the Third World would likely increase migration and refugees to the United States. In short, chaos in the Third World "will give rise to atavistic regimes whose international conduct will be far from peaceful" (Coll 1992, 47–49).

A third argument asserts that as the Third World becomes more chaotic and ungovernable, terrorist groups, nationalist insurgents, and drug traffickers will likely take advantage of "advances in global communication and transportation to engage in low-intensity conflicts that can be detrimental to the interests of the United States and its friends" (Coll, 1992:49).

Lastly, the fourth argument proposes that as economic competition increases between the United States, Western Europe, and Japan, tensions could emerge over issues such as trade and protectionist barriers and the transfer of technology to Third World countries. These tensions will require careful management to prevent them from damaging "the fabric of United States international relationships" (Coll, 1992:50).

The "Clash of Civilizations"

The theme of emergent atavistic, nationalistic, and fundamentalist regimes in the Third World that threaten fundamental Western values and norms of conduct runs through most post–Cold War U.S. foreign policy debates. It might well become, along with the fear of nuclear weapons proliferation and their use by irresponsible—not to say uncivilized—Third World fanatics, a substitute for the Cold War containment of communism. Like that argument, it may serve as the cement that unites conservatives and liberals alike within the foreign policy establishment.

In what is likely to become a seminal essay among foreign policy analysts, Samuel P. Huntington argued recently in the pages of *Foreign Affairs* that the "fundamental source of conflict in this new world will not be primarily ideological or primarily economic. The great divisions among human kind and the dominant source of conflict will be cultural" (Huntington, 1993:25). The demise of the Cold War, Huntington continued, means that the countries of the world should no longer be grouped according to their politico-economic systems but in terms of their cultures and civilizations. The civilizations that Huntington identified as constituting those likely to enter into conflict with one another include the Western, Confucian, Japanese, Islamic, Hindu, Slavic-Orthodox, Latin American, and "possibly" African (Huntington, 1993:25).

Huntington explained why the accentuation of differences among civilizations will likely lead to greater conflicts between the West and what he termed the *non-Wests*. The rise in civilizational consciousness and the spread of fundamentalist religions occurred partly in response to the power of the West, thereby leading to a confrontation between the West and those seeking to reshape the world in non-Western ways. Unlike the ideological and political cleavages that divided the world during the Cold War, the cultural differences that now divide the world are proving to be much more resilient because they embody incompatible moral or cultural values—for example, those of individualism and democracy, which are not valued in non-Western civilizations. As such, they provide individuals with their identities and lead to the formation of an us-versus-them view of the world. To prepare itself for these likely civilizational clashes, the West must pursue a policy of cooperation among the Western powers of Europe and North America; seek to incorporate Eastern Europe and Latin America into the West; prevent the escalation of intercivilizational conflicts into major wars; limit the military expansion of the Confucian states; maintain its military capabilities and superiority; exploit the differences between the Confucian and Islamic states; support other civilizations that are receptive to Western values; and strengthen those international institutions that promote legitimate Western interests and values (Huntington, 1993:41–49).

As Richard Rubenstein and Farle Crocker showed in their reply to Huntington, the only difference between his paradigm and the earlier Cold War model is the substitution of multipolar civilizational conflicts for the bipolar conflicts among states, with cultural values replacing class ideology as the point of unity. Huntington's "civilizational conflicts," which are every bit as ideological as other constructs, are no less rooted in structures of inequality than were the old conflicts among states. Furthermore, his presumption that the civilizational conflicts pit the "West against the Rest" implies, as did the Cold War assumptions, not only "that the Other was different, but that he was inferior." The inevitable conclusion is that the West is left with little choice but "to defend 'Our' inherited values against 'Theirs.'" As such, Huntington's—and, one could add, the foreign policy intelligentsia's—policy recommendations are "not easily distinguished from those inspired by the old order of competitive states and ideological blocs." Instead, they remain mired in the Cold War "realist" view whereby international politics was seen as "a struggle for power between coherent but essentially isolated units, each of which seeks to advance its own interests in an anarchic setting" (Rubenstein and Crocker, 1994:115, 118–120).

The engagement wing of the foreign policy intelligentsia, then, has identified new enemies that the United States must confront and contain, and it asserts that Washington must maintain a global and regional balance of power favorable to its interests. It must, as former Secretary of Defense James Schlesinger phrased it, "retain command of the seas or, to put it more politely, to ensure freedom of the seas . . . and, for the predictable future, needs the capability to intervene rapidly in the Middle East (or elsewhere)" (Schlesinger, 1991–1992:20). Policymakers, he continued, "should be quite clear in their minds that the basis for determining United States force structure and military expenditures in the future should not simply be the response to individual threats, but rather that which is needed to maintain the overall aura of American power" (Schlesinger, 1991–1992:20).

In 1993, it appeared that the Clinton administration shared his views and that the United States intended to maintain its military strength at about 1.4 million troops, slightly less than the Cold War level of 1.7 million. The defense budget would remain as high as it was during the Cold War and called for spending $1.3 trillion between 1993 and 1998. Endorsing the Bush administration's post–Cold War military doctrine, the Clinton defense plan justified its proposed extraordinary level of spending by arguing that the United States must be prepared to fight successive regional wars similar to Desert Storm against would-be Third World hegemons. Thus, the United States must increase its ability to project its power quickly anywhere in the world. Moreover, since the United States may not be able to rely on its allies to fight such wars, it may have to pursue a go-it-alone strategy (Gordon, 1993; Borosage, 1993:346; Klare, 1993:348).

Ideology and Power

A state seeking to maintain or extend its hegemonic dominance cannot justify its power-projection on defensive and containment grounds only. It needs a system of rationalization and must cast its objectives in broader, more universal and noble terms. As Noam Chomsky put it:

> Imperialism cannot operate without a system of rationalization and propaganda, [which], once construed and internalized, may come to be a factor influencing policy decisions as ideology overwhelms interests. . . . A close analysis of policy will generally unearth a structure of rational calculation based on perceived interests at its core, but in the complex world of decision-making and political planning, many other elements may also intervene, sometimes significantly, including the system of

self-serving beliefs that is regularly constructed to disguise—to others and to one-self—what is really happening in the world (Chomsky, 1985:56).

For the foreign policy intelligentsia, the defense and promotion of democracy and the free market serve as the "grander vision" underlying U.S. policy objectives in the new world order. First, they argue, the United States must seize the "democratic moment" created by the collapse of communism and the absence of any major ideological or geopolitical rivals to the idea of democracy (Diamond, 1992:26). Second, though not all countries in the world may be suited for an American-style democracy, the United States must nonetheless promote the spread of democracy and support those who are struggling to establish it (Diamond, 1992:27). Third, democracy is not likely to take hold unless its corollaries—a free market economy and a free trade system—are also fostered. In addition to favoring the United States in its global competition, only an open market economy and a free trade system, not socialism or statism, can create the conditions for economic development and distribute resources to make political competition possible, hold the state accountable, and observe "elemental standards of order, justice, and human rights" (Coll, 1992:52–53; Diamond, 1992:28). As Seymour Martin Lipset put it, "Democracy has never developed anywhere by plan" (Lipset, 1994:4).

The New World Order Reconsidered

In contrast to the foreign policy intelligentsia's views of the new world order, this book advances ten hypotheses on the characteristics, tendencies, continuities, contradictions, and possibilities of that so-called new order. Some of these hypotheses are broad generalizations, and their relevance to the case study of Haiti may not be readily apparent. Nonetheless, they provide a context and a framework within which to analyze U.S. foreign policy toward Haiti, as well as the constraints faced by those who seek to retain or change the status quo there.

Thesis One

Like the Cold War containment doctrine, the new world order doctrine seeks to create a bipartisan consensus behind the renewed objectives of the United States to preserve its unchallenged military status, if not also its economic and political hegemony, and prevent the emergence of any power or political movement that could threaten the post–Cold War status quo. The foregoing discussion presents a clearly defined agenda for continued U.S. dominance in the post–Cold War era. It identifies a new set of dangers (nuclear proliferation, political instability and chaos) and enemies (Third World fanatics, anti-West fundamentalists, and pre-modern, undemocratic states and civilizations). And it offers a vision of the new world order that the United States must attempt to create and the broad policies it must implement to achieve its objectives. The United States is bound to lead in this new world order, according to this view, not only because it stands for what is right, for freedom, and for order but also because it is the only superpower with the capability to project its power globally to protect this new world order from its enemies.

Thesis Two

The world is now truly unipolar: Only one superpower is hegemonic, and there are no longer two rival politico-economic systems competing for influence in different parts of the world. The demise of the Soviet Union and the Soviet bloc means that all those countries of the Third World that relied on the Soviet bloc as an alternative source of trade and economic and military aid to experiment with state capitalist, socialist, or noncapitalist models of development must now realign themselves with the West and reinsert their economies in the international capitalist division of labor (Freedman, 1992:26; Cummings, 1991:198; Sweezy, 1991:3).

If the world is unipolar with the unchallenged dominance of the capitalist system, it is still multipolar in terms of competing capitalist economic blocs. The Group of Seven advanced industrial economies that dominate the world economy can be subdivided into three regional blocs, namely, the European Economic Community, North America, and East Asia. Each of these blocs dominates its respective zone economically and serves as a magnet for the countries in its region. Within each of the three blocs, one country vies for hegemonic dominance over the others—the United States in North and South America, Germany in the European zone, and Japan in East Asia (Freedman, 1992:27).

If by "hegemony" one means the ability of a great power to "impose its rule and its wishes (at the very least by effective veto power) in the economic, political, military, diplomatic, and even cultural arenas" (Wallerstein, 1985:38), then clearly the United States can no longer be considered hegemonic in the post–Cold War era. Between 1945 and the middle to late 1960s, U.S. transnational corporations (TNCs) operated virtually unchallenged. All this began to change after 1968 when (1) transnational corporations from the core countries of Western Europe and Japan began to gain control over production and distribution networks once dominated by U.S. transnationals, and (2) Japanese investments abroad began to overtake U.S. investments in extent and in scope (Arrighi, 1991b:148–149). The relative equality between the economies of Western Europe, Japan, and the United States today means that the major decisions that affect the global economy can no longer be made by Washington alone; instead, they must be made by agreement between the core capitalist powers (Ahmad, 1992:312).

Chief among the structural factors that played a role in the relative decline of U.S. hegemony, by undermining U.S. competitiveness, are the costs of world leadership and world empire and the high price of relative peace and stability in the domestic arena with both organized labor and the professional and managerial classes. After the onset of the Cold War in 1947 and particularly after the Korean War, the United States spent vast sums to create its military-industrial complex. This involved not only the production of a massive military apparatus and sophisticated weaponry but also the deployment of a worldwide and expensive military bureaucracy (Cummings, 1991:216; Wallerstein, 1993:146). Although this allowed the United States to make significant breakthroughs and assume leadership in military technology, success came at the expense of competitiveness in civilian and commercial technology; ultimately, this caused the United States to fall behind its major European and Japanese rivals in the fields of microelectronics and robotics and possibly in biotechnology, fiber optics, and computer technology as well. The United States is now relying on its competitors to supply it with some of the technology it needs, not only for commercial purposes but also for some advanced weaponry (Sanders, 1991:241).

The wage concessions made to organized labor between 1945 and 1970 were exchanged for labor's decreasing militancy in the form of strikes. Just as important—though much less frequently considered, as Immanuel Wallerstein pointed out—was what could be called the higher cost of the professional-managerial classes in the United States as compared to Western Europe and Japan. This refers, on the one hand, to the higher wages paid to the expanding professional-managerial sector and the professional strata it relied on for its services, such as lawyers, doctors, psychiatrists, restaurateurs, and so on. While the wages of the professional-managerial class continued to rise between 1970 and 1990, union wages stagnated. On the other hand, the ratio of administrative and managerial positions to total employment is higher in the United States than in Germany or Japan and even doubled between 1970 and 1990. All this simply means that the cost of production rose faster in the United States than in Western Europe and Japan. This, in turn, led to higher productivity growth in those countries and made it more difficult for the United States to cope with what Wallerstein called the "vicissitudes of the world-economy," expressed in such symptoms as shrinking global profits, national fiscal crises, and higher unemployment rates (Wallerstein, 1993:146).

To overcome these impediments, U.S. firms must be "downsized," their productivity must be improved with more efficient technology, and their overall operating costs must be lowered. In addition to depressing wages for domestic workers, U.S. firms, especially the transnational corporations, can lower costs by relocating branch plants or subsidiaries to low-wage countries. Mexico, Central America, and the Caribbean are particularly attractive to U.S. corporations because they pay their workers substantially lower wages, offer tax and other exemptions to foreign corporations, and are close to the U.S. market. As such, Washington has sought to facilitate U.S. investments and the relocation of TNC subsidiaries in the region through such strategies as the Caribbean Basin Initiative (CBI) under the Reagan administration, the Enterprise for the Americas Initiative (EAI) of the Bush administration, and the North American Free Trade Agreement (NAFTA) of the Bush and Clinton administrations.

Thesis Three

Given the relative decline of its hegemony vis-à-vis the nations of Western Europe and Japan, the United States seeks to continue to exercise leverage over those nations by preserving its military superiority. One of the unspoken or hidden agendas of the Cold War was to contain the Western allies, primarily West Germany and Japan. Washington accomplished this goal by depriving both countries of their military strengths after World War II and by making them dependent on the United States for their own defense and the flow of essential raw materials and other natural resources to their economies. Some foreign policy analysts have suggested that "containment of the risk of conflict among the economic superpowers must replace the Cold War's containment of military risk as a primary purpose of United States foreign policy" (Bergsten, 1992:11).

Thesis Four

It is from the preceding standpoint that one can best understand the importance of the Persian Gulf War in the post–Cold War strategy of the United States. Many analysts have shown that the Bush administration's decision to reject all diplomatic initiatives and opt early for a military response to Iraq's invasion of Kuwait had nothing to do with Washington's aversion to unprovoked aggression. It also had nothing to do with its concern for human rights or even with Iraq's control over Kuwait's oil (see Alterman, 1992; Brenner, 1991; Chomsky, 1992; Hitchens, 1991; Klare, 1990). Instead, the Gulf War made it possible for the United States to (1) demonstrate that it remains the only superpower capable of projecting its military strength globally, and (2) remind its major European and Japanese competitors that they must still rely on the United States to preserve and ensure stability and the continued flow of vital resources, without which their economies would be imperiled (Cummings, 1991:216; Klare, 1990:418; Mead, 1991: 382).

In short, military supremacy remains a principal asset for the United States. Furthermore, its ability to retain its relatively dominant economic position rests on its success in convincing its economic rivals that their future prosperity depends on the stability of the world economy and that only the United States can guarantee that security. As James Petras and Arthur MacEwan argued, however, this strategy will not likely pay off for the United States. It will not allow Washington to dictate economic policy to Western Europe and Japan. And it will not create stability in world financial markets or interest rates favorable to the United States. It will not reduce the U.S. trade deficit and the increasing reliance of the United States on foreign banks and foreign capital. And it will not increase the competitiveness of U.S. multinationals in relation to those of Germany and Japan that have penetrated U.S. and other markets because of their superior technology and more effective management and marketing strategies (Petras, 1991:515; MacEwan, 1992:154–155).

Thesis Five

The dissipation of the Cold War containment ideology revealed that, along with the rivalry among the core capitalist powers, the contradictions between those core capitalist countries ("the North") and the countries of the Third World ("the South"), as well as the struggles within the Third World for basic needs and human rights, remain the fundamental sources of conflict and destabilization. This does not mean that other contradictions and conflicts (such as the many ethnic wars in the Balkans, in the former Soviet Union, and in Africa) are not extremely destabilizing. But the North-South divide and the inequalities between and within the countries of these poles remain, in my view, the most salient contradictions. The relations of exploitation that characterize this divide and that produced the immiseration of the vast majority of the world's population are the root cause of the conflicts within the South and between the South and the North. As Rubenstein and Crocker remarked, "Serious social conflict is not generated by individual aggressiveness or international lawlessness as much as by the failure of existing systems to satisfy people's basic needs" (Rubenstein and Crocker, 1994:125).

Confining the discussion to the post–World War II period, two opposite trends can be observed in the world economy: a growing equality in incomes and living standards between the advanced or core capitalist countries of Western Europe,[2] North America, and Japan, on the one hand, and a growing inequality in incomes and living standards between these advanced countries and the underdeveloped countries of Africa, Asia, and Latin America, on the other hand. Between 1938 and 1988, the developed countries of Western Europe and North America underwent a process of leveling their living standards as measured by gross national product (GNP) per capita. Income inequalities between them are currently at their lowest level. Japan, whose GNP per capita was 14.5 percent of the GNP per capita of the core capitalist countries in 1948, surpassed the GNP per capita of those countries by about 20 percent in 1988 (Arrighi, 1991a:42–46).

Meanwhile, the income gap between the core capitalist countries and the underdeveloped parts of the world economy increased, particularly after 1960.

Between 1960 and 1989, the share of global GNP for the richest 20 percent of the world's population increased from 70.2 percent to 82.7 percent, and the share of the poorest 20 percent of the world's population decreased from 2.3 percent to 1.4 percent. Stated differently, the top 20 percent of the world's population received thirty times more than the bottom 20 percent in 1960, but by 1989, it received sixty times more. If one takes income distribution between rich and poor people rather than the average per capita incomes between rich and poor countries as a measure, then the global ratio between the richest and poorest people is estimated at over fifty to one (UNDP, 1992:34). The World Bank estimated that in 1991, more than 1 billion people in the poorer underdeveloped countries lived in absolute poverty on an income of less than US$1 a day, a standard of living that the core countries of Western Europe and the United States reached 200 years ago (World Bank, 1991b:1).

In Latin America specifically during the 1980s, the total number of people in poverty increased from 120 million (39 percent of the total population) in 1980 to approximately 183 million (44 percent of the total population) at the end of the decade. Nearly half of those 183 million people lived under conditions of extreme poverty (Vilas, 1992:14; Castañeda, 1993:5–6). In Brazil, the most developed country in Latin America, it is estimated that 1,000 children die each day of starvation and disease (Galeano, 1991:253). In Haiti, the poorest country of the Western Hemisphere in 1989, more than four-fifths of its nearly 7 million people were estimated to be living in absolute poverty.

The disparities in living standard between the advanced and the underdeveloped nations also reflect real differences in the consumption levels of the core capitalist countries in contrast to those of the rest of the world. The developed capitalist countries, which include about one-fourth of the world's population, consume 60 percent of the world's food, 70 percent of its energy, 75 percent of its metals, and 85 percent of its wood (UNDP, 1992:35). No matter how one looks at this picture, it appears that the capitalist system is incapable of resolving its most fundamental structural contradictions.

Thesis Six

The struggles to overcome conditions of underdevelopment and poverty will continue and will cause unrest and instability in different parts of the Third World. As this happens, the core capitalist countries and the United States in particular will be compelled to intervene to preserve order. The absence of the East-West rivalry that partly defines the new world order, however, means that the core capitalist powers are now fully hegemonic within the United Nations Security Council. Rather than acting unilaterally to maintain order in the Third World as they did during the Cold War, the core capitalist powers can now call upon that organization to assume much of the burden of world police force, thereby giving its interventions a mantle of legitimacy that the unilateralist approach of a superpower often lacked in the past. Since 1990, the UN has been involved in mediating conflicts, with or without the use of armed forces, in a dozen or so countries in the Middle East, the Balkans, Africa, Southeast Asia, the Caribbean, and Central America. The UN's involvement in these countries is not limited to peacekeeping or peacemaking efforts but extends to institution-building as well.

The demise of the bipolar East-West antagonism in effect created a new interventionist division of labor within which at least two tendencies can be observed. The first is the relatively high degree of unity among the core capitalist powers that dominate the United Nations Security Council on how to respond to crises in the Third World in contrast to other parts of the world where particular core powers have interests at stake, such as the civil and ethnic wars in the Balkans. The second tendency is the attempt by the United States to use its overwhelming military power to exert its hegemony within the UN Security Council, pursue its unilateralist options with UN cover, and in essence deprive the UN of its ability to carry out those missions that call for the use of force independently of the United States.

Thesis Seven

The UN has emerged as a major political actor in relation to the Third World. As the UN assumes a greater policing and nation-building role in Third World countries, the criteria under which it intervenes in the internal affairs of those countries have also changed. The secretary-general of the United Nations, Boutros Boutros-Ghali, described these new criteria in his 1992 report to the United Nations, entitled *An Agenda for Peace* (Boutros-Ghali, 1992). Most critical is his redefinition of the principles of national sovereignty and self-determination. That redefinition consists of a reinterpretation of the famous Article 2(7) of the United Nations Charter that explicitly prohibits UN member states from interfering in the internal affairs of any state, which served as the cornerstone of the movement against imperialism by the Non-Aligned Movement.

Asserting that the principle of national sovereignty was never matched by reality, Boutros-Ghali declared that the time of "absolute and exclusive sovereignty . . . has passed" (Boutros-Ghali, 1992:9). Stronger states in both the North and the South, as well as in the socialist bloc, routinely violated this principle vis-à-vis weaker states. Critics of the international capitalist system have pointed out the many ways in which the imperialist countries and their regulatory institutions dictated economic policies and political reforms to Third World governments that effectively rendered the ideas of national sovereignty and self-determination meaningless. Nevertheless, these twin principles played an important role in the anticolonial and postcolonial struggles of Third World countries. Even if their invocation did not deter foreign intervention, they at least scored occasional ideological points against an aggressive imperialist power, unmasked its real motives, and sometimes galvanized domestic and international opposition to its policies.

The UN secretary-general's obituary for the principle of "absolute and exclusive sovereignty" is a double-edged sword, however. To be sure, it deprives progressive Third World governments of an important ideological weapon against imperialist intervention. But it also undermines the ability of repressive right-wing governments in the Third World to escape international scrutiny for their human rights violations. Furthermore, the UN Charter contains many exemptions to Article 2(7) that grant the secretary-general the authority to bring to the Security Council issues that he or she considers threatening to international peace and security and that may occasion interference in intrastate affairs. In my view, the most important of such provisions are those that refer to the international community's obligation to protect basic human rights. Primary among those rights, as Australian Foreign Minister Gareth Evans pointed out, is the protection of life. But also included are traditional civil and political rights and economic, social, and cultural rights (G. Evans, 1994:9–11). Thus, even though Third World progressives correctly interpreted and used Article 2(7) as a protection against the violation of national sovereignty, Secretary-General Boutros-Ghali also correctly argued that sovereignty was never absolute: It was always contingent on states observing certain fundamental and universal principles, such as basic human rights, in their internal affairs. As Evans pointedly remarked, "It is one thing to construct a rationale to justify international interest and ultimately intervention in intrastate as well as interstate disputes or conflicts; it is quite another thing to determine when and how it would be appropriate for that interest to be expressed, or the intervention mounted, in particular cases" (G. Evans, 1994:10).

Haiti serves as a test case for Evans's cautionary remarks. The worsening human rights situation in Haiti after the coup d'état of 1991 led the UN Security Council to declare that it constituted a threat to peace and security; the council then authorized the United States to organize and lead a multinational force to intervene in Haiti in September 1994.

Thesis Eight

The demise of the Soviet Union, the hegemony of the Western capitalist powers within the United Nations Security Council, and the ideological onslaught against national sovereignty have effectively silenced progressive Third World governments or popular movements within the Security Council. Thus, they cannot serve as counterweights or deterrents to intervention. The dismantling of the Soviet Union not only illegitimated socialism as an alternative to capitalism but also spelled the end of the Non-Aligned Movement that found its raison d'être in the context of the bipolar geopolitical rivalry between East and West. Aware of the absence of alternatives and with nowhere else to go for support, socialist or progressive nationalist Third World governments are left with few alternatives but to reorient their economies to those of the capitalist West. Those movements still struggling for power in the Third World must seek negotiated solutions and compromises that inevitably advantage the dominant classes allied to the core capitalist powers. Nicaragua, El Salvador, and Haiti can be cited as examples.

The end of the East-West bipolarity and the death knell of national sovereignty affect repressive right-wing military dictatorships in Latin America as well. They can no longer count on the unconditional support of the United States because they are no longer considered essential to keeping the countries of the region within the capitalist fold. The Cold War ideology of containing communism offered a ready-made justification for maintaining large armies that rarely if ever fought foreign wars. The Latin American military is facing an identity crisis: Throughout the region, it is being forced to accept civilian rule, while having no clear definition of its post–Cold War mission and basis of power (Benitez Manaut, 1993:15–16).

To be sure, the transition to democracy has been accompanied by a shift to a laissez-faire version of capitalism and, hence, to an intensification of capitalist exploitation. The version of liberal democracy that is fostered by the United States in particular is one in which citizens have formal rights to protect and pursue their individual or organized self-interests by pressing their claims against their elected government. But, as Ellen Meiksins Wood argued, liberal democracy also creates a separation between the political and economic spheres, whereby significant powers are transferred from the state to the holders of private property and the coercion of the market. The definition of liberal democracy as involving a separation of the economic from the political sphere renders

> the economic sphere [invulnerable] to democratic power. Protecting that invulnerability has even become an essential criterion of democracy. This definition allows us to invoke democracy *against* the empowerment of people in the economic sphere. It even makes it possible to invoke democracy in defence of a *curtailment* of democratic rights in other parts of "civil society" or even in the political domain, if that is what is needed to protect property and the market against democratic power (Meiksins Wood, 1995:235, emphasis in original).

No doubt, these tendencies will increase social tensions, which governments will attempt to contain. But citizens will also be able to organize to counter these restrictive and repressive practices, expand democratic rights, render their governments accountable, and, in combination with greater international monitoring of human rights violations, undercut the ability of the military to act with impunity as it so often did in the past.

A corollary of the shift to civilian rule is the illegitimacy of the coup d'état as a means of settling conflict between classes and between factions of the dominant classes vying for power. The OAS, for example, adopted a resolution in June 1991 that made representative democracy a condition of membership in that regional organization. In December 1992, it went even further by declaring that a member state could be suspended from the organization if its democratically elected government was removed by a coup d'état (Halperin, 1993). The reactions of the United States, the OAS, and later the UN to the military coup in Haiti in 1991 served as a test case for this hypothesis and indicated a hemispheric shift in the balance of power against the military.[3]

One must not consider the transition to democracy to be a given and irreversible process. Insofar as it is accompanied by an intensification of capitalist exploitation, the transition will likely increase social tensions and demands for reforms that may not be confinable through the politics of class compromises, as occurred in the advanced countries of Western Europe. Chile under Salvador Allende from 1970 to 1973 and Haiti under Aristide from February to September 1991 are cases in point. The outcome in each case was determined by power relations between classes and class factions within each country—the military, the business elites, the middle classes, and the working and peasant classes—as well as power relations within and between factions of the dominant classes of the United States and each respective society in a specific historical and geopolitical conjuncture. In the full swing of the Cold War, the military toppled Allende's government and reestablished a military dictatorship with the full support of the Chilean bourgeoisie and the U.S. government. In the post–Cold War period, the military overthrew Aristide's government with the support of the Haitian bourgeoisie but not that of the U.S. government. The Haitian junta, therefore, could not consolidate its power and reestablish a military dictatorship as happened in Chile. Extending the general hypothesis of Dietrich Rueschemeyer, Evelyne Huber Stephens, and John D. Stephens to Latin America, it may be argued that the consolidation of democracy in those countries with histories of military dictatorships ultimately depends (1) on the balance of power between factions of dominant and subordinate classes within each country, (2) on the structure of the state and its relations with civil society, and (3) on the balance of power between factions within the dominant classes of the United States and their impact on relations between the United States and those countries (Rueschemeyer, Stephens, and Stephens, 1992:5).

Thesis Nine

For U.S.–Latin American relations, the demise of the Cold War means that the United States no longer must foster or support coups d'état to prevent governments from challenging domestic or U.S. interests. With the enhanced mediatorial role of the United Nations, Washington can support the growing but precarious and reversible trend toward democratization in the region insofar as this trend no longer threatens the class structures and geopolitical alignment of these societies. This may explain why, for example, the United States agreed to UN-OAS-supervised elections in Nicaragua and in Haiti in 1990 and why it accepted a UN-negotiated solution to the civil war in El Salvador (Burbach, 1993:17).

To be sure, the interventionist impulse of the United States remains strong. In many ways, it may be easier now for Washington to intervene because it need no longer fear a retaliatory move by the Soviet Union elsewhere in reaction to a U.S. move in the Western Hemisphere (Lowenthal, 1993:66). It is also clear that the right wing of both parties in the U.S. Congress, the State and Defense Departments, and the Central Intelligence Agency (CIA) feel uneasy about abandoning their reliance on the Latin American military and fear the possibilities opened up by the democratization process. Eduardo Galeano may have been right to remind us that the United States intervened in Latin America more than a hundred times this century and that the imperial system above all wants humbled countries, not democratic ones (Galeano, 1991:252).

Yet, though stability and a climate conducive to the free flow of capital remain priorities for the United States in the Western Hemisphere, the demise of the Cold War will make it increasingly difficult for Washington to justify bolstering a right-wing dictatorship or fomenting a coup d'état in the name of freedom or containing communism. Again, Haiti is a case in point. Unable to invoke the traditional anticommunist argument to justify its support for the Haitian military coup d'état against Aristide, the Bush administration and the Right in Congress that opposed his restoration to power were compelled to go after his character and his purportedly grim human rights record. Failing to find a solution that excluded Aristide, the Clinton administration sent U.S. troops into Haiti to depose the military junta and return Aristide to power but not until the latter had embraced the Haitian bourgeoisie and accepted a U.S. occupation and Washington's neoliberal agenda. Although this supports Galeano's point, it also reflects a shift in the traditional U.S. attitude toward right-wing military dictators.

There are still other reasons why the United States may move away from its historical reliance on military dictatorships and armed intervention in Latin America. The Left is currently in retreat throughout the hemisphere and has, with few exceptions, rejected armed revolution in favor of gradual reforms arrived at through the rules of liberal democracy. Governments everywhere in the hemisphere are moving away from the statist policies of the past and are embracing the free market, structural adjustment, and privatization policies advocated by the World Bank, the International Monetary Fund (IMF), and the United States Agency for International Development (USAID). It behooves the U.S. government to solidify these trends to the extent that they support the interests of U.S. capital—or at least those sectors based in the transnational corporations and dependent on foreign markets and foreign trade.

The shift in U.S. policy toward Latin America, then, has both a geopolitical motive and an underlying economic motive. The formation of the three competing blocs among the core capitalist powers has led the United States to turn increasingly to Latin America as a source of investment, cheaper labor, trade, and markets. This is why the Bush administration launched the Enterprise for the Americas Initiative in 1990 and why the Clinton administration, taking over its predecessor's agenda, sought and won congressional backing for NAFTA with Canada and Mexico.

The economic setbacks suffered during the 1980s in Latin America as a result of the crippling debt crisis, as well as the adjustment policies and austerity measures adopted by most regional governments, make the nations of Latin America attractive new sources of investment and trade, especially in the new growth areas of finance and energy. Latin America is thus becoming an important market for U.S. exports, especially as the United States faces increasing competition from Western Europe and Japan and finds it more difficult to penetrate those markets (Sanchez Otero, 1993:20; Burbach, 1993:18; Lowenthal, 1993:74).

At the same time, it should not be surprising that the free market, structural adjustment, and restructuring policies are being pursued without regard for the growing unemployment, underemployment, and disparity between rich and poor in the region. From a class perspective, the policies advocated by the international bourgeoisie and adopted by the regional bourgeoisies are successful only if they secure the maximum conditions for the exploitation of labor as a necessary condition for the accumulation of capital. Contrary to the expectations of neoclassical economic theories, the success of these policies does not depend on reducing unemployment, inflation, or the balance-of-payments deficit (Ruccio, 1993:39). Thus, the failure of the regional bourgeoisies to address the consequence of these policies is a measure of their success rather than the reverse. As Roger Burbach concluded:

> The refusal to address the fundamental structural problems that the hemisphere faces . . . while the United States continues to cultivate free trade and economic policies that primarily benefit the multinationals and the economic elites of the hemisphere . . . does not mean that these problems will go away. The Central American wars of the 1980s may be winding down, but political and social explosions cannot be ruled out in any one of a number of countries (Burbach, 1993:22).

The recent uprising by the Zapatista National Liberation Army in the Chiapas Province of Mexico stemmed directly from the immiseration and repression of the peasants of that region, adding weight to Burbach's contention.

Thesis Ten

Despite its political defeat and its current retreat, the Latin American and Caribbean Left could find an unexpected benefit in the end of the Cold War. It has been freed from the Soviet-proxy handicap, and with the democratic opening in the hemisphere, it enjoys an unprecedented opportunity to contest elections openly and possibly win control of government. This nearly happened in Brazil in 1989, and it did happen in Haiti in 1990. At the same time, the hands of elected Left governments are tied more tightly than ever, and it is increasingly difficult for these governments to implement reforms. This is so for several reasons.

First, as mentioned in the second thesis, the demise of the Soviet bloc and the unchallenged supremacy of the capitalist world system severely restrict the options of a nation-state seeking an alternative to capitalism. Moreover, as Michael Manley argued, the globalization of production, consumption, finance, and communication makes the idea of the nation-state increasingly obsolete in the Third World. This is because "national boundaries [now] merely delimit the platforms of production" and can no longer be seen as "an arena for independent economic development." The subordination of these economies to transnational corporations and the deliberate diffusion of the various branches and processes of production, distribution, communication, and finance "reduce the capacity of any one nation to affect or even significantly influence the outcome of economic activity" (Manley, 1991:110).

A few Third World countries—such as South Korea, Taiwan, Singapore, and Hong Kong in East Asia and Argentina, Brazil, and Mexico in Latin America—succeeded in establishing what Alain Lipietz referred to as "peripheral Fordism." These so-called newly industrialized countries (NICs) used a combination of state intervention and import- and export-substitution strategies to generate relatively significant levels of industrialization and create a growing domestic market for consumer durables for the bourgeoisie, the middle classes, and a segment of the working class. These economies are still peripheral, however, because their industrialization continues to depend on importing most of their capital goods from the core capitalist economies and exporting to them their manufactured products (Lipietz, 1987:78–79). Nonetheless, a Left government coming to power in any of these Latin American NICs would have more to work with and greater room in which to maneuver than it would in any of the region's less developed nations.

Second, the division of labor between the core capitalist countries and those of the Third World, including the NICs, disadvantages the latter. This is because their export-led development strategies are based on the establishment of mainly labor-intensive and lower-cost production processes to supply primary or intermediary goods to other branch plants located in more developed countries where final processing occurs (NACLA, 1993:16). The transnational corporations with their headquarters in the core capitalist countries centralize the management and control of capital, technology, and financing, and they regulate trade, prices, and profits within and between their firms. By the early 1980s, for example, intrafirm trade among the largest 350 transnational corporations accounted for about 40 percent of world trade. More than 30 percent of U.S. trade was between U.S.-based transnationals and their foreign subsidiaries; and one-fourth of Japan's trade was between its transnationals and their East Asian affiliates (Henwood, 1993:26).

Third, most governments in Latin America and the Caribbean are now pursuing a strategy of economic integration with the core capitalist countries and the United States in particular and are consciously abandoning independent development policies. NAFTA, it must be remembered, was a Mexican and not a U.S. government initiative. A corollary to this strategy and a further indication of the weakening of the nation-state as an arena of independent decisionmaking over economic policy is the surrender of development policy formulation by governments in Latin America and the Caribbean to international aid and regulatory institutions such as the World Bank, the IMF, and the USAID (Sanchez Otero, 1993:20). The paradox of the current conjuncture, then, is this: Even as the democratization process is taking root in the hemisphere, the power to determine the agenda of the region's societies is being transferred away from the citizenry to international institutions that are not subject to democratic control and accountability. The challenge for the Left in the region is to figure out how to reverse this process and expand the scope of participation and decisionmaking in order to exercise greater popular control over the agenda.

Notes

1. "Foreign policy intelligentsia" refers to all those who are based within universities, policy think thanks, and the national security and foreign policy apparatuses of the U.S. government whose primary concerns are the analysis and formulation of U.S. foreign policy.

2. These include Austria, the Benelux countries, France, Great Britain, Switzerland, the Scandinavian countries, and the former West Germany.

3. One could also cite the reactions of the OAS to President Alberto Fujimori's coup against the Peruvian parliament in 1991, the successive attempts to overthrow President Carlos Andres Perez in Venezuela in 1992, and President Jorge Serrano's self-generated coup in Guatemala in 1993.

2

A NEOLIBERAL MODEL
FOR POST-DUVALIER HAITI

Between 1986 and 1988, the USAID, the World Bank, and the IMF renewed their efforts to have the government of Haiti adopt a program of fiscal and economic reforms to encourage private sector development, create a more open market economy, and integrate the Haitian economy more fully with that of the United States. Though this program of reforms had been recommended before 1986, the prebendary and exclusionary interests of the Duvalier dictatorship, in collaboration with a small monopolist faction of the Haitian bourgeoisie, successfully blocked its implementation. Despite the demise of the Duvalier dictatorship in 1986 and the formation of a new partnership among foreign capital, the Haitian entrepreneurial class, and the post-Duvalier military-led governments, the prebendary state system could not accommodate the most important components of the free market reforms advocated by the international aid and regulatory agencies.

By prebendary state, I mean a political regime in which those who held office or political power lived off politics. In addition to their regular salaries, these officials received perquisites of office either as bribes or by siphoning (i.e., stealing) public moneys from the various government agencies or state enterprises for private ends. In essence, as Max Weber argued, "prebendary officials" assume the character of "entrepreneurs" when they treat their public offices as they would private businesses, that is, as sources of personal enrichment (Weber, 1968:86–95, 207–209). Or, as Peter Evans put it, the objective of those who control such predatory states is simply to plunder resources "without any more regard for the welfare of the citizenry than a predator has for the welfare of its prey" (P. Evans, 1989:562).

This chapter is a revised version of a previously published article: "Free Trade and Underdevelopment in Haiti: The World Bank/USAID Agenda for Social Change in the Post-Duvalier Era," from *The Caribbean in the Global Political Economy*, edited by Hilbourne A. Watson. Copyright © 1994 by Lynne Rienner Publishers, Inc. It is reprinted with permission of the publisher.

The prebendary state is a prototype of a political system based on control of the state apparatuses by a power bloc formed around and loyal to a dictator. It often exhibits the characteristics of personal rule and its attendant clientalistic networks. As Robert Jackson and Carl Rosberg showed in their study of systems of rule in postindependence Africa, personal rule is a system insofar as it functions to "regulate power in the state and thereby provide political goods or carry out political functions," but it is not a system of *"public* governance or of *rationalist* decision-making." This is because the system of personal rule does not respond to "public demands and support by means of public policies and actions," and the ruler does not "aim at policy goals and [does not steer] the governmental apparatus by information feedback and learning." The system of personal rule is "more a matter of seamanship and less one of navigation—that is, staying afloat rather than going somewhere" (Jackson and Rosberg, 1982:18, emphases in original).

Such a form of political rule, Jackson and Rosberg pointed out, is fundamentally antidevelopmental and therefore resistant to rationalization measures and the implementation of public policies aimed at combating the ills of underdevelopment (i.e., poverty, disease, and ignorance) (Jackson and Rosberg, 1982:18). The system of personal rule is "more of a game in which individuals and factions struggle for power and place rather than an arena in which groups or parties compete for policies and the constitutional right to command the ship of state" (Jackson and Rosberg, 1982:18–19). As a prototype of personal rule, therefore, the Duvalier regime could not implement the reforms and the rationalization measures advocated by the international regulatory agencies without undermining the very sources of the wealth and power its officials enjoyed.

The Free Market Model

The "free-marketeers" or neoliberals argue that Haiti's salvation lies in orienting production as much as possible toward the export market and in adopting free trade policies for the domestic market. I will argue that the policies of the USAID and the World Bank contain some positive recommendations that are compatible with progressive reforms. But if implemented, the overall free market strategy they propose will reinforce the extant structures of inequality without overcoming dependency and underdevelopment. In the end, therefore, an alternative development strategy will be needed.

The World Bank, the IMF, and the USAID argue that the best hope for the poorest developing countries to escape their plight is to pursue what the World Bank calls a "market-friendly approach." This involves the notion that only market incentives—combined with appropriate social and political institutions, infrastructure, technology, and social services—can unleash the potential productivity of labor (World Bank, 1990b:3–6, 1991b:9). The World Bank downplays the experience of the "high-performing Asian economies" (HPAEs), also known as the newly industrialized countries, whose economic successes came largely as a result of the strong interventionist and dirigiste role of the state in guiding economic development.[1] Instead, the World Bank recommends a weakened role for the state in the economic development of Third World countries (World Bank, 1991b:5).

Essentially, the World Bank argues, the state must "do less in those areas where markets work, or can be made to work, reasonably well [and] do more in those areas where markets alone cannot be relied upon." The areas where the state must play a larger role than the market, though often in partnership with the private sector, encompass the standard neoclassical provisions: primary education, basic (preventive) health care, nutrition, family planning, poverty alleviation, infrastructural expansion and services (physical, administrative, legal, and regulatory), environmental protection, and building a stable macroeconomic foundation (World Bank, 1991b:9–11). The overall macroeconomic foundation the World Bank considers essential is one that will stimulate the private sector and production for export by observing the doctrines of free trade and open competition. The basic premise here is that unequal development among countries in the world economy stems from market conditions that are made worse by bad state policies and that can be corrected by pursuing free trade policies (Dietz and Pantojas-Garcia, 1994:24).

In relatively small economies like those of the Caribbean, production for export and open trade policies are especially important because domestic markets in the Caribbean countries are deemed too small to consume their own products. Expanded production, therefore, can be achieved primarily by targeting the export market and attracting foreign transnational corporations to the area. It follows that to achieve economic growth through production for export via the transnational corporations, the Caribbean economies must implement several structural reforms. These include not only the privatization of public sector industries but also and equally important the adoption of sound fiscal policies that will produce the needed trade balances between exports and imports. This, in turn, means that to prevent or overcome trade deficits (caused when imports exceed exports in terms of value) and thus avoid indebtedness to foreign lenders, governments must adopt certain adjustment programs. Typically, they involve: restraining wages; curbing social spending; deregulating the economy and devaluing the currency; abolishing price controls and subsidies to public sector enterprises that are not privatized; reducing consumption through higher taxes, interest rates, and credit restrictions; opening the economies to foreign investment by lowering business taxes; eliminating inappropriate legal codes on employment and bankruptcy; freeing private sector industries from cumbersome health, safety, and environmental standards; and removing inadequate property rights and industrial licensing (George, 1990:52; A. Martin, 1985:9; C. Thomas, 1988:330; World Bank, 1991b:7–11; Dietz and Pantojas-Garcia, 1994:26).

Many of the adjustment policies recommended by the neoliberals, such as curbing social spending, reducing business taxes, and deregulating private enterprises, contradict the World Bank's call on the state to spend more on health, education, nutrition, poverty reduction, and infrastructure. The World Bank seems aware of this contradiction and of the fact that the policies of the industrial countries negatively affect the development efforts of the developing countries. Consequently, the World Bank calls on the industrialized nations to further open their markets to exports from the developing countries, to increase voluntary private lending to developing countries while making more debt rescheduling concessions to the poorest debtor countries, and to expand debt forgiveness (World Bank, 1991b:9). But though the World Bank wields influence in the Third World nations through its ability to withhold financial aid to them, it has no way of affecting the policies of the advanced countries (especially those of the United States) that dominate the World Bank and determine its policy recommendations to the Third World. Thus, the bank's halfhearted appeal to its patrons to change their behavior toward the developing countries rings hollow.

The Free Market and Export Strategy in Haiti

It is not surprising that the proponents of the free market and export-oriented development strategy in Haiti accepted uncritically the recipes for Latin American. and Caribbean development formulated in the 1970s and 1980s by the World Bank, the IMF, the USAID, and the Reagan administration's 1983 Caribbean Basin Recovery Act (popularly known as the Caribbean Basin Initiative). But it is remarkable that this strategy was endorsed by an influential sector of the Haitian business class.[2] This acceptance represented, at least in theory, a dramatic break with the import-substitution and the monopolistic and protectionist practices of the past, which were based on a close collaboration between the business class and the regimes in power.

It is now a familiar refrain that Haiti is the poorest country of the Western Hemisphere. In 1989, more than four-fifths of its 6.4 million people were estimated to be living in absolute poverty. Life expectancy was fifty-two years. Per capita food intake was 80 percent of the daily requirement in calories and 30 percent in protein. Only 59 percent of the urban population and 30 percent of the rural population had access to safe water, and 45 percent and 35 percent, respectively, had access to electricity. The adult literacy rate was 62 percent. The per capita income was US$394, but less than 1 percent of the population appropriated more than 50 percent of the national income. The balance-of-payments deficit stood at US$164.2 million, and the external debt was US$760 million (World Bank, 1991a; Bazin, 1990:19; Bread for the World, 1990:86).

The Haitian economy currently faces an acute crisis in all sectors. In 1985, the agricultural sector employed about 70 percent of the active population and accounted for 35 percent of the gross domestic product (GDP); the industrial sector employed 8 percent of the active population and represented 25 percent of the GDP; and the service sector employed 22 percent of the active population and represented 40 percent of the GDP (World Bank, 1990a:12–13). The average annual growth rate of agriculture was a mere 0.5 percent between 1985 and 1989, continuing the regressive trend that began in 1980. The decline in agricultural output and in agriculture's share of the GDP—from 47 percent in 1970 to 35 percent in 1985—was caused by a combination of deforestation, soil erosion, a degradation of irrigation systems and roads, and a lack of capital and infrastructural investments, even though land and labor resources devoted to agricultural production increased. As domestic agricultural production declined, agricultural imports increased. In 1988, agricultural imports (legal and illegal) exceeded exports by about US$65 million (World Bank, 1991a:I, III, 3). When combined with substantial price increases of 72 percent between 1988 and 1989 for basic necessities (such as sugar, salt, flour, cooking oil, rice, and soap), the result was an inevitable worsening of the living conditions of the already impoverished majority (Deblock et al., 1990:16).

As with agricultural production, the export assembly manufacturing sector, which became the most dynamic sector of the Haitian economy in the 1970s, also experienced a steep decline in the 1980s. It is estimated that tens of thousands of jobs have been lost since 1986 due to plant closings. The domestic manufacturing sector also experienced a decline in production mainly because of difficulties in obtaining raw materials. This, too, meant more layoffs of employees, adding still more to the ranks of the unemployed (Deblock et al., 1990:16). According to estimates, unemployment and underemployment affected about 80 percent of the adult population (Bazin, 1990:19). This generalized deterioration of the economy meant a loss of fiscal revenues for the state, which was threatened with bankruptcy and which—through its prebendary practices, its corruption, and its misappropriation and misallocation of public funds, as well as its lack of any vision regarding an alternative—was itself a major cause of the economy's general paralysis (Deblock et al., 1990:16–17).

Although there is no doubt that the overall socioeconomic conditions worsened after 1986, one must exercise caution when talking about employment, underemployment, and unemployment in Haiti. In addition to those who work in more or less permanent wage employment, an entirely distinct category comprises workers who are self-employed, and the participation rates of these workers in market activities fluctuate constantly. Most of those workers belong to the so-called informal sector, and though they produce goods, provide services, and earn some income, they easily elude census surveys that rely on more standard methods of measurement (Fass, 1988:65–72). This is not to suggest that the employment, unemployment, and underemployment situation is not grave; rather, it is to suggest that more studies of the kind undertaken by Simon Fass need to be done to provide a fuller understanding of the ways in which ordinary

Haitians eke out a living and what policies a progressive government could adopt to improve their living conditions.

The international regulatory and aid agencies operate according to the principles of conventional economic theories, and their policy recommendations reflect their dogmatic attachment to those theories. The World Bank and the USAID recommendations that Haiti adopt the export-oriented production and free trade strategy date back to the 1970s and early 1980s when these institutions, along with nongovernmental organizations (NGOs), took charge of designing and financing Haiti's development plans (Dupuy, 1989a:168–169, 173–174). As Ernest Preeg, former U.S. ambassador to Haiti (1981–1983) under the Reagan administration, put it, "By summer 1981, the stage was set for what was to be the most active period of collaboration between [the] two governments in at least twenty-five years" (Preeg, 1985:22).

Under the auspices of the CBI, the USAID reviewed and recommended changes in the laws, regulations, and policies that governed business operations in those Caribbean countries that were eligible to participate in the CBI. These steps were designed to dismantle as far as possible the public sector and import-substitution industries in those economies and replace them with private enterprises owned either locally, by foreign investors, or by joint ventures. The underlying premise of the CBI and the USAID was that the Caribbean economies could not continue to rely on the export of a few traditional commodities—sugar, coffee, bananas—and on their subsidized domestic industries to increase production and employment. The latter industries were also thought to cause trade imbalances and to drain foreign exchange because of their relatively high import contents. The alternative was for the Caribbean economies to adopt new strategies based primarily on private sector and export-oriented growth by relying on the region's comparative advantages in low-cost labor and fertile tropical soil, as well as preferential access to the U.S. market under the terms of the CBI (Preeg, 1985:49–50; A. Martin, 1985:8–10). The proponents of the CBI readily acknowledged that the initiative was designed to further integrate the Caribbean economies with the U.S. market and that its provisions presupposed major benefits to U.S. investors and traders. This was justified on the ground that comparative advantage "cannot generally be realized without the technology and marketing expertise of the American private sector" (Preeg, 1985:50).

Before the fall of the Duvalier regime in 1985, the World Bank proposed that Haiti could improve its place in the world (despite its low per capita income) by taking advantage of its low-cost labor, its basic infrastructure, its probusiness atmosphere, its political stability, and its closeness to the North American market (Hooper, 1995:128). On the basis of these premises, the USAID and World Bank strategy for Haiti emphasized linking more bilateral aid with trade ties and greater incentives for U.S. investors, on the one hand, and greater reliance on private sector development in Haiti, on the other hand. Moreover, economic assistance was tied to the Duvalier government's agreeing to try to deal more effectively with the problems of illegal emigration, fiscal management and account-ability, and human rights liberalization (Preeg, 1985:23). In effect, in return for economic and military aid, the Duvalier regime abdicated its responsibility for determining the country's development priorities; it surrendered its autonomy to the USAID and the World Bank and entered into a relationship of de facto tute-lage under them (Deblock et al., 1990:21).

The USAID proposed a twofold development strategy that called for using Haiti's low-wage comparative advantage to foster agroprocessing industries and assembly manufacturing production for export to the United States. It was prin-cipally the latter that became the late-twentieth-century mode of Haiti's inser-tion in the international division of labor. The USAID spent tens of millions of dollars to promote investment in the offshore assembly industry in Haiti (Dupuy, 1989a:174–175; DeWind and Kinley, 1988:48; Deblock et al., 1990:20; Caprio, 1993:276; Briggs and Kernaghan, 1995:138). The assembly industries accounted for 14 percent of total exports in 1971 and 58 percent in 1985. Looked at differ-ently, the total value of manufactured exports increased from US$41 million in 1973 to US$349 million in 1985 and US$364 million in 1987. After 1987, how-ever, the value of exports declined to US$347 million in 1989 and US$323 mil-lion in 1990, due largely to the increasing political instability of Haiti. The assembly manufacturing sector comprised some 350 firms and employed about half of all workers in the industrial sector. The primary products of these indus-tries consisted of electronic and electric components, textiles and garments, toys and sporting goods (e.g., baseballs, tennis balls, fishing rods), leather goods, fur-niture, and other items made with rubber, plastic, chemicals and nonmetallic minerals (Dupuy, 1989a:175–178; DeWind and Kinley, 1988:153, 156; Caprio, 1993:277; Walker and Caprio, 1991:4; World Bank, 1990a:5; Delva, 1991:298).

The manufacturing industries were attracted to Haiti through the usual con-cessions of tax and tariff exemptions on imports used in the production process, an abundant supply of cheap but productive labor, and tax exemptions on profits for five or more years (Dupuy, 1989a:176–177; Delva, 1991:294–295). There was also a division of labor in the assembly industries between foreign (mainly U.S.) and Haitian capital. Foreign capital dominated in the most important sectors, such as electric and electronic products and toys and sporting goods, and Hait-ian capital predominated in the textile and garment sectors. Foreign capital also dominated in the joint ventures with Haitian partners (Delva, 1991:299).

Despite the optimistic predictions of the advocates of export assembly indus-tries as a development strategy, these industries neither resolved the unemploy-ment problem nor continued to expand after 1984. The golden age of the assembly industries was during the 1970s and early 1980s, during which they grew by a spectacular 120 percent in real terms and induced significant growth and activities in both the formal and informal sectors (such as construction, ser-vices, commercial and banking activities, and communal and governmental ser-vices) (Caprio, 1993:278–281). In addition to being completely dependent on the fluctuations in the U.S. market for production, the assembly industries created no viable backward or forward linkages with other productive sectors of the Haitian economy. This was because they imported most of their inputs and because their products did not serve as inputs to Haitian industries (Dupuy, 1989a:178–179).

The assembly industries employed up to 43,000 workers, mostly female, in 1986, but about 39,000 new workers entered the labor market each year (USDOL, 1990:20; Hooper, 1995:132). The choice of women as the preferred employees for the assembly industries was quite deliberate and based on the presumption that women tended to be more passive and more easily disciplined than male workers (Briggs and Kernaghan, 1995:137). The assembly industries had a limited impact on both the overall employment picture and the Haitian economy generally. The enclave nature of that industry and the absence of meaningful backward and forward linkages with other sectors of the Haitian economy prevented the transfer of technology and the creation of the conditions needed for more self-sustained industrialization. For this reason, the assembly industries failed a crucial test of the World Bank's recommendations to developing countries, namely, that they promote industries whose production would have many spillover effects for the domestic economy (World Bank, 1991b:5).

Moreover, the low wages paid to the workers in the assembly industries restricted the demand and consumption capacity of the workers. Consider, for example, the situation in a "model" apparel factory where the highest-paid workers received the equivalent of US$1.48 per day in 1991. After paying for their transportation to and from work and an inadequate breakfast and lunch, they were left with US$.71 per day. This led to a total of US$4.26 (US$.71 times 6 days) per week to cover all the expenses of the worker's family (Briggs and Kernaghan, 1995:138). The assembly industry strategy, assigned to Haiti as the model to follow to generate economic development, was generally considered incapable of performing that role by the World Bank itself as well as by its other defenders in Haiti (DeWind and Kinley, 1988:200; MIDH, 1986:28–29). But if the assembly industries did not prove to be the solution to Haiti's chronic unemployment problems and its underdevelopment and poverty, they certainly made it worthwhile for their investors to locate their businesses in Haiti. Whereas 38 percent of the U.S.- and Haitian-owned electronic assembly plants, for example, reportedly saved between 20 percent and 40 percent over U.S.-based production, 20 percent of those plants saved between 40 percent and 60 percent by doing business in Haiti (Briggs and Kernaghan, 1995:137).

Two factors mitigated the employment picture in the assembly manufacturing sector. The first was the increasingly significant role played by the remittances sent to Haiti by Haitian immigrants, in the United States and Canada especially. These remittances increased from US$15 million in 1970 to US$52 million in

1980 and remained at about that level in 1985. The second factor was the growth of the informal sector since the beginning of the 1970s; Giovanni Caprio has argued that the emergence of that sector was the "combined expression of the agrarian crisis and the negligence of public government." Absorbing mainly a migrant rural labor force and based on all sorts of survival strategies, the informal sector in Port-au-Prince alone employed some 350,000 people, or 60 percent of the city's population (Caprio, 1993:283). A more recent report from the United Nation's Department of Humanitarian Affairs estimated that, for the country as a whole, the informal sector employed around 2 million people in 1988 (UNDHA, 1994:15).

The informal sector encompasses diverse income-earning activities in the rural and urban areas, from small production units of an independent operator to four or five workers. Fass distinguished three categories of workers in this sector: those who sold their labor and performed various services; those who traded (that is, bought goods in one location and sold them in another); and those who engaged in manufacturing (that is, transformed the goods they bought before selling them) (Fass, 1988:72). These activities involved primarily artisans, artists, street vendors, and shopkeepers, as well as workers in restaurants, public transport, beauty parlors, and repair shops, among others (UNDHA, 1994:16). The incomes earned from this sector did not surpass those of the manual laborers employed in the formal sector who received the minimum wage of US$3 per day in 1985 (Fass, 1988:94). The informal sector nonetheless contributed significant revenues to the economy. It was estimated, for example, that the annual value of the goods produced by the roughly 4,900 artisans working in the informal sector (1.4 percent of the total population employed in that sector) was on the order of US$32 million (Caprio, 1993:283–284).

The informal sector faces severe internal limitations and structural constraints that undermine its economic potential. These include: intense competition in localized markets; very simple and poorly adapted equipment and tools; poor qualifications of those employed and poor quality of products and services sold mostly to low-income consumers; no access to credit and very high and usurious interest rates, ranging from 20 to 25 percent monthly; low purchasing power of the consumers of these products and services; absence of adequate occupational training; no guarantee of property rights; and overall harassment of street vendors and merchants by government and other officials (UNDHA, 1994:16). With a more supportive and well-conceived public policy, the informal sector could contribute significantly to the economy, both as a source of employment and income and as a source of goods and services to the population. But as it stood in 1990 (employment and productive contributions of the informal sector notwithstanding), large numbers of people—whether they were employed, underemployed, or unemployed—continued to be poor.

The other recommendations made by the World Bank, the IMF, and the USAID that were not implemented by the Duvalier regime were those that called for: fiscal and management reforms; eliminating price-fixing and subsidies to public sector enterprises; privatizing public sector monopolies, with the exception of the public utilities; ending the protection of the import-substitution industries; and liberalizing trade by removing restrictions and taxes on exports and imports generally.

The Duvalier regime derived its revenues from a variety of excise, export, import, property, and income taxes, as well as from the profits of its public monopolies. The tax system of the regime contained both progressive and regressive features. Some features—such as automobile registration taxes, insurance premiums, passport and exit visa charges, export and import taxes, and electricity and telephone service taxes—affected primarily wealthier urban groups. But taxes on basic items—such as flour, sugar, cooking oil, and cigarettes—had a greater proportional impact on the poorer classes (Fass, 1988:8–10).

Some important changes in the composition of government revenues were notable in terms of the class most directly affected by them. Export taxes (particularly on coffee), for example, represented 24 percent of public revenues in 1980 but decreased to 5 percent in 1985 and to 0 percent in 1988, when all export taxes were eliminated. Import taxes, which accounted for 36 percent of public revenues in 1981, decreased to 22 percent in 1985 and to 20 percent in 1989. Business turnover taxes went from 10 percent of total public revenues in 1983 to 17 percent in 1985 and to 19 percent in 1988. Excise taxes on goods and services increased from 13 percent of public revenues in 1978 to 25 percent in 1982 and to 31 percent in 1988. Income taxes contributed only about 15 percent of the total. The working class paid the bulk of those taxes since the privileged classes—the professionals and the industrial and commercial bourgeoisie—for the most part avoided paying them (Delatour, 1990:14–17). By the time of the overthrow of Jean-Claude Duvalier in 1986, some 40 percent of government revenues came from indirect taxes derived primarily from the wealthy and business classes rather than from property or income taxes.

The public revenues appropriated by the Duvalier regime were not returned to civil society in the form of increased infrastructural investments in the urban or rural sectors; as health, education, employment, technical, and financial services; or as subsidies designed to promote economic growth and the welfare of the general population. Given the prebendary and clientalistic nature of the regime, 40 percent of public revenues went to pay the wages and salaries of some 32,000 public sector employees and functionaries in 1984 (or 40,000 employees if the 8,000 army personnel are added). This represented 65 percent of the budget, in contrast to 28 percent of the public budget devoted to paying the wages of 17,000 employees in 1972 (Fass, 1988:11).

The tens of thousands of employees recruited to work in the various branches and apparatuses of the Duvalierist state bureaucracy—including the military and the *tontons macoutes* militia force (the regime's terror machine, officially known as the Volontaires de la Sécurité Nationale [VSN, Volunteers of National Security])—became integral parts of the extended clientalistic network of the prebendary system. But they did not all benefit to the same degree or share the same power and privilege as the top functionaries of the regime. Like the class structure of civil society, in which 1 percent of the population appropriated more than 50 percent of the national income and 4,000 families had a per capita income of more than US$90,000 (Midy, 1991:83), only a small fraction of the high functionaries of the Duvalierist regime received the largest salaries. Seventy-five percent of the public employees earned less than US$300 per month in 1989, and 15 percent earned between US$300 and US$500 per month. At the other end of the scale, 1.2 percent of the high functionaries earned between US$1,200 and US$2,000 per month, and 0.3 percent earned more than US$2,000 per month. These high functionaries were concentrated in the most powerful ministries of the regime, such as the Foreign Affairs and Interior Ministries (in charge of the security forces) (Delatour, 1990:28–29). It is estimated that Jean-Claude Duvalier, his wife Michèle Bennette, and their closest collaborators siphoned more than US$505 million from the public treasury revenues (Hooper, 1995:125). Yet this tiny fraction, made up of high functionaries and the members of Duvalier's family, encompassed the dominant elements of the Duvalierist state.

The clientalistic system at work in the state and the public sector bureaucracy meant that increases in the number of employees became a means of buying political loyalty to the regime. As the number of public sector employees increased, the regime also had to augment its indirect taxes and raise the prices of the goods and services of the public sector monopolies. Whereas in 1972 the net revenues of the five main public sector enterprises accounted for 5 percent of total public revenues from domestic sources, they represented 22 percent in 1984. This was an increase of 30 percent in real resources to the public sector in 1984 relative to 1972 (Fass, 1988:9–10). Given the absence of any redistributive policies to subsidize the purchasing power of the impoverished majority, the rise in demand for public revenues to pay the salaries of the inflated public sector and the military, support the macoute forces, and enrich the potentates of the regime translated into a contraction of private consumption. In real terms, private consumption declined by 3.3 percent between 1978 and 1980 and by 6 percent between 1980 and 1984. Though there was an increase of 10 percent between 1984 and 1988, the level of private consumption in 1988 was below that of 1980. As Leslie Delatour concluded, given a population increase during this period, that meant "an enormous erosion of the per capita private consumption," a fact that contributed to declining support for the regime among sectors of the middle class (Delatour, 1990:30).

In other poor countries, governments usually subsidize private consumption, and IMF-imposed structural adjustment policies often spark strong popular protests because they result in cutbacks on public spending and subsidies to low-income groups. In Haiti, such adjustment policies would have no direct impact on the poor. This was because the Duvalier regime had no redistributive policies and provided few services to the lower classes. Instead, the impact of adjustment policies would fall on public sector employment and the government payroll. This explains why those who were part of the prebendary state system or hoped to join it would be the ones to oppose such restructuring measures (Delatour, 1990:30). It is possible that in a specific context such as Haiti, some aspects of the adjustment policies advocated by the IMF could acquire a populist character. Understood properly, the absence of redistributive policies in the form of basic social services (e.g., health care, education, or nutrition) for the poorest sectors of the population could form part of the general critique of the prebendary state system and the class interests it serves. Such demands are often linked with popular struggles for a modern and democratic state that could respond to the interests of the dispossessed classes. Historically, as Carlos Vilas argued, the question has not been "whether adjustment policies are inevitable, but whether the social cost of those policies must fall on the poor. Structural adjustment may well be inevitable, but who suffers its consequences is a matter of the class nature of policy decisions" (Vilas, 1992:16). In short, a progressive government could well adopt adjustment policies that protect the interests of the poor and not only those of the propertied classes. As I will show in Chapter 5, Aristide's prime minister, René Préval, proposed a growth-with-equity or basic-needs model of development in an attempt to balance those conflicting class interests.

For its part, the Duvalier government and the state apparatuses it controlled competed with the private sector bourgeoisie for the appropriation of resources and revenues for its own ends rather than to serve the interests of the ruling class in particular and the needs of civil society generally. The principal objective of the prebendary state was to maximize the appropriation of wealth for those who held state power, irrespective of the devastating effect that this may have had on the overall economic development of Haiti or the welfare of the general population. Because of the limited degree of economic development and opportunities in the private sector, control over the state apparatuses represented the only sure avenue of wealth appropriation and social advancement for a sector of the Haitian middle class.

The prebendary practices of the Duvalier regime, then, affected private consumption negatively. Beyond that, they encroached on the interests and investments of the Haitian bourgeoisie by creating new enterprises or taking over others to compete with or undermine private sector enterprises that produced primarily for the local market. The thirty-three public monopolies controlled by the Duvalier regime included those involving with sugar, cooking

oil, cement, flour, milk, herring, codfish, wheat, soap and detergents, and cigarettes, as well as electricity, water, telecommunications, radio and television,
transportation, insurance, banking, and the lottery. As Caprio concluded, one
cannot dismiss a priori the role of the state in the management and control of
public enterprises, provided that this is done efficiently and that the resources
and revenues are used appropriately and productively. Unfortunately, as he
continued,

> such was not the case in Haiti! The state sector enterprises in fact served the inter-
> ests of a privileged stratum, heterogeneous socially but most often close to the hold-
> ers of power. . . . When the State sector is considered in its entirety, [there is] no
> doubt that [it] could have subsisted only with a waste of enormous resources. Polit-
> ical reasons are at the origin of the existence of this sector. In fact, the latter essen-
> tially served to buy the loyalty, more and more fragile to the regime in power, of the
> high functionaries. In this context, the state sector in Haiti is perceived as a con-
> straint on development (Caprio, 1993:282–283).

These antidevelopment practices, combined with an already restricted market
for secure and short-term profitable investment, have resulted in a net decrease
in private sector investment and substantial capital flight since 1981—in other
words, economic stagnation and decline. In real terms, the 1983 level of private
sector investment was 29 percent lower than in 1979, and in 1988, the level was
still 10 percent lower than in 1983. Private sector investment went from 10 percent of the GDP in 1979 to 6 percent in 1988. Rather than investing domesti-
cally, the Haitian bourgeoisie was transferring and investing its savings abroad,
especially in North America. It is estimated that between 1979 and 1989, a sum
of US$300 million, or one-quarter of the cumulative value of private investments
during that period, was transferred abroad. In other words, without the flight of
capital, private sector investment between 1979 and 1989 could have been 25
percent higher than it was (Delatour, 1990:20–22). Consequently, the economy
experienced a net decline of 1.3 percent per year in agricultural production and
2.5 percent per year in industrial production between 1980 and 1985. The official unemployment rate also increased from 22 percent to 30 percent during that
period (World Bank, 1990a:XII).

Even though the prebendary practices of the Duvalier regime had an overall
detrimental effect on the economy, a small but extremely wealthy and powerful
faction of the bourgeoisie benefited handsomely from the regime's practices.
That faction collaborated with the regime, and the dictatorship, in turn, relied
heavily on the support of this dominant segment of the haute bourgeoisie.
However, the regime did not organize the state or pursue its policies in accordance with the interests of that bourgeoisie. The dictatorship had created its
own basis of wealth appropriation, and it monopolized the means of violence;
hence, it could exercise its autonomy from the private sector bourgeoisie.

Nonetheless, the state and the dictatorship defended the general class interests of the private sector bourgeoisie indirectly by reinforcing the property rights, property relations, and repressive class practices that made possible the exploitation of the subordinate classes. The middle-class elements that formed the power bloc controlling the state did not seek to eliminate the overall economic dominance of the private sector bourgeoisie; rather, they wanted to force the mulatto haute bourgeoisie in control of the private sector to accommodate the predominantly black middle class in control of the state. This was the only means by which the latter could share the spoils of the extant economic system (Dupuy, 1989a:164).

The dominant faction of the haute bourgeoisie consisted primarily of a small number of families who enjoyed a monopolistic position in some industries that produced for the local market, as well as in the export-import sector and retail businesses. These families dominated the market in various businesses—cooking oil, poultry, textiles, automobile and truck sales, coffee, sugar, shoes, plastics, detergents, iron and steel, and others. Some among them also had interests in banking, export assembly industries, and business ventures abroad, especially in the Dominican Republic (Ridgeway, 1994a:29–30).

The monopolies controlled by these families were formed not only by the ability of a given individual or firm to forestall market competition but also by obtaining licenses from the government to export, import, or sell certain goods on the national market. Some of these monopolies, such as the coffee exporters' cartel, were formed before the Duvalier regime, but others originated under the Duvaliers. In either case, private sector monopolists had to pay a substantial fee—in effect, a political rent—to the government for the exclusive right to export, import, or distribute particular goods.

Taking the coffee exporters as an example, three firms within the twenty-five-member cartel Association des Exportateurs de Café (ASDEC, Association of Coffee Exporters) controlled 44.1 percent of coffee exports, and another six firms controlled 33.5 percent, for a combined total of 77.6 percent. Those coffee exporters bought their coffee from a network of speculators who, in turn, bought their coffee from the peasant producers. Because they controlled the prices paid to the speculators, the coffee exporters appropriated the largest profit margins; the coffee producers had the smallest margins because of the quasi-monopolistic practices of the speculators (Dupuy, 1989a:182–183, 1989b: 266–267; Girault, 1981:195).

Similarly, in 1985, nineteen families had a nearly exclusive right to import a variety of consumer goods, ranging from household items to certain foods. Some of them had a controlling share of the import of one or two items. A small number of families also had licenses to resell goods produced or imported by the public monopolies. For example, of the 222 individuals who retailed flour produced by the government-owned flour mill, 6 individuals controlled 38 percent of total sales, 9 resold 12 percent, and 17 held 16 percent of the retail sales (Fass,

1988:30). As Fass concluded, "The additive effect of restrictions on export, import, and certain kinds of domestic trade was to create and sustain substantial wealth and power among very few families, perhaps numbering between 100 and 200, and lower but nonetheless important levels of wealth and local power among a few thousand" (Fass, 1988:32).

The Post-Duvalier Regimes and the Neoliberal Model

The USAID and World Bank identified such practices as obstacles to economic growth in Haiti and sought to change them. And with the demise of the Duvalier regime in 1986 came the opportunity to implement the USAID's and the World Bank–IMF's adjustment programs. These reforms were endorsed by the sector of the Haitian business class that formed the Association des Industries d'Haiti (Association of Haitian Industries), and they became the basis for its own socioeconomic program.

The reforms, intended for implementation between 1986 and 1988, dealt with fiscal management and tax reforms, public spending, public enterprises, price-fixing and price controls, curbing corruption and contraband trade, free market competition, and inducements to investments. At the same time that government spending was to be reduced, prices and taxes on basic consumer goods were to be lowered. Income taxes were to be modified, and import taxes were to be replaced with ad valorem taxes. Quantitative restrictions on imports—with the exception of seven items considered basic—were to be eliminated, and the subsidization and protection of domestic industries (including price controls on petroleum) were to be removed to encourage free market prices and competition. Taxes on the export of coffee and other agricultural products were to be gradually lowered or completely eliminated. Two unprofitable industrial public enterprises were to be closed, and many others were to be streamlined.

In addition to these fiscal and commercial reforms, the World Bank and the USAID recommended that the government invest more in infrastructural development—such as transportation networks (e.g., roads and ports), electricity and water supplies, and health and education services—by encouraging the participation of the private sector and NGOs (World Bank, 1990a:10–11, 41–42; Walker and Caprio, 1991:13–17). In short, the World Bank and USAID objectives were to create a state that would limit, as far as possible, its intervention in economic activities and, through its fiscal and public policies, induce and sustain private sector development. The international agencies wanted to create a modern state in Haiti that would respond to the interests of capital and, simultaneously, devise and implement policies that would facilitate the accumulation of capital and open Haiti to foreign trade and competition.

By endorsing those reforms as its own socioeconomic program, the Association des Industries d'Haiti signaled that it was willing to accept the role assigned to it in the international division of labor by the core countries and their regulatory agencies. The accommodationist stance of the entrepreneurs followed the growth during the 1970s and 1980s of the export assembly industries and several hundred industries producing for the local market as well as for export. Though the industrial capitalist faction included both newcomers among the Haitian bourgeoisie and foreigners, it consisted largely of members of the traditional haute bourgeoisie who diversified their wealth from their mercantilist operations to the export manufacturing industries and other businesses. That bourgeoisie, along with foreign investors and foreign governments (namely, the United States) entered into a newly formed "tripartite" alliance with the regimes that succeeded the ouster of Jean-Claude Duvalier.

The realignment of the business class did not mean a widespread redistribution of wealth among a growing Haitian entrepreneurial class. Rather, it expressed the adaptability and versatility of the haute bourgeoisie and the diversification of the wealth concentrated between them and perhaps a few hundred families into new activities dictated by the international division of labor. By making the transition from mercantilists to industrial capitalists and accepting the principle of competition,[3] Fass argued, the "concentration of wealth may therefore have served at least one productive political purpose as well as a productive economic purpose" (Fass, 1988:37). Essentially, the reforms were seen as necessary for the successful implementation of the development strategy based on increasing Haiti's competitiveness in the production of agricultural and manufacturing goods for export. Here again, the objective was to create as many free market conditions as possible by calling on the state to eliminate its protectionist and price control policies for all the agricultural and manufactured goods produced locally.

The USAID and World Bank were aware that institutional and structural obstacles (other than those discussed earlier) impeded growth. This was especially the case in agriculture, where the patterns of landownership, the unequal distribution of land, and the agrarian class relations discouraged technological innovation, soil conservation, and overall increases in agricultural productivity. Based on 1971 figures, the last year a census was taken, the vast majority of landholdings (about 59 percent) had an average size of less than 1 hectare (or 2.47 acres); 32 percent had between 1 and 3 hectares; 5 percent had from 3 to 5 hectares; and 4 percent had more than 5 hectares. The farms with less than 1 hectare covered 21 percent of the farmland, whereas those with more than 5 hectares covered 22 percent of the farmland. The practice of subdividing these small farms resulted in the creation of approximately 1.18 million parcels with an average size of 0.8 hectare. In addition, about 19 percent of the rural population was landless (Dupuy, 1989b:267–268; Anglade, 1982:106–107; World Bank, 1991a:2).

Besides the small size of the average farm or parcel, the problem of land titles and the insecurity of landholdings represented other structural impediments to productivity. Most small peasants who possess farms do not have legal titles for them, and the majority of peasants lease their lands from other smallholders, from medium or large landowners, or from the state. The state owned between 5 and 10 percent of all cultivated farms, and it leased large numbers of its properties to officials for a minimal fee, well below the market price. These officials, in turn, parceled out and subleased these lands to farmers at or above market prices and appropriated the difference as profit. The value of such profits was estimated at between 100 million and 200 million gourdes, or between US$15.4 million and US$30.7 million, per year.[4] This was yet another mechanism of surplus appropriation by the beneficiaries of the prebendary state (World Bank, 1990a:44–45, 1991a:VI).

The absence of legal titles and the nontransferability of the leases discouraged peasant farmers from investing in better techniques of production and environmental protection measures (such as terracing and planting trees and growing perennial rather than annual crops). Both factors limited access to financial credits since the peasants lacked security in landownership and could not use their lands as collateral. The system of property rights was inequitable, and the distribution and subdivision of land among the peasants were unequal. The land tenure system was insecure, the farming methods were intensive, and modern farming techniques and technology were inapplicable to the small farms held by most peasants. At the same time, the state provided no infrastructural, technical, financial, or other services to the rural sector, and the peasants were subjected to various mechanisms of wealth extraction by the state and urban business classes. All these factors combined to cause a further degradation of agricultural production and hence the immiseration of the already impoverished majority of the peasants.

As Anthony Catanese has shown, the preceding factors also contributed to the deforestation of the Haitian countryside, which, in turn, caused soil erosion. These conditions led to further declines in agricultural productivity and thus the standard of living of the peasantry. The peasants' survival strategies compel them to cut trees from their own properties as well as from public lands: With 70 to 80 percent of Haiti's energy coming from wood, cutting trees for fuel (for personal consumption as well as for the local and urban charcoal markets) becomes a source of revenues for peasants to supplement their meager incomes from agriculture. Given that 80 percent of Haiti's topography is mountainous, deforestation, which has now left Haiti with only 2 percent of dense forest cover, causes soil erosion at a rate of about 37 million tons of soil per year, and it has stripped 40 percent of the land area of its productive soil. But with respect to this deforestation of the Haitian countryside, it is important not to confuse cause and effect:

> In considering the mutual relationship of deforestation and poverty, the factor of poverty itself must be appraised as causative. Because of their abject poverty, a sub-

stantial majority of Haitians are unwilling or unable to combat deforestation. Rural people correctly concentrate on immediate cash crops versus long-term prospects of agricultural productivity. They find it difficult, if not impossible, to consider tree farming as a cash crop. Because their needs are immediate, their time horizon is brief. If their needs are not met—now—the outcome will be slow starvation or death for themselves and their families. Reforestation, as a means of reducing deforestation, is not inviting to the majority of rural Haitians or to virtually all the urban poor. The length of time between human hunger and the maturity of a tree crop bears no relation to the facts of poverty (Catanese, 1991:28).

As the productivity per farm decreases, peasants try to farm more land by clearing more ground and cutting more trees for fuel, which then causes still more soil erosion and decreasing productivity. Unable to survive from their farms alone and given the absence of other employment opportunities in the rural areas, many rural inhabitants migrate to the already overcrowded metropolitan center of Port-au-Prince to join the ranks of the unemployed or underemployed there. The more resourceful among them also emigrate—legally or illegally—to seek better opportunities abroad. The net result of all these practices is the continued decline of agriculture and the further impoverishment of the peasantry (Catanese, 1991:12–28).

Under these conditions, Haiti cannot hope to compete on the global market with its agricultural goods. Haitian farmers, for example, could not reorient production toward the "nontraditional agro-exports" (NTAEs) that the international development agencies promoted in Latin America and the Caribbean during the 1980s to lessen dependency on the "traditional agro-exports" (e.g., sugar, coffee, and bananas). These NTAEs consist of a variety of fruits, vegetables, and flowers produced for the North American market. The experience of those countries that have embarked on NTAE production suggests that the primary beneficiaries of these ventures are transnational corporations and large domestic and foreign investors. That is because the production of these crops is a capital-intensive and technology-intensive undertaking that requires heavy initial capital investments and expensive and sophisticated marketing and transportation systems. With a few exceptions in some countries, small and resource-poor farmers, who lacked access to credit, capital, and information, found it difficult to enter and compete in the NTAE markets. And those who succeeded in entering them were eventually forced out of the competition (Thrupp, 1994).

To solve the structural problems and to modernize the agricultural sector, the World Bank recommended (1) that a mechanism to issue formal titles to the landholders be created, and (2) that the state abolish the rent transfer system by selling its lands at real market value to prevent wealthy and politically connected individuals from grabbing land at below-market value (World Bank, 1991a:VI). If these reforms were to be implemented, the World Bank argued, that could create real market relations in land and encourage the peasants and others to invest in agricultural development. It was estimated that these measures, combined with more public investments in irrigation and other technical services, could increase the yields of crops such as rice by as much as 60 percent and sorghum, maize, and beans by 15 percent (World Bank, 1991a:VIII).

Thus, the World Bank was calling for major reforms in the agriculture sector, reforms that would strike at the class interests of the potentates of the prebendary state. In the industrial sector, by contrast, only minimal bureaucratic reforms (along with the provision of better financial and infrastructural services) and the elimination of import-substitution measures were considered necessary to boost industrial production. One of the bank's primary concerns was that Haiti maintain its competitiveness with its Caribbean and Central American neighbors in the export manufacturing sector by relying on its comparative advantage—an abundant supply of low-cost labor. That implied keeping wages low, preventing wage and price inflation by devaluing the Haitian currency, and allowing the rate of exchange with the U.S. dollar to fluctuate with the market and thereby eliminate the parallel currency market and the contraband trade in food and household good imports that hurt domestic producers (World Bank, 1990a:42–44, 1991a:II–IV).[5]

Some of the consequences of the free trade policies adopted since 1986 can be discerned. Whether goods entered the country legally or illegally with the complicity of Haitian military and government officials, the opening of Haitian ports—as well as the border trade with the Dominican Republic—caused the Haitian market to become flooded with a variety of consumer goods, ranging from processed foods to household items, automobiles, and chemical and petroleum products. Haitian rice farmers were particularly hard hit by the importation of so-called Miami rice that sold for less than Haitian rice (DeWind, 1990: 71–72). The deliberate policies of both the U.S. and Haitian governments to increase food imports actually undermined domestic food production for basic crops (such as rice, vegetables, and various cereals) where Haiti has the capacity to be self-sufficient. U.S. food aid programs, such as Food for Work and Food for Peace, made it possible for Haiti to import wheat from the United States at concessionary prices, thereby making it less profitable for Haitian farmers to produce cereals for domestic consumption (Hooper, 1995:129).

As far back as 1982, the USAID recommended that 30 percent of the land being cultivated for domestic food production and consumption should be shifted to the production of export crops. This recommendation was advanced even though agency experts were fully aware that "such a drastic reorientation of agriculture will cause a decline in income and nutritional status, especially for small farmers and peasants, [and that this will cause] a massive displacement of peasant farmers and migration to urban centers" (USAID document cited in Hooper, 1995:138). The World Bank had recommended that Haiti boost domestic food production, but the USAID apparently had a different objective in mind. That was to undermine domestic food self-sufficiency, increase dependency on food imports, encourage food production for export to the United States, and create an abundant supply of cheap labor for the assembly manufacturing sector by drawing from the ranks of displaced rural farmers.

Haitian manufacturers were also negatively affected by the trade liberalization. That was especially true in agroprocessing industries producing sugar, flour, cooking oil, textile goods, and soap. Their sales dropped by 20 to 75 percent, causing massive layoffs. By contrast, the export assembly industries showed signs of recovery during 1987, particularly the garment industry, due largely to an increase in the quota assigned to Haiti by the United States. The political turmoil during that period led to a drop in the production of other assembly manufactured goods, such as machine and electric tools and accessories. But these sectors were also undercut by competition from Jamaica, the Dominican Republic, and Costa Rica, leading the World Bank to conclude that Haiti must take measures to preserve and improve its competitiveness with its Caribbean and Central American neighbors (World Bank, 1990a:18–19).

To improve Haiti's competitiveness, the Haitian government and the Association des Industries d'Haiti, which had recognized the formation of independent trade unions prohibited under the Duvalier regime, resisted the demands of workers in the assembly industries for higher wages. Haitian and foreign firms involved in the assembly sector argued that unless wages were kept low (i.e., at the US$3-a-day minimum set by the Haitian government in 1984), Haiti would lose its competitiveness in relation to other Caribbean producers and therefore would lose contracts and plants that would relocate elsewhere. To curb union activities, the assembly industry sector laid off thousands of workers—some 12,000 in 1986 alone—and fired between 1,000 and 2,500 union leaders and activists. In June 1988, after those measures failed to produce the desired result, the military government abolished one of the main trade unions involved in the assembly industry—but was forced to restore it in the face of massive popular protest (DeWind, 1990:73).

A Critique of the Neoliberal Development Model

There is no doubt that some of the reforms proposed by the World Bank could be included in any progressive program of social change in Haiti. Many of the reforms emphasized public investments in technological, educational, health, financial, and infrastructural services to the rural and urban areas. But the most important recommendations of the World Bank were those that directly attacked the class interests and the practices of the prebendary state and the monopolist faction of the private sector bourgeoisie. They included demands to streamline the bloated public sector, to end subsidies to the inefficient public monopolies, and to combat corruption and halt the practice of appropriating public funds for private ends.

There is also little doubt that the overall free market strategy advocated by the World Bank could benefit consumers generally. But rather than laying the foundation for a less dependent or integrated process of growth with equity, the free market strategy will reinforce Haiti's underdevelopment and dependence on the core countries (primarily the United States) and their regulatory agencies. That is because it will undermine the efforts at agricultural rejuvenation and greater domestic food self-sufficiency without leading to a sustainable process of industrialization. Without the latter, it will be difficult to reduce import dependency, the balance-of-payment deficit, and the public debt. And without increasing revenues, the government will be compelled by the regulatory agencies to adopt fiscal and other adjustment measures that are more stringent and regressive, inevitably resulting in cutbacks in essential services and subsidies to the poor. In other words, the classic IMF adjustment policies that protect the interests of capital at the expense of the poor would have to be put in place. If avoiding the latter outcome is a desired goal, the reforms need to go deeper and in a different direction than those advocated by the World Bank and the USAID.

The greatest indictment against the free market and export-oriented strategy recommended by the USAID and the World Bank is that it has not resulted in the creation of more NICs among the developing countries. Stated bluntly, the World Bank's assumptions about the structure of the capitalist world economy and the workings of the market system are simply wrong. Contrary to the World Bank, IMF, and USAID insistence on a free trade orthodoxy for the peripheral countries, the core countries have maintained many protectionist barriers and increased their restrictions on Third World imports since the late 1970s. This is particularly the case for those products (e.g., textiles, apparel, shoes, and electronics) advocated by the World Bank for the peripheral would-be NICs (Broad and Cavanagh, 1988:83–92).

As Kathy McAfee showed for the Caribbean region in particular, the fastest-growing industries with the greatest potential increases in trade revenues (such as petroleum and petroleum derivatives, clothing and textiles, shoes, and other leather goods) were the ones excluded from CBI duty-free status because they competed with similar goods produced in the United States (McAfee, 1991:38). The increases in the export of those goods eligible for duty-free status under the CBI (such as textiles, sporting goods, pharmaceuticals, electronics, chemicals, and coffee) represented about 11 percent of total Caribbean exports to the United States in 1986. But the gains from these exports were offset by the loss of earnings from the goods that were excluded from duty-free exemptions (McAfee, 1991:40). Thus, as McAfee concluded, the governments of the core countries adopted protectionist policies (such as import quotas, tariff barriers, reciprocal trade agreements, agricultural subsidies, price supports, and investment insurance) to strengthen their own economies and foreign trade while insisting that the Caribbean and other Southern countries eliminate all such protectionist measures for the economies of the South (McAfee, 1991:168).

For Haiti and the Caribbean region as a whole, the adoption of free trade policies had several negative consequences. First, the primary beneficiaries of the CBI have been U.S. firms, whose total sales to the Caribbean increased from US$4.9 billion in 1986 to US$8.3 billion in 1989. At the same time, imports to the United States from CBI countries fell from US$8.5 billion in 1983 to US$6.6 billion in 1989 (McAfee, 1991:42). By 1991, exports from the CBI countries to the United States amounted to just US$8.4 billion, which did not surpass the 1983–1984 level (Dietz and Pantojas-Garcia, 1994:28).

Second, the export-led strategy for the Caribbean emphasizes bilateral trade relations with the United States. This has the effect of duplicating production and encouraging intraisland competition to attract the offshore industries by offering the best package—that is, the greatest concessions in terms of tariff exemptions, profit repatriation, and labor costs. Consequently, the efforts at greater regional economic and political integration and cooperation are undercut, as are the regional institutions designed to promote them, such as the Caribbean Common Market (CARICOM), the Caribbean Development Bank (CDB), and the Organization of Eastern Caribbean States (OECS).

Third, the consequences of overemphasizing assembly production for export are already known: They do not create the conditions for integrated development because of the absence of backward and forward linkages between the export sector and other domestic sectors. The growth of an indigenous infrastructure and an agro-industrial base is not promoted, and no honeycomb of business relationships—which could allow firms to produce a higher proportion of the value-added locally—is created (Mandle, 1989:251–252).

Fourth, the export strategy is vulnerable to the fluctuations of the U.S. market since it is the demand generated in the United States that primarily determines the level of production and trade between the region and the United States.

Fifth, free trade and privatization mean opening the Caribbean economies to more imports from the United States, thereby further undermining local Caribbean manufacturers that cannot compete with either the lower-priced U.S. goods or the higher-cost luxury goods for the privileged classes.

Sixth, encouraging foreign investment and export processing or free trade zones threatens the democratic process since labor demands for improved working conditions and higher wages would have to be curbed to maintain country-by-country competitiveness. That means that popular participation in decision-making and the development of mass and professional organizations to promote the interests of peasants, women, and workers would be further weakened or discouraged. Simultaneously, the dominance of the local state and private bourgeoisies allied with the foreign interests would be strengthened (A. Martin, 1985:18–29; C. Thomas, 1988:336–338; Mandle, 1989:251–252; McAfee, 1991:38–40; Dietz and Pantojas-Garcia, 1994:27–32).

For all these reasons, it is clear that the free trade and export-led development strategy advocated by the World Bank and the USAID will not promote sustainable or integrated growth with equity in Haiti or the Caribbean region. Rather, it will reinforce underdevelopment, poverty, and dependency by making the member states mere appendages of the U.S. economy. The recommendations of the international development agencies notwithstanding, the state must play a more active and interventionist role in the development process if Haiti is to overcome its grinding poverty and travel down the long road to economic recovery. This requires devising a development strategy that targets those sectors of the population and of the economy that are most vulnerable, yet crucial, for integrated development.

Political stability, legal and judicial reforms, and a democratic government that can reverse the historical pattern of serving the interests of those who hold state power and the wealthy few at the expense of the majority are necessary preconditions for this process of reconstruction and development. There is also an urgent need for a general economic policy that prioritizes the rural sector and aims at increasing the overall productivity of the poor peasants and reducing income inequality. This can be accomplished by redistributing resources and incomes to the rural areas; promoting land reform and development programs that encourage investments in agriculture, soil conservation, and reforestation; and arresting migration from the rural areas to the urban centers (and abroad). For this to occur, priority must be given to increasing the production of crops for the domestic market and thereby reducing Haiti's growing dependency on food imports (Catanese, 1991:34–35).[6]

Kari Polanyi-Levitt reached the conclusion that Haiti could increase its food production and significantly reduce its dependency on food imports in a report written for the World Bank on Haiti's national income estimates. The World Bank suppressed that report because it found that the international aid agencies had underestimated both the value of agricultural production and the total GNP of Haiti by about 50 and 20 percent, respectively. The report is worth quoting at length:

> In the course of our research in Haiti, it became evident that the aid agencies—and most specifically USAID, which has the only comprehensive collection of economic and statistical documentation in the country—are able to prove that every type of cereal, including rice and maize, can be imported more cheaply than it can be produced domestically. Hence, these agencies pursue and support programmes which involve the substitution of domestic foodstuffs by imports, including food aid.
>
> The availability of food aid and the thrust toward the liberalisation of external trade presents a major problem. Why? Because such policies threaten and destroy the rural economy and the independence of the peasantry. They may serve to reduce the cost of living in Port-au-Prince, and keep down money wages in the assembly industry, but they will inevitably result in the impoverishment of the rural population, and in increasing the gap in income and power between the elites and the rest of the population. The exposure of domestic food production to competition from subsidized imports would, in our view, destroy the most valuable asset of the coun-

try, which is the culture of independence, initiative, dignity and co-operation of its working people. Decades of economic development have proven that it is not poverty but dependence which has destroyed the capacity of societies to provide an improving standard of living for the masses of the population (Polanyi-Levitt, 1991).

To reverse these conditions, a strategy of agricultural development that promotes food and agro-industrial production for the domestic market and reduces dependency on food aid and food imports must be given priority. This strategy could be pursued along with continued reliance on the export assembly industries and the rejuvenation of the tourist industry as ways to earn the much needed foreign exchange. A progressive taxation policy, combined with measures to raise the real wages of the working population, could also be devised. These could include subsidizing food consumption and housing costs and construction and providing essential services, such as clean water, health, basic education, and technical training. The policy could also: promote a jobs program through investments in infrastructural projects in the urban and rural areas; extend technical and financial assistance to the informal sector; and create small- and medium-size labor-intensive agro-industrial and artisanal enterprises, some of which could be export oriented.

The strategy outlined here includes many of the recommendations of the international development and aid agencies, but it differs from them in significant respects. It calls for a more interventionist state that prioritizes the needs of the majority of the population above stimulating the growth of the private sector, as advocated by the antistatist "market-friendly" approach.

Notes

1. Several recent analysts challenged the World Bank's claim that the successes of the HPAEs vindicate the free market approach to development. They argued that the reasons lie in the role of the state in the following arenas: comprehensive land reform; basic universal education; granting subsidies or low-interest loans to, and protecting selected industries with high growth potential from, foreign imports; restricting foreign investment to better control and direct economic development; and encouraging competition through high labor productivity rather than low wages (Fishlow et. al., 1994; Judis, 1994; McGuire, 1995). As McGuire concluded, "The development success of the East Asian NICs does owe something to good macroeconomic management. However, it provides not the slightest evidence for the central claim of the free-market approach: that the smaller the state's role in the economy and the more open the economy to the world market forces, the faster the rate of economic growth and (through a rise in overall affluence) the faster the rate of poverty reduction" (McGuire, 1995:207).

2. I know from private conversations with the president of one of the business associations that only one out of sixteen representative associations did not endorse the "White Paper" of the private sector. The associations of the business class had put forward their program in a "White Paper" written by the Association Professionelle des Banques (APB, the Bankers' Professional Association), entitled *Le livre blanc du secteur privé*

national: Propositions de politique économique (The White Paper of the National Private Sector: Economic Policy Proposals) (APB, 1991). Leslie Delatour, a former economist with the World Bank who served as minister of finance under the first military government formed after Jean-Claude Duvalier's ouster, also reflects the views of the business class (Delatour, 1990).

3. Given the extreme levels of wealth concentration in Haiti, it is unlikely that the passage to a free trade regime would weaken significantly the controlling position of the haute bourgeoisie discussed earlier.

4. These values were based on a rate of exchange of 7 gourdes to US$1 (July 1991). From 1919 to 1991, the rate of exchange was officially fixed at 5 gourdes to US$1. When the Aristide government took office in February 1991, it allowed the exchange rate to fluctuate with the market rate for dollars in Haiti. The subsequent military-backed de facto governments that succeeded Aristide in September 1991 continued the practice of floating the gourde, as did the new government formed by Prime Minister Smarck Michel after the restoration of Aristide to the presidency in September 1994.

5. There is no doubt that contraband trade undermines domestic producers while enriching those involved in it and that the protectionist and tariff policies of the government encourage this. Walker and Caprio contended that the growing contraband trade, whose value was estimated at US$300 million per year (about 50 percent of total imports), generated boomlike conditions in the provinces, where it has been the primary source of their recent growth. They concluded that without the reduction in tariffs and value-added taxes and other fees, it will be difficult to discourage contraband trade, even with a "stable and credible government." This is because such activities currently "provide lucrative opportunities for importers and local military and customs officials to transfer potential state revenue into illicit profits" (Walker and Caprio, 1991:15).

6. It is conceivable that with the proper structural reforms and government support to provide peasants access to credits, adequate technology, market information, and the formation of cooperatives among small- and medium-size farms, Haitian farmers could enter and compete in the NTAE markets, particularly for those fruits and vegetables for which Haiti's climate and soil are particularly well suited.

3

THE STRUGGLE FOR A
DEMOCRATIC ALTERNATIVE: 1986–1990

The Fall of Jean-Claude Duvalier
and the Rise of Neo-Duvalierism

From the fall of the hereditary Duvalier regime in February 1986 until March 1990, Haiti experienced an unparalleled political crisis marked by the rise and fall of four military-dominated governments and an unrelenting popular struggle for a democratic alternative. Complex struggles during that period lay at the root of the general crisis and paralysis of the country. On the one hand, the Duvalierist forces attempted to retain and consolidate their control over the state apparatuses and the government. On the other hand, the broad-based popular movement fought to create a strong civil society and a democratic government that would give priority to the multiple needs and aspirations of the impoverished majority for a just, egalitarian, and participatory social order. The hegemony of the United States overdetermined the struggles of the opposite camps and must be considered among the forces operating within Haiti.

Two tendencies were evident within the forces favoring democratic change. On one side were certain sectors of the Haitian bourgeoisie and the professional and managerial middle classes who had broken with the Duvalier dictatorship but feared the masses. Sensing the winds of change and believing that they stood to benefit from the creation of a democratic order, the "enlightened" sectors of the dominant class sought to establish a representative democracy to legitimate the rule of the bourgeoisie and preserve its privileges. On the other side were the many social groups and forces representing a broad cross-section of a reemergent civil society, including professional and political organizations, workers' associations and trade unions, women's groups, religious and lay community organizations, neighborhood committees, and peasant associations. This broad array of social forces represented various interests that ranged from peasant demands for land redistribution to workers' demands for union rights and higher wages. Theirs was a call for social justice, jobs, human rights, and equality. Though decentralized organizationally and ideologically divergent, these forces symbolized the broad popular movement for a more inclusive and participatory democracy; they sought to transform an exclusionary social system dominated by a small, wealthy elite and a rapacious and tyrannical dictatorship.

Those who wanted to preserve the status quo of the previous thirty years opposed both expressions of the democratic movement. Most of these individuals were from the social groups that had had total control of the military, the state, and the public sector enterprises and bureaucracy—that is, the prebendary state system. And for them, total control was essential to safeguarding the power and privileges they had acquired during the thirty-year Duvalier dictatorship. They constituted the neo-Duvalierists who fought to perpetuate Duvalierism without the Duvaliers, and they included both hard-core and more moderate factions of the ancien régime. Allied to the neo-Duvalierist forces was the tiny—but wealthy and powerful—sector of the haute bourgeoisie that benefited from the dictatorial regime and opposed any change that would threaten its class privileges.

By 1980, it had become clear that the so-called economic revolution of President-for-Life Jean-Claude Duvalier—which had followed the so-called political revolution of his father and which was redefined as "Duvalierism reconsidered, corrected, and broadened" to form an alliance with the traditional (predominantly mulatto) bourgeoisie and foreign capital—had failed to deliver on its promises (Chamberlain, 1987:17). Despite large amounts of foreign aid and the creation of an export-manufacturing enclave, the economy was in shambles. The primary beneficiaries of the regime's policies were the Duvalier family; the top government and military officials; foreign investors; the Haitian industrial and commercial bourgeoisie; the clientalistic professional, technocratic, and administrative bureaucratic cadres; and the larger base of the tontons macoutes. For the vast majority of the population, the three decades of Duvalierism had meant political repression and abject poverty.

Within this context, an opposition mass movement emerged during the 1970s, especially after the aborted political opening of 1978–1979 and the renewed waves of repression in 1980. This movement signaled that the Duvalier regime no longer monopolized the political discourse and that the opposition was beginning to reflect aloud about the country's problems and their solutions (Moïse, 1980, 1990:2, 423; Moïse and Olivier, 1992:70–72). This movement drew particular significance from the fact that it was the first major wave of political opposition since the United States occupation of Haiti (1915–1934) to emerge in the provinces before it spread to the capital city of Port-au-Prince (Nicholls, 1986:1243). The domestic opposition movement, backed by the Haitian community living abroad and encouraged by President Jimmy Carter's human rights foreign policy (1976–1980), compelled the regime of Jean-Claude Duvalier to contemplate democratic reforms. The dictatorship knew that it could not survive a free and open democratic contest for power, however, and that it could retain power only through force and by monopolizing the political space. In the dual tendency of liberalization and repression that marked the 1970s and 1980s, the latter prevailed and proved once and for all that the dictatorship could not be reformed and could not move beyond the economic, social, and political impasse it had reached (Moïse and Olivier, 1992:67–69, 85).

Once the popular movement gathered momentum in the 1980s, the Duvalier regime, which at one time had seemed so powerful and unshakable, crumbled more quickly than expected. The regime certainly had at its disposal the military means to suppress the protest movement, but the historical conjuncture of 1986 was such that the regime could no longer revert to that means. For its part, the domestic and external opposition movement, though primarily nonviolent, had gained much momentum and legitimacy. It had become a force to be reckoned with, and it gradually succeeded in eroding the alliance between the bourgeoisie, the Catholic Church, foreign capital, and the U.S. government that had support-ed the Duvalier regime.

The alliance between the regime of Jean-Claude Duvalier and the traditional bourgeoisie meant that the regime had to abandon the strident black nationalist discourse that had solidified the dictatorship of François "Papa Doc" Duvalier in the black nationalist faction of the middle class. Thus, Jean-Claude Duvalier's regime undermined its own base of support within the black middle class, giving rise to divisions between the old and the new guards. This loss of support from the black middle class also meant that the old methods of repression used by Jean-Claude's father and justified by the black nationalist crusade against the "mulatto threat" could no longer be applied effectively. Equally as important, Jean-Claude began to lose support within the ranks of the Duvalierist military officer corps, and reported threats of a coup d'état further weakened the regime (Dupuy, 1989a:155–168; Ferguson, 1987:143).

Though the regime of Jean-Claude Duvalier had served the interests of the bourgeoisie primarily by suppressing the labor and peasant movements, the growing illegitimacy of the dictatorship compelled the bourgeoisie to distance itself from the regime. The bourgeoisie and the private sector professional and managerial classes received encouragement from the mounting criticisms direct-ed at the regime by the Catholic Church's hierarchy. Indeed, the openly political role of the church after the crackdown of 1980 weakened the regime because the church had considerable influence among all sectors of the population. Pope John Paul II himself sanctioned the church's opposition to the Duvalier regime during his visit to Haiti in 1983 by denouncing the regime's violence and declaring that "things must change in Haiti" (cited in Wilentz, 1989:118).

The Catholic Church openly contested the Duvalier regime and held it accountable for its corruption and repression of dissidents. This paved the way for those in the church's most progressive sectors—in particular, the propo-nents of liberation theology and participants in the ecclesiastical base commu-nity movement known in Haiti as the Ti Kominotés Légliz or Ti Légliz (TKL, the Little Church)—to assail the dictatorship (and the entire system of exploitation that it presupposed) and to express their "preferential option for the poor."[1] By siding openly with the oppressed and impoverished population, the church and the Ti Légliz movement played a significant role in furthering the political consciousness and mobilization of the masses (Delince, 1993: 134–136; Midy, 1991:85).

As Franklin Midy showed, the "messages" that emerged from the national congresses organized by the adherents (especially the youths) of the Ti Légliz movement in 1982 and 1986 were national, collective, and democratic. Delegates from all the dioceses of Haiti attended those congresses. Transmitted by radio broadcasts throughout Haiti, the "messages" constituted a direct intervention in the national political discourse. They took a decisive stance against the existing social order in favor of a new democratic society and called on all those who wanted this change to participate in the democratic movement. As Midy put it, these messages served as "*cahiers de doléances* [list of grievances] that said what was denied, [as] manifestos that announced what was desired, [and as] invitations to engagement in favor of radical social change" (Midy, 1991:77).

For its part, the U.S. government faced two alternatives. It could continue to back the discredited Duvalier dictatorship and risk a further radicalization of the opposition and the spread of anti-U.S. sentiment, or it could abandon the regime and hope to prevent another Cuba, Nicaragua, or El Salvador in the region. The United States chose the second alternative, compelled Duvalier to step down, and turned to the military to contain the opposition with the promise of democratic elections (Ferguson, 1987:121, 152; Hooper, 1987:30–31). Michel-Rolph Trouillot best summarized the role of "international interests" in Duvalier's ouster:

> Duvalier's departure and the constitution of the first CNG [Conseil National de Gouvernement, or National Council of Government] [was] a multinational exercise in "crisis management," a calculated break in the democratic path that the Haitian people had embarked upon. We may never learn the details of the negotiations [that led to Duvalier's departure], but negotiations there were. And we need not know these details, or fully investigate ex-US Marine Colonel Oliver North's claim to have brought an end to Haiti's nightmare, to be certain of one crucial fact: Jean-Claude Duvalier was brought down by a high-level coup d'état executed with international connivance (Trouillot, 1990:226).

The international interests played the role they did primarily because the Duvalier regime was beleaguered by an opposition movement, completely isolated, and unable to surmount the impasse it had reached.

The Conseil National de Gouvernement

Formed after Jean-Claude Duvalier's departure, the Conseil National de Gouvernement was the result of a connivance involving the U.S. government, the

Haitian military leaders, and the hierarchy of the Catholic Church.[2] The hope was that the new government would appease both the Duvalierist forces who wanted to retain power and the broad opposition movement demanding an uprooting of Duvalierism. Headed by Lt. Gen. Henri Namphy, the CNG included three other Duvalierist military officers (Colonels Prosper Avril, Williams Régala, and Max Valles) and Alex Cinéas, a civilian and former minister of public works under Duvalier. Two other civilians were included because they had been known for their opposition to Duvalier and because they added credibility to the CNG. They were Gérard Gourgue, a lawyer and president of the Haitian League for Human Rights, and Rosney Desroches, a well-known and respected educator. These last two members had short-lived tenures in office, however. Gourgue resigned after two months to protest the continued killings of demonstrators by the army, and Desroches was removed a year later, along with three other liberal ministers, when the CNG abandoned its reformist facade and moved sharply to the right.

In the interim, the CNG took some measures to appear to be distancing itself from the deposed Duvalier regime. It rescinded the 1983 Constitution that provided for Duvalier's life presidency. It officially dismantled the organization of the tontons macoutes, and it replaced the black-and-red flag, adopted by François Duvalier to symbolize his black nationalism, with the blue-and-red flag created when Haiti became an independent nation in 1804. The CNG dissolved the National Assembly of the Duvalier regime and formed a new thirteen-member ministerial cabinet. The properties belonging to the Duvalier family were nationalized. And the CNG freed political prisoners and allowed political organizations to form and political exiles to return to Haiti. It further pledged to respect human rights and freedom of the press (Dupuy, 1989a:188).

The CNG introduced symbolic and nominal changes, but it did not pursue the uprooting of Duvalierist forces from the military, government agencies, and public enterprises as demanded by the popular opposition movement. This was never its objective. The formal dissolution of the macoute organization meant that the army had reasserted its historically dominant political position, but Duvalierists still dominated the armed forces. The resurgence of the regular army (the FADH) is significant in light of François Duvalier's subordination of the army to his VSN—that is, the tontons macoutes. Duvalier claimed that he "amputated" the army's role as a power broker because it vacillated between "one side or the other according to its own interests." He created the VSN as a force of "dissuasion, ready to defend to the end the stability of the government and the integrity of the nation." For Duvalier, who had equated himself with the nation[3] and linked its well-being with that of the chief executive, the VSN "only had one soul: Duvalier, only knows one Chief: Duvalier, only struggles for one goal: Duvalier in power" (Duvalier, 1969:324).

As Franck Laraque argued, Duvalier "amputated" the army to prevent it from being a power broker as it had been in 1946, 1950, and 1957—when, after consulting with Washington, it would take power and select the next president. By creating the tontons macoutes and subordinating the army to that organization, Duvalier weakened not only the regular army but also the influence of the United States on Haitian politics. This explains why, when Jean-Claude Duvalier assumed the presidency after his father's death in 1971, Washington demanded that he create the special force known as the Léopards in return for substantial economic and military aid. The Léopards, Laraque maintained, gave the army a force that was superior in "quality, mobility, communication, and heavy weapons, to that of the tontons macoutes, who retained their advantage in numbers." As he concluded, the "American government regained control over the Haitian military apparatus by reestablishing contact with army officers among whom the most gifted for suppression and repression [were] trained in the US and Panama" (Laraque, 1982:9).

Namphy's disbandment of the macoute organization, therefore, was simply the culmination of a struggle for supremacy by that faction of the Duvalierist forces that controlled the FADH and had been subordinated under the regime of François Duvalier to the VSN. Though weakened and subordinated, the disbanded macoutes were never disarmed, and many were reincorporated into the regular army. Many of the former (but still armed) macoutes, deprived of their institutionalized means of extortion, engaged in criminal activities that were not curbed or investigated by the police.

Dictatorial regimes in Third World peripheral societies often make use of armed civilian death squads or militias to assassinate their opponents and terrorize and subdue the population without giving these groups official sanction or status. This allows such governments to deny responsibility for the operation of these organizations, thereby avoiding official investigations and permitting the death squads to operate with impunity (C. Thomas, 1984:91). However, this was never the case in Haiti. Unconcerned with their accountability to civil society and unable to legitimate their rule, the successive military-led governments relied on both former macoutes and members of the regular armed forces to pursue a campaign of intimidation, violence, and assassination of political leaders, trade union activists, and organized peasant cooperatives between 1986 and 1990. The army, which had regained some legitimacy among the population for its role in toppling the Duvalier dictatorship by withdrawing its support for the regime at a crucial moment in the mass struggle, had now become completely divorced from the masses, discredited and distrusted by them (Pierre-Charles, 1988:69).

Despite the increasing brutality, human rights abuses, and widespread corruption of officials within the CNG, the United States, Canada, France, and West Germany continued to provide military and economic aid to the Haitian government. The Reagan administration repeatedly maintained to Congress that the CNG was improving its human rights record and was the best guarantor of a future democratization of Haiti (Hooper, 1987:31). The United States and the other Western powers supported the CNG because it followed pro-U.S. and free market policies and maintained "stability," meaning that it contained the opposition and prevented the Left from gaining power. The World Bank was supportive of the CNG because it believed that the appointment of economist and former World Bank official Leslie Delatour as finance minister was an indication that the CNG would implement the USAID–World Bank development plan recommended under Jean-Claude Duvalier.

But the military-dominated CNG did not represent a viable alternative to Duvalier. Instead, it was a continuation of Duvalierism—without the Duvaliers. The regular army, rather than the macoute organization, dominated militarily and politically, and Duvalierist military officers rather than civilian macoute leaders benefited directly from the new arrangements. Yet the same pro-Duvalierist groups continued to hold influential and dominant positions within the various government agencies and public enterprises.

In one important respect, the CNG differed from the defunct Duvalier regime: It tolerated press freedom and political organizing. This change was not caused by the sudden conversion of the military hierarchy to the principles of democracy. Rather, the political conjuncture and the balance of power in the immediate aftermath of the overthrow of the Duvalier regime favored the widespread and better organized opposition movement and compelled the CNG to make certain concessions to the opposition.

The popular opposition that emerged after 1986 differed in several ways from the one that confronted the Duvalier regime before 1986. This broad social movement took many different organizational and political forms. It included several political groupings, professional associations, democratic coalitions and human rights organizations, radicalized community-based religious groups, women's organizations, neighborhood committees and civic action groups, trade unions, peasant cooperatives, and a plethora of newspapers, journals, and radio programs expressing a broad range of views and agendas from the popular opposition movement. The emergence of independent media played a singularly strategic role in the opposition movement.[4] As Midy argued, the independent press, within which radio broadcasts played a prominent role, implanted the idea of independence from the absolute power of the state. It launched the struggle for freedom of information and expression by informing the population of events and issues that the government tried to suppress. By transmitting news, events, and ideas that expressed the grievances, aspirations, and critiques of the powerless and the victims of the dictatorship, the independent press became an engaged press and played a key role in the national struggle for civil society and democracy (Midy, 1991:78–80).

The national scope of the opposition movement reflected a decline in the dominance of the capital city of Port-au-Prince as the hub of political activity. Taken together, the views and struggles waged by the broad and varied opposition movement represented nothing less than a call for the restructuring of Haiti into a democratic, just, and egalitarian society (Soukar, 1987:19; Pierre-Charles,

1988:65; Ferguson, 1987:160). As Gérard Pierre-Charles put it, this popular movement was a "truly democratic revolution that began in the minds and hearts of the people prior to the mass uprisings against the Duvalier regime. It is an ongoing process born from the belly of the system of oppression that has made the Haitian people the most exploited and poorest of the hemisphere" (Pierre-Charles, 1988:65).

The characteristics of this broad and decentralized democratic movement meant that no single political organization or specific individuals emerged as the identifiable leaders. This was the most important virtue of that movement, for without identifiable leaders, the cadres and participants in the movement could not be easily targeted and eliminated. Hence, the movement as a whole could withstand and survive the repression directed against it by the would-be dictatorial governments that succeeded the Duvalier regime. The absence of a centralized organization and an identifiable leadership also meant that, short of a broadly shared consensus against Duvalierism and the neo-Duvalierist dictatorships that emerged after the fall of Jean-Claude Duvalier, the opposition movement did not articulate an alternative vision or a national political platform for a reconstructed Haiti (Moïse and Olivier, 1992:87).

The Challenge of the Democratic Opposition

It is in this context that one can measure the significance of the January 1987 creation of a broad, left-of-center social democratic coalition known as the Komité Nasyonal Kongrès Oganizasyons Démokratik (KONAKOM, National Committee of the Congress of Democratic Organizations). KONAKOM's objective was to create a popular, progressive, and democratic government as an alternative to the discredited dictatorial system that benefited the privileged few (Soukar, 1987:13, 53; Chamberlain, 1987:20). As it became the most active opponent of the CNG and the most articulate proponent of progressive alternatives, the KONAKOM prevented the centrist and right-of-center political leaders and their parties from monopolizing the political discourse.[5] The determined struggles waged by the KONAKOM and the issues that group put on the agenda played a large role in the new constitution that was drafted and approved by an overwhelming majority of voters in the March 1987 referendum. The 1987 Constitution was the most progressive Haiti had ever known. Calling for the creation of a parliamentary democracy, the constitution barred former close collaborators of the Duvalier regime from running for or holding public office for a period of ten years. Going beyond the traditional liberal provisions, the constitution embodied several social democratic principles and articles. It called for a thorough agrarian reform, and it declared that health care, housing, education, food, and social security were fundamental human rights, in addition to those of personal liberty, freedom of thought, and freedom of political association. In yet another significant acknowledgment of the historical exclusion of the majority of

Creole-speaking Haitians, the constitution declared Creole as an official language along with French, the language of the educated and propertied classes.

To deter the consolidation and indefinite prolongation of power by the president of the republic, the constitution counterbalanced the chief executive's power with that of a prime minister chosen from the party with either a plurality or a majority of seats in both houses of the National Assembly (comprised of the Senate and the Chamber of Deputies). The presidential term was set for five years; a former president could run for the same position only after being out of office for at least five years. A system of checks and balances and of power-sharing between the president, the prime minister, and the two houses of parliament was instituted to prevent the executive from monopolizing power. Ministers and secretaries of state were to be chosen jointly by the president and the prime minister, and, once formed, the government had to be approved by the two houses of the National Assembly. The president still had the power to appoint high state functionaries, but often this would have to be done with the approval of the Senate. This was also the case for nominating the commander of the army, the chief of police, and ambassadors, among others (*HO*, 20–27 March 1987; Hurbon, 1987:23; Ferguson, 1987:156; Saint-Gérard, 1988:33–34).

Since it preserved the right of individuals to hold private property, the constitution did not undermine the privileges of the propertied classes, but it did strike at the heart of the Duvalierist system and its traditional means of perpetuating itself in power. As Claude Moïse concluded, the greatest innovations of the 1987 Constitution were that it redistributed power between the three branches, redefined their relationships, and created autonomous institutions and new regional and local assemblies in order to decentralize political power to a certain extent (Moïse, 1990:2, 467). Even though the constitution embodied the principles of a representative democracy, which historically has been compatible with and conducive to the rule of the propertied classes, it opened the door to progressive reforms aimed at achieving a more equitable distribution of resources to the disempowered and impoverished majority. The constitution not only embodied lofty principles in the abstract but also registered the aspirations and the struggles of the heterogeneous forces opposed to the continuation of a dictatorship of any kind. It was a "product of all the conflicts of interests, the sociopolitical demands, and, above all, the relations of forces between the diverse social and political sectors, as well as the points of formal agreement. It [was] a project of popular participation in creating a society with a new kind of relationship between the state and the people—in other words, a democracy" (Pierre-Charles, 1988:71). In this context, the demand for its adoption and implementation was nothing short of revolutionary, and the Duvalierist forces understood it as such.

The progressive forces regrouped around the KONAKOM realized that they could not force the CNG out of office and that a progressive rebellion from within the ranks of the army was not likely. The electoral route, therefore, seemed to offer the best opportunity to oust the Duvalierist forces from the government and the state apparatuses once reform-minded and democratic forces gained control of them. At that point, fifty-seven organizations within the KONAKOM formed the Front National de Concertation (FNC, National United Front) to contest the parliamentary and presidential elections scheduled for November 29, 1987, and nominated Gérard Gourgue, the former CNG minister of justice, as their presidential candidate. Though Gourgue was a moderate and a centrist, the FNC members chose him as their candidate because they believed he could defeat the other two major candidates—Marc Bazin and Louis Déjoie II, who were more right-of-center. Nonetheless, Gourgue's choice as the candidate of the left-of-center FNC was controversial, and it reflected the conflicting tendencies within the organization (Soukar, 1987:16).

Because of these internal conflicts, the FNC never issued a political platform that spelled out its program of government. Though moderate forces had prevailed in the choice of Gourgue, several left-of-center and radical organizations, such as the Bloc Inyon Patriotik (BIP, Patriotic Unity Bloc) and the Komité Inité Démokratik (KID, Democratic Unity Committee), continued to militate within the FNC. Even though the FNC had not declared itself socialist, the fact that it encompassed the BIP and KID sufficed for the Conseil National de Gouvernement and the U.S. State Department to tag it as a leftist-communist front. Consequently, the FNC's candidates for the legislature and the presidency were seen as dangerous and thus had to be prevented from winning. Well before November 1987, it had become clear to many activists and observers of Haitian politics that the CNG would not allow the elections to take place.

A public opinion poll conducted in Port-au-Prince in August 1986 indicated that Gourgue was neither the most popular and well-known candidate nor the candidate most likely to win. To the contrary, Marc Bazin, the right-of-center leader of the Mouvement pour l'Instauration de la Démocratie en Haiti (MIDH, Movement for the Establishment of Democracy in Haiti), was seen as the most well-known presidential candidate in the country and the one most likely to prevail in the elections. He was also thought to be the favorite candidate of the United States and the CNG. Bazin was followed in the opinion poll by presidential candidates Sylvio Claude, a centrist and leader of the Parti Démocrate Chrétien d'Haiti (PDCH, Christian Democratic Party of Haiti), and Hubert de Ronceray, a former Duvalierist and leader of the Parti de la Mobilisation pour le Développement National (PMDN, Mobilization for National Development Party) (Laguerre, 1987:15–18).

These survey findings notwithstanding, the CNG, the military, and the Duvalierist forces in general considered the constitution and the elections scheduled for November 29, 1987, to pose a real threat to their continued political dominance and privileges. The Duvalierists, both within and outside the government and the military, had become socially isolated. The candidates who represented the interests of the bourgeoisie, such as Marc Bazin and Louis Déjoie II, had joined with the candidates representing other social interests and the Left to demand the application of the famous Article 291 of the 1987 Constitution, which barred former close collaborators of the Duvalier regime from seeking office for ten years. All the presidential candidates agreed that the elections should be organized and supervised by the independent Conseil Electoral Permanent (CEP, Permanent Electoral Council). The bourgeoisie as a whole, which had broken with the Duvalier regime, supported free elections because it was confident that one of its own candidates would win. And a win at the polls would allow that class to reassert its political influence, legitimate its dominance, and attract new foreign investments and foreign aid to Haiti. Moreover, the legitimacy gained from the elections would allow the bourgeoisie to contain the more radical fringes of the democratic movement (by force, if necessary) by branding them as extremists and antidemocratic.

For the Duvalierist forces, holding free elections that they could not control and that excluded their candidates represented a major threat to their continued hold on the government and the state apparatuses—and, as noted earlier, that control was the only means they had to "guarantee the continuity of the interests established by the last thirty years of dictatorship." The Duvalierists vowed to wage a civil war if their candidates were prevented from running for office, which they, in fact, were according to the list of eligible candidates published by the CEP on November 2, 1989 (Louverture, 1987:8). By early November 1987, it had become clear that the CNG intended to sabotage the elections scheduled for November 29. In addition to refusing all logistical and other support to the CEP, the CNG allowed soldiers and macoutes to unleash a wave of terror throughout the month. On election day, when the people still defied the threats and turned out to vote en masse, soldiers and macoutes opened fire on them, killing at least twenty-two and wounding another sixty-seven. The CNG immediately canceled the elections and disbanded the independent CEP. General Namphy justified the CNG's actions on the grounds that, if the elections had been held, the CEP would have handed victory to a candidate of the Left, a claim with no basis in fact (Louverture, 1987:8–16; Saint-Gérard, 1988:81–83; Chamberlain, 1988:1). Former U.S. Ambassador to Haiti Brunson McKinley sided with General Namphy when he accused Gourgue of being "at least a Communist front man, if not a Communist himself" and declared that the CEP was "being run by foreign leftists" (cited in Wilentz, 1989:327).[6]

Whoever (other than the military's choice) had won the elections, whether from the bourgeoisie or from the Left, would have been perceived as a threat by Namphy and the Duvalierists and would not have been allowed to assume power. Like both Duvaliers, Namphy understood quite well that dictatorship was the only means to retain power and that only someone who could be controlled by the military could be "elected" president. For its part, the U.S. State Department, which had historically relied on dictatorial regimes to preserve the existing social system and prevent the coming to power of elements potentially inimical to U.S. interests, mildly protested the election-day massacre and continued to defend the

CNG as the best guarantor of democracy in Haiti (*Caribbean Report*, 1988:6). The Reagan administration, always apprehensive about the Left and more partial to dictators in the region, was not willing to force the Haitian military to accept a democratic alternative, and it condoned the military's behavior.

The CNG had achieved its objective. The Duvalierists were kept in power but at great cost. The election-day massacre completely illegitimated the CNG nationally and internationally. The four major presidential candidates—Marc Bazin, Louis Déjoie II, Sylvio Claude, and Gérard Gourgue—joined together to create the Comité d'Entente Démocratique (CED, Democratic Agreement Committee) and condemn the CNG, demand the restoration of the independent CEP, and oppose and abstain from any new elections organized and supervised by the CNG. The U.S. Congress cut off all nonhumanitarian economic and military assistance to the CNG.[7] All other major foreign aid donors and the English-speaking member countries of CARICOM also condemned the CNG, canceled foreign aid to the discredited regime, and called for new free elections as a precondition for the renewal of aid.

The Manigat Presidency

Responding to foreign pressure, the CNG decided to hold new elections on January 17, 1988, but this time under its own appointed electoral council. Chosen by the CNG as its candidate after prodding by the United States and Jamaica, Leslie F. Manigat was elected president on January 17 with less than 10 percent of the electorate voting in what all independent Haitian and foreign observers agreed were fraudulent elections (Chamberlain, 1988:2). As a staunch anticommunist and a member of the International Christian Democratic Party and with connections in other Caribbean countries (notably Venezuela and Jamaica) and the U.S. intelligence and conservative communities, Manigat was seen as the perfect man for the job. As with the elections in Honduras and El Salvador, the United States, still captive to its Cold War mentality, sought elections in Haiti that would bring to power a weak president who would remain subservient to a powerful military. Despite acknowledging that the elections were fraudulent, the U.S. State Department still welcomed Manigat's election as a positive development that would "move Haiti in a democratic direction" (*Haiti Beat*, 1988:11).

Manigat's presidency lasted less than five months after he took office in February 1988. Relations between Manigat and the military soon began to sour. Contrary to expectations, Manigat was unable to deliver on his promise to win the renewal of military and economic assistance and hence some sort of legitimacy from foreign aid donors. In an attempt to increase revenues, he initiated a policy of fighting contraband trade and sought to pursue legal actions against Jean-Claude Duvalier to recoup the hundreds of millions of dollars allegedly stolen by him. Both of these actions threatened vested interests within the armed forces. Moreover, Manigat seemed unable to do anything about those powerful military officers, such as Colonel Jean-Claude Paul, who were allegedly implicated by the U.S. State Department in international drug trafficking.

Thus, in an attempt to remove some top military officers and consolidate his power, Manigat appeared to align himself with the very officers opposed by the U.S. State Department. Reacting to this apparent move against them, the same officers of the former CNG who had chosen him for the presidency backed a coup d'état organized by noncommissioned officers in June 1988. Though the Reagan administration publicly decried the coup, it was the first to recognize the new military government with Gen. Henri Namphy again as its president (Wilentz, 1989:335–336).

The Second Namphy Regime

Namphy, who claimed that Haitians were not yet ready for elections and democracy, declared that his government would rule by decree. He subsequently abolished the 1987 Constitution, which he condemned for having introduced "elements that are foreign to Haiti's history and traditions" (*HO*, 15–22 July 1988; *HM*, 13–19 July 1988). Though he had been accepted by the army as the president of the new military government, deep divisions remained within the higher ranks of the army. Several factions and factions within factions rivaled each other to capture the presidency and control the military establishment, and none of those factions favored turning power over to an elected government. As Amy Wilentz put it, the Haitian army is "a collection of gangs run by individual *gwo nègs* (strongmen)" (Wilentz, 1989:372).

Knowing the precariousness of his support within the military hierarchy, Namphy quickly moved to ally himself with some of the most notorious henchmen of the Duvalier regime—men who were responsible for countless crimes, including the election-day massacre in November 1987. He also reintegrated many former macoutes into the army to increase his base of support among the rank and file (*HM*, 24–30 August 1988; Wilentz, 1989:337–338). To intimidate the democratic opposition movement, Namphy unleashed a campaign of terror against various sectors—especially the progressive peasant organizations struggling for land reform and the radical liberation theology movement led by the influential priest Father Jean-Bertrand Aristide—that had strong roots in the urban working class and in poor communities.

Namphy's actions made it clear that he aimed to consolidate not only his own power but also that of the worst elements of the Duvalier regime. Had he been allowed to succeed, the macoutes would have regained their prominent positions in the army and in the other state agencies as well. This possibility, coupled with the increasing brutality of the second Namphy government, sparked a coup d'état on September 17, 1988. Namphy was forced to leave Haiti, and the noncommissioned officers who led the coup installed Gen. Prosper Avril as Haiti's new president.

The Avril Regime

The coup d'état of September 17 differed from the preceding coups in one major respect, namely, the series of demands issued by a faction of the noncommissioned officers who organized and led it. The demands included salary increases for the lower ranks, low-cost housing for soldiers and their families, cafeterias and medical clinics for army recruits, and medical insurance and retirement pensions for lower-echelon military personnel. These demands revealed the class cleavages existing within the military. Those in the higher ranks of the officer corps were a privileged group, and they exploited members of the lower ranks, who came from the poor and unprivileged working classes. Many among the officer class increased their modest military salaries through corruption within the military establishment. They appropriated part of the military aid funds received from the United States and part of the food rations and furniture allocated to military cafeterias and dormitories for the rank and file, then resold these goods to private merchants. They also forced the rank and file to buy uniforms more often than was necessary (T. Thomas, 1988:17).

The noncommissioned officers did not restrict their demands to redressing grievances within the army. They joined with the popular progressive forces to call for the restoration of the 1987 Constitution, the scheduling of new legislative and presidential elections, respect for human rights, the retirement of all officers who had reached retirement age (meaning all those promoted by François Duvalier), an end to corruption within all branches of government, the removal of the macoutes reintegrated in the army as attachés, the disarming of all remaining paramilitary macoute gangs, the separation of the army from the police, and an end to police brutality (Wilentz, 1989:361). As André Charlier pointed out, it appeared that some sectors of the rank-and-file soldiers finally understood Father Jean-Bertrand Aristide's message that their interests lay with the poor and the working classes, not with the wealthy, high-ranking officers and the bourgeoisie who despised and scorned them (Charlier, 1988:11–12).

In addition to issuing formal demands, the progressive noncommissioned officers and rank-and-file soldiers arrested officers in the capital city and in the provinces. President Avril took advantage of the turmoil within the army to retire fifty-seven top-ranking officers and potential rivals to his power. Seeing an opening provided by the soldiers' rebellion, citizen vigilante groups from working-class and poor neighborhoods unleashed a new effort to uproot the macoutes. All over Port-au-Prince, bands of macoutes (particularly those who had participated in the bloody Sunday massacre at Father Aristide's church at Saint Jean Bosco on September 11, 1988) were hunted down, beaten, and killed. The demand for immediate justice in the capital echoed throughout the provinces, and for a moment, it appeared as if the country was on the verge of another popular uprising (Wilentz, 1989:363; *HM*, 21–27 September/a 1988).

The soldiers' rebellion, however, proved ephemeral. General Avril in effect used the rank and file for his own benefit. By allowing them to get rid of Duvalierist officers and macoutes loyal to his rivals in the officer corps, Avril was in a stronger position to avert possible countercoups and could consolidate his own power. He did this swiftly and quickly. Having removed some of the most powerful Duvalierist officers, Avril then moved against those who helped put him in power. Charging that soldiers were plotting a coup d'état against him for October 15, 1988, Avril arrested fifteen noncommissioned officers, among them one of the leaders of the coup of September 17 that overthrew Namphy and a leader of the faction that had issued the list of progressive demands mentioned earlier. By striking at the progressive and anti-Duvalierist forces among the rank and file and noncommissioned officers, Avril appealed to his right flank among the Duvalierist officers and civilians allied to him; these individuals also opposed the democrats and saw them as their ideological enemies (Wilentz, 1989:379).

Avril, who was once a financial manager for the Duvalier family and a personal aide to the young Jean-Claude Duvalier before he rose to prominence, had no intention of breaking with Duvalierism per se. An astute politician and tactician, Avril had learned much during his long association with François Duvalier. To remain in power, he knew he had to be ready to sacrifice his friends and strike at his enemies or enlist others to do his dirty work for him. He demonstrated this skill very early in his career as president (Wilentz, 1989:379; *HM*, 21–27 September/b 1988).

In addition to his constant vigilance and political maneuvering, Avril, like many of his predecessors, kept himself in power by buying loyalty from others. This took many forms: augmenting the salaries of public employees and the soldiers of the Presidential Guard; misappropriating the profits of the public enterprises; and all kinds of favoritism, such as allowing certain officers and even enlisted men to buy goods from public enterprises or military warehouses at subsidized prices and resell them on the market at substantially higher prices. Another practice consisted of granting certain favorites of the government a share of the goods that Haiti imported, such as rice and sugar, which they could then resell to the merchant houses that offered these goods on the national market. Among the nefarious consequences of these practices was an increase in the deficit of the government budget by US$60 million in just one year (*HM*, 13–19 September 1989, 29 November–5 December 1989). These practices and the spoils they yielded were anathema to those who believed in democratic rule and to proponents of Washington's neoliberal agenda, but the White House and the State Department were not yet ready to abandon Avril for fear of the alternative to him.

The inclusion of Duvalierists, albeit less notorious ones, and non-Duvalierists in his thirteen-member ministerial cabinet also reflected Avril's attempt to placate simultaneously his Duvalierist constituency, some sectors of the bourgeoisie, and the more moderate opposition. Avril also sought to satisfy the undaunted opposition movement (which demanded the scheduling of new legislative and presidential elections) and to win renewed military and economic aid from the U.S. Congress (which insisted on free elections as a precondition for renewing such aid). In November 1988, Avril decreed the formation of an electoral council that would be in charge of drafting an electoral law and organizing and supervising the elections. Contrary to the 1987 Constitution, which required that the members of an independent electoral council be nominated by independent and representative institutions (such as the Catholic and Protestant Churches, the Association of Journalists, and the human rights organizations), the members of the new electoral council were to be nominated by Avril's government and chosen from the nine provinces of Haiti. Such a decision guaranteed that only individuals loyal to Avril would be appointed, destroying the credibility of the council from the start (*HM*, 9–15 November 1988).

When the new Conseil Electoral (CE, Electoral Council) issued its electoral calendar in September 1989, it was not at all surprising to see that it reflected Avril's expressed desire to spread out the elections into three stages, starting with the municipal, followed by the legislative, and ending with the presidential. The process was to begin in April 1990 and end with the presidential elections in November 1990. Having the voting spread out in three stages and at different times would undoubtedly make it easier for Avril to manipulate their outcomes while keeping his promise to hold "free" elections (*HM*, 27 September–3 October 1989).

The Fall of Avril and the Victory of the Opposition

The U.S. Congress refused to renew economic and military aid to the Avril regime because it remained unsatisfied with the general's performance. In addition to demanding the scheduling of new free and fair elections, Congress included many other preconditions, which Avril could not meet, for the renewal of aid. Among the more important were the reinstatement of the 1987 Constitution, respect for human rights, disarming the macoutes, an end to corruption in the public administration, greater cooperation with the United States in the "war on drugs," and acceptance by the military of the preeminence of civilian rule. Congress, at that time, was far ahead of the Reagan White House in its willingness to push for a democratic alternative and raise the cost to the Haitian military for not conforming to its dictates.

The puzzling question is, why were Congress and the members of the congressional Black Caucus who played a key role on the question of aid to Haiti so determined to press their demands with Avril when they had supported the Duvalier regimes and the CNG despite their refusal to hold elections, their deplorable human rights records, and their widespread corruption? The answer could be that having been deceived and embarrassed by Namphy, the U.S. leaders were not willing to fall for Avril's promises and wanted to see concrete and sustained action on his part before resuming U.S. aid.

Two other hypotheses are more plausible. The first has to do with the international conjuncture of 1985–1989—the emergence of glasnost and perestroika in the Soviet Union in 1985 and the momentous "democratic revolutions" in Eastern Europe in 1989 signaled the demise of Soviet communism, the fall of the Soviet bloc, and the end of the Cold War. Closer to home, the Sandinista government in Nicaragua was facing a major economic crisis caused largely by the U.S.-financed Contra war. It was compelled to move considerably to the right economically in 1988 and adopt a stringent structural adjustment program to curb inflation and the rising debt burden by cutting social spending, reducing social services, lowering wages, and increasing unemployment. The Sandinistas were also on the defensive politically and agreed to hold internationally supervised elections in February 1990.

Similarly, in a dramatic rethinking of their strategy after their early 1989 "strategic counteroffensive," leaders of the Farabundo Marti para la Liberación Nacional (FMLN, Farabundo Marti National Liberation Front) in El Salvador decided to seek a negotiated end to the civil war and form a broad, multiclass coalition with the aim of participating in national and presidential elections. This left Cuba as the only socialist government in the region, and U.S. policymakers wanted to isolate the Castro regime as the only nondemocratic government in the hemisphere. The U.S. Congress, therefore, did not want to allow a dictatorship to reestablish itself permanently in Haiti. And it saw free and fair elections as the only way to legitimate governments in the region. The Congress, if not yet the White House and the State Department, began to understand that military dictatorships were no longer needed to assure U.S. hegemony in the hemisphere and that the Cold War containment ideology could no longer serve as an ideological cover for supporting such dictatorships. The premises of Washington's post–Cold War, new world order foreign policy guidelines were beginning to be formulated by the U.S. Congress in shaping policy toward Haiti.

The second hypothesis is that in Haiti, the democratic Left had not yet reorganized itself to face new elections by coming forth with a presidential candidate capable of offering a challenge to the other center-right candidates. If elections were held soon, one of those candidates was likely to win, and there was a good chance that the winner would be Marc Bazin, Washington's favored candidate. Bazin, who had shown his willingness to compromise with the military, would not likely pursue widespread criminal indictments against military officers and might not even challenge the preeminence of the military as an institution in Haitian politics.

Even if the Left won the elections, it would be powerless to implement the social and economic reforms that, when adopted by other progressive governments in the past, had irritated the United States and provoked its covert or overt interventions to undermine or overthrow these regimes. The beginning of the end of the Soviet bloc, the discrediting of socialism as an alternative to capitalism, and the global shift to antistatist and pro–free market policies advocated by the United States and the international regulatory agencies all meant that a left-of-center government in Haiti would have little choice but to come to terms with the rules of the game of international capitalism. It would have nowhere else to turn for support. Even if the Left in Haiti had not yet understood that the principles of self-determination died along with the Cold War, for the U.S. Congress, the United States had nothing to lose and everything to gain by pressing for elections in Haiti. So it decided to distance itself from the Avril regime.

Avril could not meet the demands of the U.S. Congress. Controlling the government, the state apparatuses, the military, and the public bureaucracy was the principal base of power, privilege, and social promotion for the Duvalierists and their middle-class supporters. To allow free elections that would inevitably end in victory for some sector of the democratic opposition—which could then introduce reforms in public administration and the military to curb corruption and disarm the paramilitary macoute bands—was tantamount to class suicide for the neo-Duvalierist forces. And without the neo-Duvalierists, Avril was nothing.

Avril sensed that Congress might be serious about its conditions for the renewal of financial aid and that his government was becoming increasingly isolated from the bourgeoisie, the Catholic Church (which had renewed its criticism of the government's human rights abuses), and the moderate opposition once willing to enter into a dialogue with him. Consequently, he reinforced his ties with the Duvalierist old guard. At the same time, in a move reminiscent of Namphy's tactics to strengthen his own power, Avril talked of defending the nation's sovereignty against foreign interference in the internal affairs of Haiti, an obvious reference to his displeasure with the U.S. Congress's recalcitrance on the aid question. He also hinted that the soldiers of the army might hold a plebiscite to have him remain as president for five years or more. No one, however, took Avril's nationalist pronouncements seriously. His regime, like those of his predecessors, had no legitimacy. As with the previous dictatorships, only force, not rule by popular mandate, could maintain Avril in power. The end of his administration was marked by a renewed wave of random murders, armed robberies, and repression of targeted sectors of the democratic opposition by the military and paramilitary gangs of attachés. These crimes included the arrest, torture, and assassination of leaders of independent trade unions, political organizations, and peasant cooperatives. (*HM,* 20–26 September 1989; *HO,* 15–22 November 1989, 29 November–6 December 1989).

The insecurity created by these practices was designed to spread panic among the population and disarm the opposition. These tactics were similar to the ones adopted by the CNG when it faced an opposition movement determined to struggle for the election of a civilian government as a precondition to a transition to democracy—precisely the situation confronting Avril. The opposition had launched a call for unity against dictatorship, and different organizations formed alliances to consolidate their forces. Twenty-five political organizations, including many of the left-of-center and radical groups, joined together to form the Common Front Against Repression. Marc Bazin's center-right party, the MIDH, formed an alliance with the center-left Parti Nationaliste Progressiste Révolutionnaire Haitien (PANPRA, Progressive Revolutionary Nationalist Haitian Party) led by the socialist Serges Gilles, and the Mouvement National Patriotique—28 Novembre (MNP—28, National Patriotic Movement—28 November) to form the Alliance Nationale pour la Démocratie et le Progrès (ANDP, National Alliance for Democracy and Progress). Six other parties also called for the unconditional departure of the Avril government and the temporary transfer of power to the Cours de Cassation (Haiti's highest court of appeal) in accordance with the constitution (*HM*, 6–12 December 1989; *HO*, 1–8 November 1989, 29 November–6 December 1989).

Avril responded by stepping up his attacks against the opposition between November 1989 and January 1990 in a manner that revealed the true Duvalierist colors of his regime. He also sought unsuccessfully to obtain financial support from Taiwan. Rebuked by all sectors, Avril eased up on his repressive measures and called for a dialogue with the "moderate opposition" but to no avail. Washington and Paris remained silent and indifferent to these moves, with the former insisting on its demand to restore constitutional rights and the electoral process and the latter canceling a planned visit to Haiti by the French minister of cooperation and development. Most sectors of the opposition renewed their call for unity and for Avril's departure, and the ANDP, which was most moderate in its demands and once willing to dialogue with the regime, was steadfast in maintaining its conditions for participation in the elections. These included respecting the constitution, allowing the return of exiled political leaders, modifying the electoral calendar to hold presidential and parliamentary elections simultaneously, and having those elections supervised by the United Nations. More damaging still for Avril was the resignation of his ambassador to Washington, who declared that the regime's recent violations of human rights made free elections and a transition to democracy impossible in Haiti. Similarly, in a sermon delivered on February 14, 1990, the bishop of Jérémie, Msgr. Willy Romélus, declared that elections were impossible under Avril and called for his departure (*HM*, 21–27 February 1990; Maguire, 1991:11–12).

Completely isolated, discredited, and illegitimated, Avril received the famous "phone call" from U.S. Ambassador Alvin Adams,[8] who compelled him to resign as president and leave Haiti on March 12, 1990 (*HM*, 14–20 March 1990).

The Council of State and the December 1990 Elections

The fall of the Avril regime was a major defeat for the neo-Duvalierist forces and a significant victory for the broad democratic opposition and for U.S. diplomacy.

Had the White House and the U.S. State Department decided to oppose Congress vis-à-vis Avril and renew economic and military assistance to his regime, Avril might have weathered the storm of the opposition movement with stepped up repression and consolidated his power. Likewise, had the popular opposition movement not been united against Avril and the preceding regimes and had it not shown its determination to press for a democratic alternative despite the brutality and large-scale repression it suffered at the hands of the successive military governments, the concentration and prolongation of power by the Duvalierist forces after 1986 would have been a fait accompli.

It was not a given that the fall of Avril would lead to the formation of an interim civilian government and the organization of democratic elections under international supervision. Here again, the unity of the opposition movement, at least in terms of its desire for a democratic alternative, allowed it to seize the moment and take advantage of the opening created by Avril's defeat. Moreover, the internecine conflicts within the higher ranks of the army split it in such a way that no military officer dared seize power. The combination of the absence of another military strongman capable of taking power and the momentum of the democratic opposition led to the creation of an innovative transitional power-sharing formula that neutralized the neo-Duvalierists (for a time) and paved the way for the December 1990 elections.

The democratic opposition, temporarily unified under the umbrella of the Assemblée de Concertation (the Unity Assembly), formed a transitional government. The government comprised a provisional president chosen among the Supreme Court justices, a nine-member ministerial cabinet, and a council of state that included representatives of the eleven political parties that formed the Unity Assembly, plus the Komité Tèt Ansanm pou Onè Respè Konstitisyon (Unity Committee to Honor and Respect the Constitution) headed by Father Antoine Adrien. An accord signed on March 4, 1990, between Provisional President Ertha Pascal-Trouillot, a former justice of the Cours de Cassation, and the Council of State made it clear that the latter would exercise overall control and vigilance over the government.

The Council of State was empowered to approve most decisions taken by the provisional government before they could take effect. They included: the nomination of the ministerial cabinet; all decrees issued by the president; all treaties, agreements, and international conventions that were negotiated by the provisional government and that were not binding for the democratically elected government-to-be; and the overall economic and political orientation of the provisional government. Equally as important, the Council of State retained the right to veto presidential decisions and the right to a vote of no confidence against the government (by a two-thirds majority of the members of the Council of State). By contrast, the provisional president did not have the power to dissolve the Council of State (*HM*, 7–13 March 1990).

In actual practice, relations between the president and the Council of State soured as President Pascal-Trouillot tried to usurp the prerogatives of the council and exercise power independently. Contrary to the stipulations of the March 4 accord, Pascal-Trouillot nominated members of her cabinet and heads of state agencies and even issued presidential decrees without consulting the council. The greatest rift between the executive branch and the Council of State occurred over the return to Haiti of some notorious exiled henchmen of the Duvalier regime—namely, Roger Lafontant, former interior minister under Jean-Claude Duvalier (1982–1985) and head of the tontons macoutes, and Gen. Williams Régala. Haitian and international human rights organizations accused Lafontant of supervising the torture of prisoners and persecuting members of the clergy and the press. Régala was accused of complicity in the massacre of voters in the November 1987 elections (French, 1990; Chamberlain, 1990a:7; *HM*, 15–22 August 1990).

Standing behind the principle that the separation of powers prevented the interference of the executive branch with the judicial system, Provisional President Pascal-Trouillot deferred the enforcement of the warrants to the courts. The courts, in turn, passed the responsibility on to the police, who refused to act. Infuriated by this game of passing the buck, the Council of State responded by issuing a deadline for the provisional president to resign if she did not take action against Lafontant and Régala. The intervention of the U.S. ambassador and a split within the Council of State, however, allowed Pascal-Trouillot to survive. Those members of the council who were also presidential hopefuls believed, along with the CEP and the U.S. ambassador, that to force the resignation of Pascal-Trouillot and dissolve her government was a dangerous adventurism that would set back the electoral process. They therefore dissociated themselves from the call for her resignation (Chamberlain, 1990b:7).

For their part, the Duvalierists understood quite well the significance of the Council of State at that point in Haiti's history. It was a product of the popular struggles and an expression of the aspirations of the democratic forces. As such, the council's primary objective was to create the conditions needed for organized elections and the transition to democratic government. To this end, the council intended to be guided by the articles of the 1987 Constitution—including Article 191, which called on the independent Conseil Electoral Permanent to develop electoral laws and organize and supervise elections. This the council did: It reinstated the CEP that Namphy had dissolved in 1987. The president of the CEP declared that the conseil would apply the famous Article 291 of the constitution that barred former close and zealous collaborators of the ancien régime from exercising any public functions for a period of ten years following the adoption of the 1987 Constitution. When this article had been strictly applied in 1987, the Duvalierists responded by massacring voters in the November 1987 elections, and it was anticipated that they would do so again this time around.

Taking the offensive, the neo-Duvalierists attempted to deepen the rift between President Pascal-Trouillot and the Council of State. They revived the "color question" and depicted Pascal-Trouillot as an heiress to Papa Doc Duvalier and the Council of State as the representative of the reactionary mulatto bourgeoisie.[9] Not satisfied with propaganda alone, the neo-Duvalierists also stepped up their violence by attacking the Council of State and assassinating one of its elder members in a failed attempt to kill the council's president (*HM*, 2–8 May 1990; Chamberlain, 1990a:7). The CEP was not to be intimidated, however. The Council of State was encouraged by the U.S. government's willingness to finance many of the election costs and its warnings to the Haitian military high command that it would not tolerate another coup d'état or interference with the electoral process. In early October 1990, the UN and OAS decided to send unarmed observers to supervise and provide security during the voting process, and the CARICOM countries offered support and practical help as well. With such international backing, the CEP finally set the presidential and parliamentary elections for December 16, 1990 (Danroc, 1990:109–111, 306; Chamberlain, 1990b:7).

Notes

1. The concept "preferential option for the poor" will be discussed more fully in the next chapter.

2. The section covering the first CNG to the second Namphy presidency is derived from Dupuy (1989a:185–199).

3. Duvalier's equation of himself with the nation did not stem from any attachment to the notion of democratic representation, however distorted, but rather from an essentialist and racist notion of being the "authentic" representative of the black masses. Duvalier, who claimed to be the heir of President Dumarsais Estimé (who had led the first so-called black nationalist revolution in 1946), formulated his views of Haitian history and politics when he was an active member of the Griots group that emerged within the Indigéniste movement of the 1930s. The Griots argued that there was a specifically African psychology and culture that was biologically determined and that expressed itself in the collective personality of the Haitian population. Accordingly, the solution to Haiti's ills lay in transferring political power to the "authentic" representatives of the black majority and reorganizing the institutions of society to express the African-derived cultural values of the masses (see Dupuy, 1989a:147–148).

4. The term implies independence from government control.

5. It is more accurate to speak of political groupings, rather than political parties, in the context of Haiti. As Delince explained, although the political groupings define themselves as political parties, they do not, in fact, embody the characteristics of conventional political parties. Rather, they are "voluntary association[s] of political activists, constituted at the initiative of an influential leader, with the aim of participating in national politics. . . . [The political grouping] is an *ad hoc* social grouping, which specializes in the accomplishment of a specific and temporary political objective. Generally, it competes, directly or indirectly, in expressing universal franchise. . . . [The] political grouping represents the

basic collective unit of the national political system, the preponderant form of association of the political actors. As much as possible, the ensemble formed by these partisan structures fulfills . . . a fundamental role which presents certain analogies with that of the political party system which functions in democratic regimes" (Delince, 1993:144).

6. The Central Intelligence Agency (CIA) had also been involved in the 1987–1988 elections. In an attempt to undermine the political influence of Aristide, who was not a candidate in those elections, the CIA had a covert plan to channel money to support particular candidates. Even though Congress blocked the plan, the CIA was more than likely already operating in Haiti under a previously approved covert-action program (Mann, 1993).

7. According to a report in the *New York Times*, the CIA trained, financed, and equipped an "intelligence service" within the Haitian military from 1986 to 1991. It was allegedly supposed to fight drug trafficking, but it evolved instead "into an instrument of political terror whose officers at times engaged in drug trafficking." At the same time that Congress had cut off aid to the Haitian military, the CIA provided up to US$1 million a year to the Service d'Intelligence National (SIN, National Intelligence Service) and continued to pay key members of the Haitian military who were involved in the overthrow of President Aristide until shortly after the coup d'état in September 1991 (Weiner, 1993).

8. Ambassador Adams, in fact, went to Avril's residence to tell him to leave Haiti. Be that as it may, the "phone call" (or "visit") from a U.S. ambassador has come to be used as a euphemism in popular Haitian political discourse to mean the decision taken by the White House to oust a particular dictator from power. It represents a tacit acknowledgment among Haitians that real power in Haiti rests with Washington and that nothing of major significance happens in Haiti without the consent of the United States. The long history of U.S. meddling in the internal affairs of Haiti lends credibility to this claim. But the ability of the United States to influence events in Haiti also tends to be taken as a given, ascribing omnipotent powers to the United States and serving as a substitute for critical analyses of concrete situations and changing power relations within and between the two countries.

9. The "color question" refers to the historical conflict between the black nationalist wing of the middle class and the predominantly mulatto bourgeoisie to control the state. For a fuller analysis of this history, see Dupuy 1989a, Trouillot 1990, and Nicholls 1979.

4

The Prophet Armed:
Jean-Bertrand Aristide's
Liberation Theology and Politics

Enter Jean-Bertrand Aristide

The scheduling of elections for December 1990 demonstrated the resolve of the opposition movement and the prodemocratic forces to put an end to dictatorship and build a modern and democratic Haiti. Not everyone in the prochange camp, however, saw the upcoming elections in the same light. For the sectors of the privileged classes who understood the necessity of a democratic government, the elections represented an opportunity for a probourgeois candidate to gain political power and form a legitimate government that could also contain the more sweeping demands for change emanating from the grassroots movement. For the more progressive and left-of-center organizations, the elections represented a major dilemma. Some activists opposed the elections altogether and argued instead for the formation of a coalition government that would reflect the various sectors of the progressive popular movement. Other organizations and activists engaged in a divisive debate about the desirability and possibility of democratic elections, given the continuing violence against the Council of State and the popular democratic forces by uncontrolled sectors of the military and macoute thugs who acted with impunity. While that debate went on, the neo-Duvalierist party, l'Union pour la Réconciliation Nationale (URN, Union for National Reconciliation), put forward its standard-bearer, Roger Lafontant, as its candidate for president.

At that point, Aristide responded to the challenge by declaring himself a candidate for the presidency. He did not withdraw when, as anticipated, the CEP later disqualified Lafontant and several other candidates, including former President Leslie Manigat. Over the years since the overthrow of the Duvalier regime, Aristide had emerged as the single most important symbol of resistance to the ignominious, larcenous, and barbaric neo-Duvalierist dictatorships. His humble origins also set him apart from most other candidates, who were from well-to-do backgrounds, and played a major role in his identification with the impoverished majority and their allegiance to him.

Born in 1953 to a property-owning peasant family of modest means in Port Salut in southern Haiti, Aristide soon moved to Port-au-Prince, where he began his education with the Salesian Brothers at the age of five. Having decided to become a priest very early in his life, he entered the Salesian seminary in Cap Haitien in 1966. After completing his seminary studies at the age of twenty-one, he spent his novitiate in the Dominican Republic and went on to study philosophy, psychology, and theology in Haiti, Canada, Greece, Israel, and Italy. By 1975, long before his ordination in 1982, Aristide had defined his position vis-à-vis the traditional church: The top priority of his pastoral work would be the poor (Aristide, 1990:33–58).

This "preferential option for the poor" is a basic tenet of liberation theology. It implies not only identifying with the poor and their suffering but also and more important the commitment to work alongside them and join them in their struggle for liberation (Boff and Boff, 1990:2–9; Gutiérrez, 1990:12–14). This commitment is grounded "in the social analysis we use, or in human compassion [and] in the final analysis, in the God of our faith. It is a theocentric, prophetic option that has its roots in the unmerited love of God and is demanded by this love" (Gutiérrez, 1990:14).

In this context, Aristide's option for the poor led to the "unfolding of the connecting thread of a theological view which surely brings one back to the one God, that of the excluded, manipulated by the more privileged to maintain an ancestral domination over the poor" (Aristide, 1992a:69). This stance inevitably put Aristide on a collision course with the Catholic Church hierarchy, for it led him to another conclusion, namely, that the Catholic Church in Haiti either compromised with the dictatorships or at least preached acceptance of their regimes. Henceforth, his relationship with the church in Haiti and with the Vatican would be marked by increasing divergence and confrontation. Returning to his homeland in 1985 after nearly six years of study abroad, Aristide found a country "in a state of general mobilization for change" (Aristide, 1992a:66). Already an ardent proponent of liberation theology, he soon emerged as one of the most outspoken leaders of the radicalized ecclesiastical base community movement Ti Légliz.

The fusion of mysticism, martyrdom, and antimacoutism added a messianic character to Aristide's leadership and immediately won him the devotion of a population that—crushed by the abject exploitation of the dominant classes and the violence of the dictatorships and steeped in its own religious mysticism—was ready to accept a savior (Pierrre-Charles, 1991:18; Moïse and Olivier, 1992:147). Through his words and actions, Aristide revealed a charismatic authority. He had developed what A. W. Singham argued was needed by a charismatic leader: a keen understanding of the cultural and social relations that governed the lives of the ordinary people, coupled with the ability to express their grievances in national terms and to exploit his personal relationship with them to build a mass movement (Singham, 1968:148).

As sociologist Max Weber argued, the charismatic hero does not obtain his authority from established orders or official enactments. Rather, it is through actions—by performing "miracles" or heroic deeds—that the charismatic leader proves his powers. The recognition of a charismatic leader by the followers "derives from the surrender of the faithful to the extraordinary and unheard of, to what is alien to all regulation and tradition and therefore viewed as divine." When thus established, this charismatic authority is not subject to formal laws and regulations but derives its "objective laws" from "the highly personal experience of divine grace and god-like heroic strength and rejects all external order solely for the sake of glorifying genuine prophetic and heroic ethos" (Weber, 1978, vol. 2:1114–1115).

A leader acquires and exercises charismatic authority in concrete social contexts and at specific historical moments. As such, charismatic authority is always socially and historically contingent. Aristide developed his charismatic powers in the specific context of the post-Duvalier period, the democratic opening occasioned by the dictator's departure, and the popular movement for a democratic Haiti. That opening made it possible for Aristide to deliver his sermons at Saint Jean Bosco Church and in his radio broadcasts, through which he inspired his followers, gave them hope, explained to them the nature of the system that imprisoned and impoverished them, and galvanized them into action against the Duvalier regime and its military successors. His attacks were not limited to the Duvalierists and the macoute system; they were also directed at the United States (which he referred to as the "cold country to the north"), the Catholic Church hierarchy, and members of the bourgeoisie for their collaboration with the dictatorships and their roles in the exploitation and oppression of the people (Sontag, 1990; Wilentz, 1990:x–xx).

Aristide likened Haiti to a prison, where the rule of the game was that the "prisoners" (i.e., the poor and oppressed) were presumed guilty by virtue of being poor. They had to accept their plight (i.e., their "prison sentence") without protest, without discussing their social conditions with their fellow prisoners, and without organizing to defend their rights and their interests for fear of worse cruelty or death (Aristide, 1990:34).

In Aristide's view, the Duvalierists intended to maintain power at any cost, and to that end, they deployed systematic violence and repression against the population. The Duvalierists sought to preserve power not simply for its own sake but also because it enabled them to plunder the public treasury for their own benefit. The state and the government were run like an organized gang, with the Duvalier family originally at its head. Yet even with the Duvaliers gone (Aristide had likened them to the "king" and "queen" in a chess game), the "bishops," "knights," and "rooks"—meaning the lower officials of the regime— remained to perpetuate the system. The military commanders linked to the system had become a mercenary force. And the lower echelons of the military, particularly the rural police and section chiefs, benefited from the system principally by extortion and by terrorizing the population (Aristide, 1990:26, 1992a:70–71).

The Duvalierists, whom Aristide often simply referred to as the macoutes, formed an alliance with the moneyed and propertied oligarchy and protected its interests. In return, part of the profits of the oligarchy went to finance the macoutes. The Haitian bourgeoisie, which includes the landed and commercial-industrial oligarchy and represents a tiny fraction of the population, is in reality nothing more than a comprador bourgeoisie that mediates between foreign capital and the national economy. Its primary concern is to enrich itself by exploiting the people as much as possible and without regard for their welfare (Aristide, 1990:6–9, 1992a:71, 74–76). The whole system was shored up by the imperialists from the "cold country to the north" through their military and financial aid. In short, the government and the oligarchy were devoid of any meaningful development or social project save that of enriching themselves and maintaining the population in a state of ignorance and misery (Aristide, 1990:7–8, 1992a:71, 76).

Aristide reserved his most detailed and biting criticism for the hierarchy of the Catholic Church. As a liberation theologian and a leader of the TKL movement, he opposed and struggled against the church hierarchy because it colluded with the bourgeoisie and the dictatorships to exploit and oppress the poor and working people. The church leaders also sought to suppress the growth of the TKL movement among the rebelling rank-and-file priests, as well as the work they were doing among the poor (Aristide, 1992a:58–60).

The structure of the church, Aristide maintained, is similar to that of a multinational corporation, such as United Fruit, Gulf & Western, or National City Bank. The pope, as the chief executive officer, presides from the headquarters in Rome over the branch plants—the churches—all over the world. The principal task of the pope qua chief executive officer is to protect the international interests of the corporation and to ensure its efficient operation, uninterrupted growth, and profitability. He also must maintain cohesion and prevent dissension among the shareholders and the managers (the archbishops and the bishops) and the rank-and-file employees (the priests and nuns who execute the orders from above). What sets this multinational corporation apart from all the others (and, in a sense, makes it more powerful) is its possession of a secret weapon that allows it to secure the allegiance and passivity of the final consumers, who are the people. "That weapon is belief, the long-established belief of the people . . . in the word of the Church" (Aristide, 1990:20–21). Aristide continued:

> The man in Rome and his colleagues are able to wrap company policy up in the proud yellow and white [flag] of the Church. They can pronounce and prettify effi-

ciency actions using the beautiful words of the Bible. They can dress up their offi-cers and parade them around the Church as men of God. They can take the policies of United Fruit, Gulf & Western and the National City Bank, all multinational cor-porations like the Church—with the same interests—and package them along with their own policies, and call that package truth (Aristide, 1990:21).

The reactions of the church hierarchy and the dominant classes to Aristide's views further reinforced the bond between him and his followers. As the popu-lar struggles against the post-1986 military rulers intensified and Aristide gained a prominent leadership role in them, the church hierarchy, the conserv-ative sectors of the bourgeoisie, the United States, and the military governments saw him as a dangerous, radical firebrand. The church authorities tried to silence him by transferring him to a parish outside Port-au-Prince. But each time an attempt was made to silence Aristide, his supporters responded by occupying his church at Saint Jean Bosco and the Port-au-Prince Cathedral, forcing the authorities to back down. Failing to achieve their objective with these measures, the Salesians, with the approval of the Vatican, finally expelled Aristide from the order in 1988 for preaching violence and class struggle (Sontag, 1990; Wilentz, 1990:xv). In response to his expulsion, Aristide drew an analogy between him-self and Jesus Christ and said that "it doesn't really matter whether I have a church or an order, after all. Jesus Christ, you'll remember, was not a priest" (cited in Sontag, 1990).

Aristide's defense against the government and the church accusations that he was preaching class struggle and revolution was that, under certain circum-stances, it was legitimate for the people to defend themselves against the brutal-ity and systematic attacks of the powers that be. As Aristide saw it, the condi-tions that existed under the post-Duvalier military governments, which had reacted viciously to the popular movement for social change and democracy, demanded that the people defend themselves. Aristide maintained that it was the privileged classes (including the military rulers and the church hierarchy) who, through their greed, selfishness, indifference, and unwillingness to share wealth and power with the poorer classes, bore responsibility for the "class warfare" they accused him of advocating (Aristide, 1990:15–17).

Turning the argument against his accusers, Aristide offered a simple choice to the privileged classes (i.e., those he referred to as "eat[ing] at the great table"): Either they could avoid class warfare by agreeing to share their wealth and power with the poor or they could accept the alternative. "They must accept the simple fact that it is they, and not I and my colleagues, who are advocating war" (Aris-tide, 1990:17). One image that Aristide often evoked in his discourse was that of the bourgeoisie sitting "at a vast table covered in white damask . . . and eating steaks and pâté and veal flown in from across the water . . . while the rest of my countrymen and countrywomen are crowded under that table, hunched over in the dirt and starving" (Aristide, 1990:9). This situation, he argued, was violent and one day would lead the people under the table to "rise up in righteousness, and knock the table of privilege over, and take what rightfully belongs to them. Brothers and sisters, it is our mission to help them stand up and live as human beings" (Aristide, 1990:9).

Pushing his analysis further and in keeping with the materialist or historico-structural perspective that liberation theology borrowed from Marxism (Boff and Boff, 1990:27–28), Aristide sought to explain the "laws" that governed human communities in the extant relation of forces:

> Life unveils a politics that does not look for the common good but which is based on the relations between exploited and exploiters. The exploiters justify and legalize the exploitation of a majority by a minority. From this human reality whence emerges a negative force, because it does not correspond to the common good and is opposed to justice, there also emerges an opposite force. We thus have the force of politics in which the weak suffers the exploitation of the strong, and the divine force from which the weak rises to reestablish an equilibrium of justice. In other words, theology and politics bring us at the heart of history (Aristide, 1992b:17).

Aristide's view here corresponds to the classic tenets of liberation theology, which locate the primary cause of poverty and oppression in the socioeconomic organization of capitalist society. Within that society, some (the workers) are exploited, and others (the underemployed, unemployed, and other marginalized groups) are excluded from the production process. Due to this exploitation and exclusion, the poor are denied access to adequate food, housing, health care, and education, as well as respect for their personal dignity, self-expression, and freedom (Boff and Boff, 1990:26; Gutiérrez, 1990:8).

At this point, it may be useful to make a distinction between liberation theology and Marxism. For Marx and Engels, the working class was the only class that could emancipate all of human society because its structural location in the relations of production enabled it to abolish its own and all other modes of wealth appropriation. All dominant social classes in history, Marx and Engels argued, sought to consolidate their rule by subjecting the rest of society to their forms of wealth appropriation. They succeeded in becoming ruling classes and subordinating other classes because theirs were either movements of emergent minorities or movements led in the interests of minorities. By contrast, the proletariat, because it was the "lowest stratum" in capitalist society with no other classes below it to exploit, "[could not] stir, [could not] raise itself up, without the whole superincumbent strata of official society being sprung into the air" (Marx and Engels, 1978:482).

As Meiksins Wood also argued, the working class and its struggles remain at the center of the Marxist theory of social change because that theory locates the exploitation and political oppression of the working class in the relations of production characteristic of capitalist society. The Marxist proposition that the working class is potentially the revolutionary class is not a metaphysical abstraction; rather, it stems from the materialist premises of the theory (Meiksins Wood, 1986:14). From this, it also follows that:

> 1) the working class is the social group with the most direct objective interest in bringing about the transition to socialism; 2) the working class, as the direct object of the most fundamental and determinative—though certainly not the only—form of oppression, and the one class whose interests do not rest on the oppression of other classes, can create the conditions for liberating all human beings in the struggle to liberate itself; 3) given the fundamental and ultimately unresolvable opposition between exploiting and exploited classes, *class struggle* must be the principal motor of this emancipatory transformation; and 4) the working class is the one social force that has a strategic social power sufficient to permit its development into a revolutionary force (Meiksins Wood, 1986:14–15, emphasis in original).

Marxism is concerned first and foremost with the creation of a socialist society. The liberation of the working class, by the working class itself, is the necessary (if not sufficient) precondition for the emancipation of other oppressed groups. Only by becoming "masters of the productive forces" (Marx and Engels, 1978:482) can the working class carry out fundamental, structural changes in the social relations of production as well as in the political relations of domination.

Although liberation theology is also concerned with the this-worldly social emancipation of the poor and the oppressed, it remains committed to the spiritual or prophetic aspects of liberation. This is, in fact, its guiding principle. In its more "classist" interpretation, liberation theology borrows heavily from the Marxist tenets and emphasizes the exploitation, oppression, and struggles of the "socio-economically oppressed" over other forms of oppression and discrimination, such as racist, ethnic, or sexual oppression. In the words of Leonardo and Clovis Boff:

> The socio-economically oppressed (the poor) do not simply exist *alongside* other oppressed groups, such as blacks, indigenous peoples, women—to take the three major categories in the Third World. No, the "class oppressed"—the socioeconomically poor—are the infrastructural expression of the process of oppression. The other groups represent "superstructural" expressions of oppression and because of this are deeply conditioned by the infrastructural. . . . This shows why, in a class-divided society, class struggles—which are a fact and an ethical demonstration of the presence of the injustice condemned by God and the church—are the main sort of struggle (Boff and Boff, 1990:29).

Today, being poor has increasingly come to mean standing up and struggling for justice, peace, freedom, and more democratic participation in society, as well as "organizing 'to live their faith in an integral way,' and being committed to the liberation of every human being" (Gutiérrez, 1990:8). Liberation theology is "about liberation of the oppressed—in their totality as persons, body and soul—and in their totality as a class: the poor, the subjected, the discriminated against" (Boff and Boff, 1990:28–29). The "selective affinity" between liberation theology and Marxism reflected in these ideas means that, like the Marxist premise that the workers themselves must be the agents of their own liberation, liberation theology defines the poor not simply as objects of charity or as passive victims of their oppression but also as the active agents of their own liberation (Löwy, 1993:36; Boff and Boff, 1990:25–28).[1]

The selective affinity or compatibility between liberation theology and Marxism does not mean that liberation theologians cease being concerned with their prophetic mission or that they abandon their faith in Jesus Christ or in the Catholic Church's magisterium (see Dussel, 1992; Löwy, 1993). As Boff and Boff put it, because of its materialism and atheism, Marxism "can be a companion on the way, but . . . never *the* guide, because [there is] only one teacher, the Christ" (Boff and Boff, 1990:28, emphasis in original). So, although liberation theology and Marxism may be compatible at some level, they remain at odds in other essential respects.

There are, then, at least two currents within the liberation theology movement. In the first or more "classist" current, liberation theologians like Boff and Boff see the working class as the primary agent in the emancipatory project. In the second or more populist current, proponents like Aristide view the poor, the exploited, the excluded, and the marginalized—not the working class—as the agents of social change. Whereas the "classist" interpretation implies that nothing short of a socialist society organized primarily in the interest of and led by the working class will result in human liberation, the populist interpretation permits compromise. It adopts what could be called an "agnostic" position on the type of alternative social order that could render justice and equality to the poor and the oppressed.

Aristide not only adopted the populist and agnostic version of liberation theology but also tended to emphasize its prophetic side in his writings and sermons. He used it to justify the this-worldliness of the liberation of the oppressed Haitian masses. As he put it:

> The liberating faith allows the believer to be in deep communion with the God who is present, in good as in bad times. . . . God of life, he lives for all. Such is the God of Jesus Christ in whom we believe. This theological dimension certainly sustains a people struggling against corruption with neither economic nor arm power. It is thus fair to believe that the relation of forces . . . manifests itself clearly at the heart of this drama. It is the theological force resisting the political forces which use money and weapons to fight the poor. The God of the Haitian people is called the force of resistance, resistance against the *macoutes* and against all wrongs (Aristide, 1992b:67).

The fact that he advocated social justice and equality for the poor and the oppressed earned him the bitter enmity of the military rulers, the bourgeoisie, and the church hierarchy. These groups were not in the least interested in the subtle theoretical differences between the classist and the populist tendencies within a doctrine that they considered dangerous and threatening to their interests. To them, Aristide was simply a communist and nothing more.

On three occasions, the government of General Namphy tried to assassinate Aristide, but he always escaped unharmed.[2] For Aristide, these failed assassination attempts were a powerful demonstration of the ability of a weak force to vanquish a strong force, and they represented a victory not only for Aristide himself but also for the Haitian people in general (Aristide, 1990:62). Put another way, they represented God's energy manifesting itself in the people. In reference to the assassination incidents, Aristide wrote:

> Thus would God have us walk through the valley of death and find ourselves, our voyage at the end, at the sunlit crossroads of life; so would God have us travel nightmarish highways of rain and gloom and murder only to pull into a carefree village at sunrise in our exhausted car with four tires flat; so would God have us fight for life in the battlefields of blood and entrails, and harvest life from fields of bones and ashes. There in the wasteland when you had not thought to find life, you will suddenly find the signs of God's renewal, blooming and flowering and bursting forth from the dry earth with great energy, God's energy (Aristide, 1990:64).

The Triumph of the Prophet

Aristide emerged stronger than ever from his confrontations with the church and the military, and he earned a reputation as the nemesis of the macoutes and Duvalierism. He came to be seen, in fact, as the icon of antimacoutism. Equally important, by appearing to be undaunted by the assassination attempts, Aristide proved his prophetic quality to his followers: He confronted the forces of evil and emerged victorious. It was understandable, then, that he galvanized the population behind him when he decided to run for president. For them, Aristide, already known through his radical sermons and his pastoral work, was the only one who could stand up to and not compromise with the macoutes and who, guided by the light of God, could rid the country of the Duvalierist scourge that had terrorized and devastated the entire society (Moïse and Olivier, 1992:147).

The decision to run for president represented a major about-face for Aristide. As recently as April 1990, Aristide asserted that he was free of the disease known as "presidentialism"—that is, the "incurable sickness" manifested in the desire to become president of Haiti—that afflicted many Haitian politicians. Up until two weeks before he declared his candidacy, he was stating that the elections, desired by the United States, would solve nothing for the Haitian people. He had remained one of the strongest proponents of "linkage" among the Left opposition leaders, meaning that genuinely democratic elections could not be held until the criminals of the Duvalierist regime had been brought to justice (Aristide, 1992a:136; Hérard, 1990:3).

The entry of Lafontant in the presidential race and his own rethinking of the political conjuncture of September-October 1990 led Aristide to change his mind. He offered three reasons for his decision to run for president. First, he argued that, by insisting on the arrest and trial of Duvalierists accused of crimes and by boycotting the elections until this demand was met, the Left would inadvertently allow one of the "acceptable" and "electable" conservative candidates (supported by moderate Duvalierists like Provisional President Pascal-Trouillot, the privileged bourgeoisie, and imperialists) to win. The United States wanted the elections, and a sector of the bourgeoisie wanted to revive the dictatorship for its own benefit. Aristide believed that, despite her failure to take action, Pascal-Trouillot was more moderate than the hard-core Duvalierists such as Namphy or Avril. And even if Pascal-Trouillot's intentions regarding the elections were unclear, the Council of State and the United States were determined to hold them.

As Aristide saw it, the elections would be held and unless a candidate "from the people" entered the race, the field would be open only to those opposed to changing the status quo. He also realized that because these elections would be supervised by international observers, their outcome—and the winner—would have unprecedented legitimacy. In his words, "Woe betide the non-participants!" (Aristide, 1992a:138). But without a strong candidate from the people who could galvanize and unify the masses, the bourgeoisie could establish a formal democracy that would exclude the lower classes, allow that bourgeoisie to form an alliance with the moderate neo-Duvalierists, and enable it to rule without any vision for a reconstructed Haiti or any commitment to justice and equality. Aristide concluded that, in this way, the "obscure forces, relieved of their mafia components, could dominate anew and perpetuate themselves" in power (Aristide, 1992a:138–141).

The second reason Aristide gave for participating in the elections pertained to the divisions he saw within the prodemocratic and antimacoute camp. Splintered into various factions, the prodemocratic forces would divide the electorate and thus facilitate the victory of the promacoute forces. That is why, in his view, there was a need for a candidate chosen from among the people, an individual who would move forward with the people and in the same direction. "Only one solution imposed itself to us: unity. The unity of all those men and women who had said no to the return of the *macoutes* to power and yes to the democratic transition" (Aristide, 1992b:30).

The third reason stemmed from Aristide's sense of his own role as a political leader and his relationship with the oppressed masses. Even though it had been suggested to him (long before 1990) that he run for president, Aristide maintained that he had always refused because he considered himself a spokesman for the oppressed, a man whose role was to raise their political consciousness (Aristide, 1992a:140). Because the Left parties had not advanced any candidate who could defeat Lafontant and the other Duvalierists or the other candidates, Aristide believed that he had an obligation to the people to declare his candidacy— even though his aversion to the presidency and his sense of himself as an opposition leader pushed him toward saying no. The people, with whom he had formed a close bond long before and who considered him "a shield, [and] a free and disinterested spokesman," would consider it a betrayal if he declined. "My candidacy was akin to a reflex of self-defense," Aristide claimed. "My place at the heart of the popular demands was reassuring. . . . I would accept the responsibility, I would be the candidate of all my known and unknown companions of misery" (Aristide, 1992a:143).

Although Lafontant's candidacy was the precipitating factor in his decision to run, Aristide made it clear that his own candidacy was more of a counterforce to the Duvalierist system as a whole, not to any particular Duvalierist candidate. This is why he decided to stay the course even after Lafontant and Claude Raymond, two of the most hard-core "barons" of Duvalierism, were disqualified by the CEP from running for president.[3] Aristide had a problem with "the system that produces these individuals. Even if Lafontant leaves, we cannot say that we are saved. It is like with Jean-Claude Duvalier. Article 291 is not for Lafontant only, it is to ban all Duvalierists" (*HM*, 31 October–6 November/b 1990).

As a charismatic liberation theologian, Aristide ultimately came to see his candidacy as a messianic mission. "It has often been written that I considered myself more and more as a prophet," Aristide wrote, but "I only had the impression of obeying the word of God and of being the representative of communities which, themselves, were certainly prophetic" (Aristide, 1992a:143). Denying that he was the Messiah and asserting that he owed whatever political vision he possessed to "those who have walked beside me," Aristide nonetheless went on to draw an analogy between Jesus Christ and himself, as he had done on earlier occasions. Unlike others who saw Jesus as a divine being, Aristide viewed him as a fully human being from whom the divine emerged. "He was so human that he was God. . . . That is why I accepted finally to discover, to experiment with the complimentarity between the priest and the president. If the people put forth so much energy for their priest-candidate, it is because they distinguish the human capable of bringing about a new political partition and to advance toward another land of justice, love and respect" (Aristide, 1992a:143–144).

Aristide made the same point in still another way. The historical irruption of the poor onto the political scene, he argued, was actually God rising up in the lives of those individuals. It was a process whereby the [people's] faith in God transformed itself into a lever that lifted a whole people against a whole range of false promises made by the traditional candidates. Having found the crystallization of this God at the center of its own reality, that of the poor fighting for liberty; having discovered the communion of the poor building a whole new world, the people transformed itself into a theophany which was the manifestation of this God. This living God that guides. The God who advises. The God who accompanies. The God who anthropomorphises himself so that the Haitian people can theomorphise themselves (Aristide, 1992b:20).

With this fusion of politics and theology (or of the secular and the sacred), the enlightened people chose the one who simultaneously incarnated the political authority and the power willed by God. Aristide continued:

It is this collective thrust that imposes a political choice. Theology is no longer an ensemble of credos, but a force which pushes toward a better world. One does not recite credos, one lives by this force. Lived in this manner theology goes beyond the singular to articulate the plural. The ensemble of the Haitian people found a voice that expressed the different dimensions of a history, while making of the collective the sign of each. They all wanted to find a candidate who responded to their taste, to their choice. The gaze of all, brothers and sisters, converged in the same direction. . . . The light of God had to be discerned to render unto God what God was due. Reality had to be scrutinized to find in it the concrete gestures expressing this unity to be offered to a unique God. Thus, the people found a candidate to provoke with it the irruption, the manifestation of this divine face reflecting the human reality. On the 18th of October, the chosen candidate understood that he also had to live this theological density by accepting to espouse the collective causes and demands, thereby rejecting his first choice [i.e., turning down the candidacy] (Aristide, 1992b:21).

These lengthy citations from Aristide are necessary to make the point that his decision to become a presidential candidate was not based solely on secular reasons. Primarily, it was based on his conviction that it was his theological duty to accept that role. Aristide, in other words, could have chosen to remain true to his earlier stated position and not run for office, instead throwing his support behind another candidate. Or had he decided to enter the race to counter the threat posed by Lafontant, he could have withdrawn after the latter was disqualified. However, Aristide justified his decision to stay in the race even after Lafontant's disqualification on the grounds that his opposition was to the Duvalierist system as such, not only to some of its ardent adherents.

It does not follow, however, that only by running for president could he successfully challenge that system and cause its demise. It could be argued, in fact, that given his stature as a clergyman and a popular and charismatic leader revered by the masses, Aristide could have played a far more constructive role in the struggle for change by exposing the crimes and the brutality of the regime or by mobilizing the masses to press the regime to make more concessions to the prodemocracy forces. An opposition leader can adopt uncompromising stances precisely because he or she does not have the responsibility to govern and, especially in a democratic order, be held accountable (ultimately to and by the voters) for his or her decisions and actions. By contrast, an elected president must make compromises with opponents to neutralize their opposition, win their support, and govern effectively. Occupying public office would necessarily place constraints on Aristide's actions; he would have to accommodate the very social forces that controlled the social system he and his movement sought to change, in order to prevent them from undermining or even toppling his government. Aristide said many times that he rejected the idea of running for president because he considered his role to be a formative one, raising the people's political consciousness and struggling beside them to achieve their liberation. Did he also reflect on the implications of his candidacy along the lines suggested here? Or did he believe that as president he could govern without compromising his beliefs and goals and coming to terms with very obstinate and predictably hostile opponents?

The only viable explanation for Aristide's decision to run for president is that he really believed he had a theological responsibility to do so and that this belief led him to put aside potentially restraining arguments. To understand this point, it may be necessary to return to the meaning of the phrase "option for the poor," which lies at the root of liberation theology. As Gustavo Gutiérrez explained it, the commitment to the liberation of the poor is not an "option" in the sense that an adherent of liberation theology is free to make or not make this commitment. Rather, it is the sine qua non of liberation theology, for its ultimate objective is to achieve "salvation in Christ in terms of liberation." The praxis of liberation theology is one of "solidarity in the interest of liberation and is inspired by the gospel." This is what allows liberation theology to remain faithful "to the message of the God who acts in history to save a people by liberating it from every kind of servitude." Liberation theology implies three kinds or levels of liberation: liberation from conditions of oppression and marginalization "that force many to live contrary to God's will for their life"; personal transformation that allows one to "live with profound inner freedom in the face of every kind of servitude"; and "liberation from sin, which attacks the deepest root of all servitude; for sin is the breaking of friendship with God and with other human beings" (Gutiérrez, 1990:12–13, 16, 24–25).

It is precisely his adherence to these principles that led Aristide to claim that

> we had said many times for many years, notably since 1985, that we were not a candidate [for political office], but that we were ready to respond to the people's will and thus to the will of God. Walking with the people and in communion with it, our faith, on the 18th of October, transformed itself into a political choice fed at the source of a theological life. . . . Son of the people, united with the people,

with the people during the past five years, we refused to take part in the activities of the political parties as far as being a member of political parties or a supporter of a political leader. But, having gotten to the 18th of October, a choice had to be made to remain faithful to its [the people's] theological and political choices (Aristide, 1992b:22).

By invoking the will of the people as an expression of the will of God—the poor as the "elect" of God who will save those who listen—and citing that as the underlying justification for his candidacy, Aristide gave his decision to run the air of inevitability and, indeed, of obligation. This justification becomes all the more significant in light of the fact that before he declared his candidacy on October 18, there had been no known organized voices among the people that called for Aristide to run for president. In fact, two of the base organizations from Aristide's parish of Saint Jean Bosco—Solidarité ant Jèn (SAJ, Solidarity Among Youths) and the Konbit Véyé Yo (Vigilance Committee)—joined with others like Tèt Kole pou Yon Mouvman ti-Peyizan (Solidarity with the Small Peasant Movement) to criticize publicly Aristide's decision to participate in the elections (*HM*, 31 October–6 November/b 1990).[4] Aristide seemed to have been aware of this problem. He stated that, though the voices calling for his candidacy over the radio airwaves were few, those that reached his heart and ears directly but silently were much more numerous. He continued:

The more we tried to touch the roots of this depth, the more we found ourselves at the heart of a collective soul, that of a people which expresses itself in gestures, in words, but equally in eloquent silences. One must know this people to understand it. One must know its psychology to touch the conscious and unconscious mechanisms which underlay its silently eloquent discourse (Aristide, 1992b:25).

Aristide, in fact, did not need to point to a groundswell of support for his candidacy to justify his decision to enter the presidential race. Since he claimed that he was doing so because he believed that was what the people wanted, he only had to explain why such a demand was not expressed publicly and massively before October 18, 1990. And the only explanation he had was rooted in the mystical and theological argument. Recourse to this type of argument, however, is dangerous and open to demagogy: Any leader can claim to be in touch with and understand the "soul" of a people and to "hear its silent discourse" and thereby justify any number of acts without having to account to anyone or follow democratic principles and practices. Indeed, succumbing to the temptation to "go it alone" with the people behind him would later prove disastrous for Aristide the politician and president.

Aristide substantiated his claim to be the people's choice by offering this proof: Soon after he agreed to become a candidate, voter registration increased from 35 percent to 90 percent in the space of a few hours. (Actually, the surge in voter registration did not happen as quickly as Aristide claims, but an estimated 92 percent of the 3.2 million eligible voters ultimately did register, and there is no doubt that this was caused by Aristide entering the race for the presidency [Chamberlain, 1990a:5].) Another expression of his popularity could be seen in the throngs that attended his campaign rallies throughout the country. Aristide, in short, gambled on his popularity, and he won incontestably. For him, this was yet another demonstration of God's work: "The hand of God was not hidden that day. . . . Guided by him and in communion with him, our theological reality was able to project the choice of the people and of a man. Choice of a man, choice of his people; choice of the people, choice of its man. People of God, man of God, together they only obeyed their God, by rendering unto him what was due him" (Aristide, 1992b:25).

Whatever justifications he offered for his decision, Aristide could not run for office without the cover of a political organization. He had not yet formed his own and therefore had to find a home in one already active on the political scene. The recently formed Front National pour le Changement et la Démocratie (FNCD, National Front for Democracy and Change) had asked Aristide to run under its banner. The FNCD, which regrouped fifteen left-of-center organizations (including KONAKOM and KID), had initially chosen the leader of the KONAKOM, Victor Benoit, as its presidential candidate. However, it became evident that Benoit lacked the popular appeal to defeat the other well-known candidates, particularly Marc Bazin (the leader of the well-financed and well-organized right-of-center MIDH) and the candidate of the ANDP, who was then considered the front-runner.

Aristide, for his part, wanted to avoid being seen as an opportunist and was reluctant to displace Benoit as the FNCD's candidate unless Benoit withdrew his name (Aristide, 1992a:142). Pressured by the KID, the FNCD apparently went over Benoit's head to nominate Aristide and compelled Benoit to agree (reluctantly, if not angrily) to withdraw his candidacy. He reportedly did so "for cause," that is, because of the need to counter the threat posed by the macoute forces, not because he favored Aristide. Benoit and his organization, KONAKOM, then left the FNCD (*HM,* 24–30 October 1990; Charlier, 1990:9; Chamberlain, 1990a:5; Sontag, 1990).

Though he became the candidate of the FNCD, Aristide never considered himself beholden to that organization. In fact, he had a jaundiced view of the existing political parties, even those on the Left like the FNCD that shared many of his political views. He saw them basically as "talk shops" that held congresses and engaged in legitimate but byzantine discussions in which he did not participate; he believed that they had difficulty coming up with unified candidates— individuals whom the different left-of-center groups could support—and that their proliferation rendered them ineffective (Aristide, 1992a:141). Thus, for Aristide, the FNCD served merely as a conduit and a legal cover for his candidacy, nothing more. His allegiance was only to the people and to his soon-to-be baptized Opération Lavalas movement (OL, Operation Lavalas, meaning "cleansing flood"), which he believed was more significant than the FNCD (or any other political organization then in place) and of which he was the self-proclaimed leader.

The issue went deeper than Aristide's sense of the limitations of the extant political parties. He also believed that he had formed a special bond with the masses and that he embodied their aspirations and had become their spokesman. Since he believed that the will of God was manifested in the will of the people, it follows that accepting their call to become a candidate was an expression of God's will. He further believed that he stood above all other political actors or organizations, who lacked this symbiotic relationship with the masses. In short, Aristide became persuaded that the "prophetic" people had propelled him onto the historical stage and that only he and his Lavalas movement could bring about the transformations that the people demanded.

For Aristide, Lavalas was not to be confused with a political party restricted only to those who adhered to its principles. Rather, it was a movement open to all who wanted to join with the people to bring about change, regardless of their class location or institutional affiliation.[5] "The idea of Lavalas—the torrent that cleans everything in its path—was growing in the [peoples'] opinion: unity, the unraveling, the cleansing of a shameful past, eradicating the roots of the Macoute system. To unravel. To uproot. To be born again" (Aristide, 1992a:142). He went on to say: "Our program is simple. . . . We say no to the corruption and terror of the past and yes to the mobilization of the people— yes to change, change that we undertake ourselves" (cited in Sontag, 1990). From these ideas came the slogan that would become the refrain of the Lavalas movement, heard for the first time on October 8, 1990, in a broadcast on Radio Antilles: "*Yon sèl nou fèb; ansanm nou fò; ansanm, ansanm nou sé Lavalas*" ("Alone we are weak; united we are strong; altogether we are a cleansing torrent"). Lavalas had its roots in the ecclesiastical base communities, or TKL, movement. Its principal sociological and demographic base was among the urban youths and the marginalized and urban poor but not among the working class as such. Lavalas also regrouped diverse grassroots organizations from the rural areas and provincial cities that were formed after 1986, peasant organizations and principally among them the Mouvman Peyizan Papaye (MPP, Papaye Peasant Movement), as well as many civic and political-educational networks, professional cadres, and progressive elements from the private sector and from the Haitian diaspora (Pierre-Charles, 1991:16–17, 1993:222–223). Lavalas, in short, could be thought of as a broad popular front that aimed to dismantle the prebendary and discredited dictatorship and build a democratic state that made the demands of the excluded and exploited majority a priority and sought their full participation in setting the agenda of their communities and the nation.

Even though Lavalas regrouped many political organizations and tendencies and relied on the mobilization of the organized and unorganized popular sectors for its eventual electoral success, it was not at all clear how the various constituents of Lavalas expressed their ideas and their demands within the movement. No efforts were made before or after the elections to create a structure that coordinated and integrated the groups that were part of the Lavalas movement (Oreste, 1992:4). To be sure, the movement published its vision of a new and democratic Haiti and the economic development model it would adopt in two documents, *La Chance qui passe* (The Passing Chance) (OL, 1990a) and *La Chance à prendre* (The Chance to Take) (OL, 1990b).[6] But these documents were known by only a small circle of intellectuals, the literate members of political organizations, and other literate political observers. The leaders of Lavalas held no congresses to discuss, amend, and ratify the program of government proposed in these two documents. Moreover, Lavalas never revealed its internal organizational structure to the public. In fact, it had no structure. It was neither a political organization nor a political party with clearly defined principles of membership, rules of decisionmaking, methods of choosing the party leadership, and a set of responsibilities assigned to the leadership and to the constituent members. As such, it is difficult to know the mechanisms by which it developed its ideas and its overall orientation or to identify which individuals spoke for the movement and with what authority.

To be sure, one may attribute this failure to the fact that it was impossible to develop an organization that followed democratic principles and procedures given the legacy of more than thirty years of dictatorship, the climate of violence in which the electoral campaign occurred, and the campaign's short duration (only two months). It could be argued also, as Kern Delince did, that political parties have never existed in Haiti because the extant dictatorial system would not tolerate autonomous political organizations that could challenge its political monopoly. Even if they were not always banned legally, political organizations in Haiti have historically existed in an environment averse to their evolution. This explains why Haitian citizens and political activists have traditionally thrown their support behind an influential or powerful leader whose authority they accept and from whom they expect assistance and protection in return (Delince, 1993:142).

This latter tendency prevailed in the case of Aristide and his Lavalas movement. The primary social base of Lavalas came overwhelmingly from the urban youths (especially from Port-au-Prince), the marginalized, and the urbanized poor. As Alain Gilles argued, the members of these "marginalized cities" confront conditions of permanent poverty and other factors such as illiteracy and inadequate health care, housing, and employment. Moreover, these cities are characterized by a perpetual movement of groups of rural migrants from different regions and social backgrounds. Under such conditions, the sense of social-rootedness or neighborliness is either absent or weakly developed, as are the bonds of solidarity that workers often form in the process and unit of production. Consequently, Gilles concluded, the populations of these marginalized cities tend not to develop a specific class consciousness, and they typically do not analyze society in terms of group or class conflicts but in terms of a generalized opposition to society as a whole. They are thus more open to a religious or messianic interpretation of their social problems and become very receptive to populist, charismatic leadership (Gilles, 1991:109).

It should not be surprising, then, that Lavalas recruited its mass base from the marginalized cities of Haiti, that it was a fluid and loosely knit organization, and that Aristide's charismatic and messianic leadership was precisely the sine qua non of his symbiotic relationship with the impoverished masses. This much was candidly admitted by the leadership of the Organisation Politique Lavalas (OPL, Lavalas Political Organization) in an internal document written in June 1992, nine months after the September 1991 coup d'état that overthrew Aristide and Prime Minister Préval's government. The characteristics of Lavalas, they argued, emerged from the "impulse of a powerful popular movement in favor of change and democracy and from the personalistic and charismatic nature of the political leadership. . . . They rest on the force of popular demands and the popularity of one man, who incarnated it, and not on adherence to an explicit political group or program" (OPL, 1992:6).

In the absence of such mechanisms of control and accountability and a program debated and approved by the rank and file of the movement, there was a danger that anyone could speak and anything could be said in the name of Lavalas. Given the personalistic nature of the leadership, however, it is reasonable to conclude that Aristide, along with a cadre of close advisers and intellectuals, made all the decisions, wrote the documents, and spoke for the organization and the movement it claimed to represent. While ostensibly representing the aspirations of the majority and struggling for an inclusive democracy, Aristide and Lavalas did not depart from that all-too-Haitian and all-too-Caribbean tradition of "one-manism." Under that tradition, class politics and factional interests become personalized, and leaders substitute themselves for those they claim to represent and arrogate to themselves the right to speak and set goals for their followers (G. Lewis, 1987:165–166). More universally, this phenomenon is simply known as the cult of personality. This phenomenon would have occurred in Haiti regardless of the fact that Aristide was popular, that his candidacy was backed by some of the best-organized groups as well as the unorganized sectors who together represented various cross sections of the population, and that his progressive theological and secular views corresponded to the real aspirations and demands of the excluded majority.

Despite its unquestionably democratic aspirations, Lavalas was not a democratically structured organization. Within Lavalas, Aristide and a close network of advisers led without direct accountability to a defined constituency vested with definite powers and responsibilities. Even more dangerous, Aristide justified his leadership in theological terms before his ratification by the people in the December elections. And furthermore, Aristide and the Lavalas leaders decided on programs and goals without subjecting them to popular debate and ratification by the constituent organizations or groups ostensibly represented within the movement.

Before the elections, then, the most that can be said is that Aristide benefited from the support of many sectors of the popular opposition movement, centered around the desire to rid the country of the macoute system and its legacies. The demand for an inclusive democracy, social justice, land reform, equality, dignity, jobs, health care, education, and welfare services—in short, for a strong interventionist and social democratic state—were very much part of the political discourse. These demands were shared by many organizations that considered themselves leftist, not only by those who adhered to the Lavalas movement. Nevertheless, Aristide's landslide victory in the December 16, 1990, elections—capturing 67.48 percent of the popular vote[7]—confirmed his unquestioned popularity. It was a popular mandate for him and the government of his prime minister-to-be to implement the hoped-for transformations of the old regime and create a just, equal, and democratic Haiti.

The analysis thus far of Aristide as a liberation theologian and charismatic leader points to the following conclusions. Aristide and his Lavalas movement symbolized and expressed the hope of the Haitian masses for a just and democratic Haiti, freed of the yoke of the tyrannical and rapacious Duvalier dictatorship and its successors. Aristide had become the prophet who "looked at reality with the eyes of God, . . . the one who after having discovered the truth in reality was not afraid to unveil that truth, to proclaim that truth at the risk of his own life" (Midy, 1988; also cited in Moïse and Olivier, 1992:151).

As Claude Moïse and Émile Olivier argued, Aristide's liberation theology linked an interpretation of the gospel with a radical stance in favor of the poor and their struggle. This discourse identified not only the actor (Aristide) and the subjects for whom he spoke (the impoverished masses) but also the enemies who had to be extirpated in order for justice to be done (Moïse and Olivier, 1992: 151–153). Aristide had clearly identified the enemies of the people as the Duvalierists and the macoute system they created, the bourgeoisie, the hierarchy of the Catholic Church, and the imperialists from the "cold country to the north." In short, Aristide had become "the savior, the redeemer. . . . Henceforth the protagonists expressed themselves in terms of justice, of morality, of dignity, of change that transcends social classes. To echo these demands, to give voice to the voiceless, rekindle hope, take into account the will of the masses to accede to the status of citizen, these are the manifest aspects of the Aristidian discourse" (Moïse and Olivier, 1992:153–154).

As Moïse and Olivier acutely observed, the danger of a mass movement that relies on the mediation of a charismatic leader is that, though that individual may serve a useful purpose in defining a political project and in galvanizing popular support for its realization, this can quickly lead to disaster if the charismatic leader turns into an idol. To prevent this from happening, they argued that two conditions must be met. The first is that a structured organization, controlled by enlightened and responsible individuals, must exist between the leader and the masses. The second is that the charismatic leader must be an "enlightened visionary" who understands the complexity of the present conjuncture and, conscious of his or her limits and essentially formative role, exercises his or her responsibilities without losing sight of the democratic objective—to allow the citizens to take charge of their problems and propose their own solutions (Moïse and Olivier, 1992:154).

A third argument can be added. To ensure that the citizens take charge of their problems and determine their own political agenda, a political party must be democratically structured. This means that accountability of the leadership to the rank and file, the demos, must be built in, as must the mechanisms by which the leaders are chosen and changed by the party rank and file.[8] This is the only way to prevent leaders, no matter how enlightened or noble their intentions, from substituting themselves for the masses and becoming a vanguard that speaks and acts in the name of the masses but is not controlled by or accountable to them. This point is amply demonstrated by the experiences of the vanguard parties that transformed themselves into ruling parties and ultimately imposed the dictatorship of the party (i.e., in the former Soviet bloc countries, as well as in China, North Korea, and Cuba).

It is clear that the conditions for democracy did not exist within the political organizations in Haiti in 1990. No leader, including Aristide, had succeeded in federating and democratizing the various political tendencies and organizations that claimed to be part of the democratic movement. Aristide drew his inspiration from and behaved according to the tenets of liberation theology. He was a charismatic leader who had a direct relationship with the masses whom he had galvanized, and they, in turn, idolized him and became his faithful followers (Moïse and Olivier, 1992:154–160). Both he and his Lavalas movement claimed to be above ordinary politics and political parties because they responded to the will of the deified people and hence the will of God.

As Midy put it, the real question was whether Aristide, the priest turned prophet, would also be able to make the transition to become the prince: "Yesterday, the inspired prophet appeared to be in conflict with the appointed priest. Tomorrow, will the prophet be able to coexist with the prince, the man of the Word with the man of action?" (Midy, 1990–1991:3). Put differently, how would Aristide resolve the antinomies of his beliefs and his politics? There is no doubt that his candidacy and subsequent election raised serious fears among various groups: the hard-core Duvalierists; the black middle classes that held positions in the public sector bureaucracy and enterprises (thanks to the Duvalier regime); the traditional Haitian haute bourgeoisie that loathed the masses and resisted any tampering with its privileges; and the United States, which instinctively opposed any expression of anticapitalism and anti-imperialist (i.e., anti-U.S.) nationalism in the hemisphere.

To assuage these fears, Aristide made it clear during the campaign that all social sectors (excluding the barons of Duvalierism), from the repentant "small" macoutes to the bourgeoisie to foreign capital, would have their place in his new government. The private sector's capital, know-how, management skills, dynamism, and creativity would be essential for the country's rejuvenation, he maintained. "We are under no illusion," Aristide said in a speech in Miami in early November 1990. "We are not making a revolution, although what is going on could reveal itself to be a revolutionary stage. Our role is to unleash the possibilities that will allow each sector to play its part, dialogue together, make its contribution." He went on to say that within this context of participation, one partner remained the common denominator: the people. That is why, Aristide insisted, the "popular mobilization" could never lower its guard so that the primacy of the popular demands could be safeguarded against any deviation (*HM*, 7–13 November/a 1990).

How would Aristide resolve these seemingly antagonistic objectives? Would he follow the path of conciliation and bring in the other sectors that were more moderate and ideologically opposed to him to form a broad coalition government and hence remain faithful to the principle of unity against the macoute forces that was the principal justification of his candidacy? (*HM*, 31 October–6 November/a 1990). As Midy also asked, would Aristide continue to behave as the prophet and leader of an opposition movement when he became president? Would he be able to balance his political convictions with his responsibilities as chief of state? (Midy, 1990–1991:4). Or would he, instead, adopt a "go-it-alone" strategy premised on the belief that, with the people behind him, he and his Lavalas movement were invincible?

Notes

1. For a useful and succinct discussion of the distinctions between liberation theologians and the relationship and differences between Marxism and liberation theology, see Löwy 1993 and Dussel 1992.

2. The first incident occurred in August 1987 at Pont Sondé when gunmen opened fire on a crowd attending a mass celebrated by Aristide to commemorate the peasants who had been massacred by the military and agents of the large landholders at Jean–Rabel in July 1987. Several shots were aimed directly at Aristide, missing each time. Then, on the way back to Port–au–Prince that same evening, Aristide and the other priests who had accompanied him to Pont Sondé were ambushed by armed gun-

men at an army post near the village of Freycineau, but they managed to escape. The third and most bloody attack against Aristide occurred in September 1988, while he was celebrating mass at his church at Saint Jean Bosco. Gunmen opened fire on the worshippers during the ceremony, attempted to kill Aristide, and burned down his church. The Sunday massacre left between ten and twenty dead and eighty wounded. Here again, Aristide, protected by his followers, escaped unharmed (Aristide, 1990:37–46, 52–55; Sontag, 1990).

3. The CEP gave several reasons for disqualifying Lafontant and Raymond other than the famous (or infamous, if one was a Duvalierist) Article 291 of the 1987 Constitution. For Lafontant, the reasons given were that he did not have his birth certificate and was not discharged from other public administrative duties; for Raymond, the reason was that he was not recognized as the candidate of a party before the deadline for registering his candidacy (see *HM,* 7–13 November/b 1990).

4. SAJ was created in 1985 to unite the youths from the poor neighborhoods of Port-au-Prince in the struggle against the Duvalier dictatorship, and the Konbit Véyé Yo was created in 1986 to work on political education and uprooting the macoute system (Aristide, 1994a:205–206).

5. As Aristide wrote, "One does not adhere to *Lavalas* as one becomes a card-carrying or a dues-paying member of a party. One joins freely a movement which transforms the eternal vassals, the serfs into free human beings. We are all free human beings. *Lavalas* was the chance of all men and women. . . . It was the opportunity for the army, a mercenary institution yesterday, to become united with its people. It was the chance of the bourgeoisie to opt for a democratic transition rather than a violent revolution. It was the chance of the Church to come closer to its people" (Aristide, 1992a:150).

6. The Lavalas socioeconomic project will be analyzed in the next chapter.

7. Marc Bazin, the candidate favored by the United States and supported by the bourgeoisie, came in second with 14.22 percent of the popular vote. Louis Déjoie, a member of the wealthy mulatto elite, followed with 4.88 percent. Hubert De Ronceray received 3.34 percent, Sylvio Claude got 3.0 percent, and René Théodore got a mere 1.83 percent. The other five candidates shared the remaining 5.26 percent of the vote (Pierre–Charles, 1991:11). There is no doubt about Aristide's massive victory or that he was unquestionably the most popular leader in Haiti.

8. To be sure, no amount of rules and regulations can prevent a leader from usurping the democratic process and establishing complete control over an organization. But these rules and regulations provide a mechanism by which the members of an organization can enforce democratic practices by legitimately sanctioning those who seek to violate them. The same principle applies in society at large. Democratic practice can be sustained insofar as there are institutions and actors with sufficiently binding authority and legitimacy to enforce compliance and make the cost of noncompliance higher than conformity to the rules of the game.

5

AN ALTERNATIVE DEVELOPMENT
MODEL FOR HAITI

The Lavalas Socio-Politico-Economic Model

Before assuming power on February 7, 1991, the Lavalas leaders wrote an analysis of Haitian society and advanced concrete proposals for change in two documents, *La Chance qui passe* (OL, 1990a) and *La Chance à prendre* (OL, 1990b). These two documents served as the principal guide for the policy objectives that President Aristide's prime minister, René Préval, presented to the bicameral parliament (the National Assembly) in February 1991 (*HO*, 20–27 February 1991). The new government also outlined its objectives in the *Cadre de politique économique et programme d'investissement public* (Economic Policy Framework and Public Investment Program) that the Ministère de la Planification de la Coopération Externe et de la Fonction Publique (Office of Planning for External Cooperation and Civil Service) and the Ministère de l'Économie et des Finances (Office of Management and Budget) submitted to the IMF in April 1991 (Haiti, 1991). Henceforth, the ensemble of propositions contained in these documents will be referred to as the Lavalas Project.

It is wrong to say, as Moïse and Olivier and others have, that "Aristide had no program" and that the "*Lavalas* team was not prepared to govern" (Moïse and Olivier, 1992:160–161). In fact, there is consistency between the general political principles and objectives enunciated by Aristide, the two documents written by the intellectual cadres of Lavalas (*La Chance qui passe* and *La Chance à prendre*), the general policy guidelines presented by Prime Minister Préval to the National Assembly, and the *Cadre de politique économique et programme d'investissement public* of the two government ministries. But to have an agenda is one thing. To be able to translate it into specific public policies and then implement them is yet another.

The Lavalas Project was to be implemented over Aristide's five-year mandate. Aristide and his government, however, lasted only seven months. No government anywhere could be expected to implement its program in such a short time, no matter how well crafted or how well prepared its leaders were. It also takes time for any new administration just to get organized. This is certainly true in a democracy where the government in power must engage in the give-and-take of parliamentary politics. And it was even more true in a country such as Haiti, where the people had just elected their first democratic government; where there was no tradition of democratic governance to draw upon; and where the government that came to power by majority vote was despised by political-military and economic elites, groups who had depended upon dictatorships for their existence and who now sought to undermine and overthrow the newly elected government. This does not mean that the Lavalas government was simply a passive victim of the forces of reaction or that its contradictory actions did not exacerbate the tensions with its enemies. Rather, the Lavalas government came to power under foreboding conditions, which resulted from the contradictions and conflicts between the contending forces as well as those within the Lavalas government itself.

In a speech at the United Nations on September 25, 1991, just five days before he was toppled by the Haitian military, Aristide outlined his views on democracy in the form of "ten democratic commandments." He started from the premise that the pedagogy of a democratic praxis enlightened by liberation theology was informed by the lived experience of the poor (the second democratic commandment). Then Aristide listed three rights he considered to be fundamental human rights, alongside the universal rights to life, liberty, and the pursuit of happiness. They were: the right to eat and the right to work (the fourth commandment) and the right of the impoverished masses to demand what they are owed (the fifth commandment). This meant justice and respect for all and an end to the social injustices suffered by Haitians nationally and internationally (Aristide, 1992a:193–223, 1994b:128–147).

To guarantee these rights, Aristide argued that his government would be based on the principles of "justice, participation, and openness" and that it would "respect the individual and individual rights; respect private property and private initiatives; and respect the rights of workers" (Aristide, 1994b:158–160). In addition, three conditions had to be met to implement the government's economic objectives over the following five years. Collectively characterized as components of a "transition from misery to poverty with dignity," they included (1) the decentralization of political structures to increase popular participation in decisionmaking at the rural, communal, departmental, and national levels; (2) a literacy campaign; and (3) agrarian reform (Aristide, 1994b:160–161).

The Lavalas development model is a variant of the basic-needs or growth-with-equity model that emerged in the Caribbean during the 1970s and 1980s. It also conforms to the classic vision of West European social democracy, adapted to the poverty and underdevelopment of Haiti. The growth-with-equity model emerged in the Caribbean as an alternative to the free market capitalism found in most societies of the region and the state socialism established in Cuba since 1961. There are basically two variants of this model in terms of the extent of state intervention in and control of resources and enterprises and state regulation of the economy.

In the first variant, state intervention in and regulation of the economy are extensive, and the state is moving in the direction of a mixed economy. Here, the state is seen as controlling the "commanding heights" of the economy and as being responsible for macroefficiency. The private sector plays a less central role in directing economic development and is left to handle microefficiency. With some variation, the state controls sectors such as banking, marketing (especially external commerce), and mineral resources. It also has a strong presence in services and industrial and agricultural production, as well as in those sectors considered strategic because they involve the production of goods and services deemed essential for national development. All told, the public sector controls as much as one-third of the GDP in this scenario (Gorostiaga, 1985:30; Mandle, 1989:256).

In the second variant, the state limits its ownership of assets to a minimum of key or strategic enterprises and ascribes a much greater role to the private sector and the market. Nonetheless, the state plays a significant regulatory and redistributive role by determining which sectors of the population and economy are in greatest need of support and by redirecting resources to them. Whether a country opts for the first or second variant is determined by the historical conjuncture and the combined effects of struggles between internal and external forces. The most important factor is not the extent of state intervention as much as it is "the class and social interests [the state] serves or seeks to serve. . . . The interpretation of development advanced here is intended to subject the functioning of the state, as well as the development of society as a whole to what has been aptly termed the 'logic of the majority'" (C. Thomas, 1988:361).

The basic-needs approach begins by redefining development in class terms since it assumes that the development process is not neutral vis-à-vis the class interests it primarily serves. In contrast to the World Bank's free market model, which clearly promotes the interests of foreign capital and the domestic dominant classes, the growth-with-equity model gives preeminence to satisfying the basic needs of the majority—the peasants, workers, women, unemployed, poor, and small traders and entrepreneurs. It is they who bear the heaviest burdens of underdevelopment and poverty in the Caribbean region (Gorostiaga, 1985: 27–28; C. Thomas, 1988:356).

The "logic of the majority" also implies that social, economic, and political changes cannot occur without the active involvement of the majority, who must become "the subject, and not the object, of their own history" (Gorostiaga, 1985:28). The logic of the majority principles of the basic-needs model are synonymous with liberation theology's option for the poor. This means that democratic participation and control must be extended to various hitherto excluded social groups, such as tradespeople, peasants, members of professional organizations, residents of villages and towns, and workers. Extending participatory democracy, however, must not be substituted for the representative form of democracy characteristic of liberal democracies. The two forms must be seen as complementary rather than as opposites (C. Thomas, 1988: 358–359).

As James Dietz and Emilio Pantojas-Garcia have argued, the proponents of the basic-needs model emphasized politics and political change in favor of the poor majority, but they paid little attention to the effects of these policies on external imbalances, such as exchange rates and balance-of-payment deficits. Absent from these alternative development theories "was a grasp of how necessary, if at times distasteful, is compromise, both economic and political, if meaningful change ultimately is to be achieved" (Dietz and Pantojas-Garcia, 1994:23).

The development model presented by Opération Lavalas fell within the contours of the basic-needs model, albeit a moderate version of the second variant. It is not clear if its architects in Haiti were conscious of the earlier formulations and failures at implementing this development strategy elsewhere in the Caribbean region. In any case, they tried to balance their commitment to the logic of the majority or the option for the poor with the neoliberal policies of the IMF–World Bank and, in so doing, avoid the negative effects that the internal policies might have on external imbalances. As such, the Haitian variant of the basic-needs model remained within the logic of capital. Despite the balanced and moderate approach, however, the model clashed with the class interests of the Haitian bourgeoisie and foreign capital, which exacerbated tensions between them and the Lavalas government, on the one hand, and between the Lavalas government and its mass base, which expected more sweeping reforms, on the other hand.

Claiming that the Lavalas movement was based on the principles of popular participation, openness in government, and social justice, the creators of the Lavalas development model gave priority to the needs of the most destitute and neglected sectors of the population and the economy to make possible a transition from "misery to poverty with dignity" and to equate development with democracy (OL 1990a, 15–30). They sought to create not only a state of laws that respected individual liberties but also a just and equitable society that targeted the most basic needs of the population (Haiti, 1991:2–4). As Suzy Castor put it succinctly, the Lavalas Project could be viewed as a modernizing economic development project based on social justice and a politics of redistribution (Castor, 1991:34).

The alternative development program proposed by Opération Lavalas presupposed a thorough uprooting of the Duvalierist system in all branches of the state and public sector as a requisite of a reconstructed and democratic Haiti. This uprooting was the "pillar of the popular mobilization and of the national consensus around the [new] government. It [was] the cement that unite[d] all strata of the nation" (Castor, 1991:25). The government also intended to increase public revenues by collecting taxes on profits, tariffs, and patents on the principle of equity; by eliminating all favoritism to the wealthy and powerful; and by combating corruption and curbing waste in government spending (Aristide, 1994b:166–167; Haiti, 1991:8). All subsequent propositions of the project rested on these fundamental premises.

The project offered an original reconceptualization of the Haitian economy and the principal sources of its wealth and culture.[1] The core of the Haitian economy and society, it was argued, were the rural and agricultural sectors, centered around the *bourg-jardin*, that is, the link between the market town and the microfarms cultivated by the peasants. Yet those sectors were the most neglected and would require the most massive intervention on the part of the state to unleash the new processes of growth with equity (OL, 1990a:56–58).

The degradation and impoverishment of the rural and agricultural sectors resulted directly from the process of increasing urbanization and centralization of power and resources in one large metropolitan center, Port-au-Prince, during the twentieth century. The process of centralization reached its apogee and entered a period of crisis beginning in 1980, not only in Haiti but also in most other underdeveloped Third World countries. This still unresolved crisis of centralization in the underdeveloped parts of the Third World stemmed from the insertion of the principal urban centers of these societies into the networks of international exchange. The processes of underdevelopment that resulted from the patterns of insertion of the peripheral countries into the world economy meant that the urban centers of the Third World derived their economic significance more from their relations with the urban centers in the developed or core countries than with the hinterlands of their own countries (OL, 1990a:34–35).[2] Thus, as the hub of economic activities in Haiti, Port-au-Prince was much more integrated with the markets of North America and Western Europe than with the provincial towns and cities of Haiti.

In Haiti, the transformation of Port-au-Prince into the principal metropolitan center and the accumulation and concentration there of material, social, and cultural resources occurred at the expense of the provincial cities and their hinterlands. The formation of a principal and centralized metropolitan zone happened simultaneously with the impoverishment and displacement of the peasantry and with the ghettoization of neighborhoods in and around Port-au-Prince and in the secondary cities throughout Haiti. The catastrophic environmental degradation that Haiti has undergone during the second half of the twentieth century resulted equally from (1) the social and spatial distortions caused by the processes of centralization and accumulation by the metropolitan center, and (2) the country's exploitation of the human and material resources of the hinterland (OL, 1990a:35–36).

It is not at all surprising that the nationwide mass protest movements that emerged in the early 1980s and paved the way for the downfall of the Duvalier regime had their beginnings in the ghettos of provincial cities like Gonaives, Cap Haitien, Cayes, and Jérémie, among others, before reaching Port-au-Prince. There was also an explosion in the contraband trade of basic-need items imported from abroad and destined principally for urban consumers (such as rice, sugar, and used clothing); this was used as a palliative by the political authorities, who could not resolve the crisis. This contributed to the worsening of domestic agricultural production and lay at the root of the conflicts between the poor consumers from the ghettos, who benefited from the lower prices of the imported contraband goods, and the peasant producers of local crops, who could not compete with the cheaper illicit imports (OL, 1990a:39). The policies of the U.S. and Haitian governments to increase food imports also undermined the domestic production of basic crops (such as rice, vegetables, and various cereals) where Haiti had the capacity to be self-sufficient. The U.S. food aid programs (e.g., Food for Work and Food for Peace) encouraged the importation of wheat from the United States at concessionary prices, thereby discouraging Haitian farmers from producing cereals for domestic consumption.

Any program of economic and political modernization in Haiti must begin by identifying the root causes of the crisis that resulted in the immiseration and marginalization of the vast majority of the population, both urban and rural. Only then can appropriate solutions be devised. From this perspective, priority must be given to reversing the flow of migration from the rural hinterland to the urban ghettos by revitalizing the provinces economically and modernizing and energizing the agricultural sector.

According to the Lavalas development model, the point of departure for a reconstructed and democratic Haiti lay in addressing the peasant question and considering the peasants' interests and points of view as primary. To that end, the project advocated new structures to allow the peasants to participate directly in the decisionmaking process, such as having representation in the proposed Institut National de la Réforme Agraire (INRA, National Institute of Agrarian Reform), as well as in the new Conseils d'Administration de la Section Communale (CASEC, Administrative Councils of Communal Sections). Basic services such as health care, a literacy campaign, education, and drinking water were to be extended to the rural areas, and the road and transportation networks were to be built up and improved.

To release the peasants from the claws of the moneylenders and the powerful landlords, credit and savings institutions needed to be created, and the laws and other legal mechanisms that discriminated against peasants had to be revised or abolished. This included, above all, the most oppressive institutionalized extortionary force in the rural areas, the infamous *chèfs seksyon* (section chiefs) system; the various other methods of directly and indirectly taxing the peasants; and the laws regulating the operation of the notary publics, the surveyors, and the judges (OL, 1990b:26–27).

The project considered these propositions to be necessary preconditions to improve immediately the daily lives of the peasants and remove the repressive sociopolitical relations to which they were subjected. On a longer-term basis, the modernization of the agricultural sector and the stimulation of economic growth in the rural and provincial hinterlands demanded more changes in the relations of production and the distribution of land and other resources. The Lavalas Project envisioned a land reform program with the objective of making entrepreneurs out of farmers and encouraging others to invest in the agricultural sector. In addition to redistributing state-owned lands to the farmers, granting land titles to the tenant farmers, and preserving for the state the right to purchase and redistribute farms larger than a predetermined size, the project contemplated new forms of property ownership and agro-industries, such as communal enterprises and cooperatives.

This reorganization was designed not only to produce more and better crops but also to promote agribusinesses that could produce for the local market and for export. The agribusinesses could also be integrated with other sectors of the economy—for example, those that could produce appropriate technologies for the farms and industries that could use agricultural outputs as their inputs. Such a reorganization of agriculture also could generate research and lead to the development of new and better methods of soil preservation, seed production, and other crop cultivation techniques. Agriculture, in short, would play the leading role in the general transformation of the economy (OL, 1990b:44–45, 62; Haiti, 1991:26–29; *HO,* 20–27 February 1991; *HP,* 15–21 May 1991).

In addition to laying the foundation for an integrated infrastructure, with agriculture playing the leading role, the project proposed forming other industries that produced primarily for the national market. Attacking the "excessive protection" granted to the import-substitution industries by past regimes, which prevented those industries from modernizing their equipment and methods of production, the new industrial policy was intended to provide incentives to industries to modernize and become more open to international competition. The industrial policy would promote the formation of small- and medium-size enterprises by offering them technical assistance, information about market outlets for their products, greater access to credit, and inducements to create backward linkages with enterprises that could supply local raw materials. In sum, the overall policy sought to make Haitian industries more competitive by improving their productivity and quality and the prices of their products (Haiti, 1991:30–31). The new industrial policy also proposed to support the informal sector, which performed an important role in the economy in terms of employment, training, and income generation. The effort here would be to increase the informal sector's productivity by providing greater access to credit and technical assistance, upgrading the skills of its labor force, and better utilizing the savings and investments it generated (OL, 1990b:68; Aristide, 1994b:164).

Although the Lavalas Project gave priority to creating industries that produced primarily for the national market, it did not abandon or neglect production for export. It considered the export subcontracting sector important because that sector could play a greater role in the transfer of technology and in industrial development generally. The project leaders understood that this sector must be kept competitive with those in other Caribbean and Central American countries. Rather than coming at the expense of worker's salaries, however, competitiveness had to be achieved by means of technological innovation, better methods of production, decreased losses associated with poor transportation and infrastructural services, and improved the qualifications and productivity of workers. In addition, the right to work had to become a priority, as did the right to collective bargaining, worker representation within the bargaining units, and the democratization of the workplace itself (OL, 1990b:26–38, 63).

As for the public sector enterprises, the new policy was designed not to privatize government-owned industries but to streamline them to eliminate corruption and waste. In addition to rationalizing their operations, the policy was aimed at creating new relations between these enterprises and the state by granting the businesses more financial autonomy and even privatizing their management to make them more market responsive. According to the policy, the public enterprises were expected to be financially solvent, and they would be taxed like all other industries. The state and other stockholders would be paid dividends after deducting the funds needed for reinvestment (Haiti, 1991:15–16).

Although the Lavalas program was nationalist in its conception and priorities, it recognized that Haiti existed in the context of U.S. hegemony and that its economic survival depended on the preservation of commercial relations between the two countries. Nonetheless, the project redefined the way in which Haiti would relate to the advanced countries by emphasizing that foreign assistance and foreign investments would have to conform to its broad objectives of greater self-reliance and independence in domestic and foreign policy. The project also called for establishing better relations with other countries in the region to diversify trade partners and form new alliances that together could reduce Haitian dependency on the United States and the other developed countries (OL, 1990b:81–84).

The overall objective of the model was to lay the foundation for a more independent, integrated, and equitable development. This strategy neither opposed private property ownership nor sought to assign to the state the leading role in economic development through extensive nationalization of key sectors and control of the commanding heights of the economy. Nor did the project imply that class and social inequalities would cease to exist. Rather, it sought to minimize the most negative consequences of the free market and capitalist system by (1) calling on the state to play a greater protective and redistributive role in favor of the agricultural sector, the peasantry, the working class, the informal sector, the small entrepreneurial petty bourgeoisie, women, the young, and the poor, and (2) mediating the conflicts between the various classes in general (OL, 1990b:21–25).

In the context of the experiences of Cuba after 1961, Jamaica under the prime ministership of Michael Manley (1972–1980), Grenada under the New Jewel government of Maurice Bishop (1979–1983), and Nicaragua under the Sandinista government (1979–1990), the Lavalas development model appeared quite moderate. However, in the context of Haiti, which has known nothing but dictatorships and the most abject forms of exploitation since its independence in 1804, the Lavalas development model seemed quite radical.

It must be reiterated that, though it stressed the need for a redistributive policy to improve the living standard of the impoverished peasantry and urban majority, the Lavalas Project did not challenge the institution of private property and the leading role of the private sector in economic development. Rather than substituting state or collective property for private property, it promoted the expansion of the latter among the small farmers through the creation of small- and medium-size agro-industrial and craft enterprises. It also gave priority to those industries that produced primarily for the national market but without downplaying the significance of production for export and of the assembly manufacturing enclave. The project leaders recognized the existence of divergent and contradictory class interests. However, they believed that, by assuming the burden of the project's redistributive policies, the state could mediate between those competing interests and satisfy both the particular concerns of the bourgeoisie and the general interests of the majority through a program of national development.

The Lavalas development model was essentially a moderate version of social democracy. It emphasized the redistribution of income and resources rather than the nationalization and/or socialization of the means of production that is characteristic of socialist or Marxist thought. The project leaders believed in the continued existence of private ownership of the means of production and in cooperating and compromising with the owners and managers of the means of production. As Michael Kaufman argued in the case of Jamaica in the 1970s, the social democratic project shares with modern liberalism the view that the injustices of capitalism can be corrected through the actions of a state under the control of enlightened and technocratic leaders (Kaufman, 1985:59–60). The creators of the Lavalas model agreed with the liberal view that capitalists had a right to appropriate the profits of their enterprises because they would presumably save and reinvest them productively (Przeworski, 1985:43). It fell to the state to assume the role of redistributing wealth and resources to other social strata. The social democratic model envisioned by the architects of the Lavalas Project, like the authors of the democratic socialist program proposed by Michael Manley in Jamaica, insisted on class reconciliation as a "vehicle for the gradual reduction of class divisions" (Kaufman, 1985:60).

The Lavalas Project incorporated the liberal democratic premise that the bourgeoisie, especially the sector that invested nationally, had an essential role to play in the new democratic order because the private sector was best capable of generating economic development. The class compromise it called for, therefore, would occur primarily on the terms of the bourgeoisie since it was the logic of capital, efficiency, and profit that would guide the expected reforms. Rather than the bourgeoisie being asked to make concessions, the liberal state with its progressive, technocratic intelligentsia would assume the role of redistributor and modifier of class injustices and the conflicts they generated.

The Lavalas model sought to defend the interests of all sectors of society while remaining faithful to the rules of the game established by the owners of capital and the international capitalist system. Although the project conformed to many of the tenets of the World Bank, the IMF, and the USAID, it differed from them in some fundamental ways as well. It was designed to streamline and rationalize the public sector to make it more efficient, more market responsive, financially solvent, and less reliant on government subsidies. It assigned a leading role in economic development to the private sector rather than to the state, and it kept Haiti open to free trade and production for export through the assembly manufacturing industries. Its authors wanted to grant land titles to the peasants who held state-owned lands, thereby divesting the state of its holdings and creating market relations in land. Moreover, the Lavalas government was determined to curb corruption and waste in the public sector, implement a better and fairer system of taxation, reduce the rate of inflation, rationalize the public administration and service agencies, eliminate tax exemptions on imports, and impose a minimum tax of 3 percent on all previously exempted imported goods. In short, the government hoped to reduce the public deficit by controlling and restricting spending as much as possible and increasing revenues through various reform measures.

But the project also differed significantly from the overall orientation and recommendations of the international regulatory agencies. In contrast to the latter, the Lavalas Project did not call for selling state enterprises to private buyers; rather, it would primarily privatize the management of those enterprises to make their operations more fiscally independent and more market responsive. The project leaders emphasized the needs of the most neglected sectors and impoverished strata of the population and intended to reallocate resources and services to them. They focused on the necessity of reforming and supporting the agrarian sector as the basis for Haiti's version of growth with equity, and they stressed production for the domestic market over production for export. They sought to improve the competitiveness of Haitian agriculture and export industries by increasing the efficiency of the enterprises. They also intended to raise the wages and productivity of workers rather than rely on the low-wage strategy of the USAID. Lastly, though the project leaders recognized the need to maintain Haiti's ties to the U.S. economy, they advocated greater regional and South-South economic and political relations as an alternative way to increase Haiti's autonomy and counteract the hegemony of the United States.

Although the project leaders did not advocate state control over the commanding heights of the economy and although they assigned the leading role to the private sector, they contemplated playing an interventionist, dirigiste, and even protectionist role in economic development. Theirs was not a state-led or state-dominated model, but it was more interventionist and more social democratic than the "market-friendly" model advocated by the World Bank. Just as the social democratic project sought to balance the interest of classes within Haiti, it aimed to negotiate the nation's historical subordination to foreign capital and the rules of the international capitalist division of labor by balancing those interests with its own model of growth with equity. This was decidedly a novel approach that would test whether the so-called new world order would allow a hitherto client state of the United States to experiment with its own homegrown model of democracy and economic development.

Walking a Tightrope

At first glance, the Lavalas development model appeared to be very moderate and feasible because it remained compatible with the apparent interests of the Haitian bourgeoisie and would later win the approval of regulatory agencies in the core capitalist countries. One could go further and claim that the Lavalas development model would have strengthened the dominance of the Haitian bourgeoisie in the long run by creating a modern state dedicated to providing essential services to the population and improving the country's infrastructure. This, in turn, would have created more opportunities for investments and economic development led by the private sector. What, then, stood in the way of implementing the project? And why would Aristide be overthrown in September 1991 by the military, with the support of the bourgeoisie?

For a democratic system to survive, all the important contending political forces within the system must be convinced that it is in their interest to play by democratic rules. That is, the political forces must be assured that they can compete and that their interests and values have a fair chance of winning occasionally. They must also come to realize that, even when they lose, they are better off under a democratic regime than they would be under an undemocratic one (Przeworski, 1991:33). Haiti never had democratic regimes precisely because the most important political forces—the military, the prebendary state bourgeoisie, and the private sector bourgeoisie—always believed they had more to gain under a dictatorship and more to lose under a democracy. The latter would inevitably have meant competition for public office and the right to rule legitimately. A democracy would also have raised issues of the effectiveness of government, public accountability, fairness, justice, and equality—all or any one of which would have threatened the interests of the beneficiaries of the prebendary state system. Under such conditions, when powerful actors believe that they would be worse off under a democratic government and that there are no more powerful institutions or forces that could sanction their veto over the democratic process, the chances of democracy winning out over dictatorship are slim (Przeworski, 1991:26–33; Lipset, 1994:7–12).

It could be said that the likelihood of a successful transition to democracy in Haiti, even to a democratic government that would seek to preserve the interests of the powerful and propertied elites, was very remote. This was so if only because democracies, no matter how conservative and repressive they may be, are unpredictable: They may create opportunities for social forces that stand to benefit more from such a regime to advance their interests and challenge established privileges. Events from 1986 to 1990 made this point very clear to the privileged classes in Haiti as the popular forces seized on the slightest democratic openings to further their agenda, culminating with the election of Aristide in December 1990.

Aristide symbolized the worst fears of the prebendary state and the propertied bourgeoisie because he was not preaching a democracy that would protect the interests of all sectors of Haitian society equally. Rather, he advocated a democracy that would rectify past injustices and promote the interests of the impoverished and excluded majority more than it would those of the privileged classes. From the outset, the most powerful political actors in Haiti feared Aristide's objectives, and they lined up against him. Yet he needed to win some of these actors over to his side to have the slightest chance of success.

Because it called for the creation of a liberal social democratic state, the Lavalas Project threatened the most fundamental interests of the Duvalierist state, which was antimodern, antidemocratic, and antidevelopmentalist. Consequently, it was to be expected that the Duvalierists would oppose the Lavalas government and seek to overthrow it. For its part, the Haitian bourgeoisie generally (and especially the small but powerful monopolist faction that collaborated with the Duvalier and post-Duvalier dictatorships) feared and despised Aristide. Therefore, it was imperative for the Lavalas government to convince the bourgeoisie and the professional strata that it was in their interest to break with Duvalierism and side with the new government; they had to be convinced that they would have more to gain under the new system than they would ever obtain by staying with the old regime.

Aristide had a chance of succeeding only if he could neutralize the business elite and prevent it from undermining his government by withdrawing its financial support and opposing the government's initiatives. To do this, Aristide had to woo the business leaders by forming as broad a consensus and as inclusive a government as possible but without abandoning his commitment to the reforms outlined in the project. The Lavalas government also had to speak frankly to the masses about the nature of the project: to tell them that this was a liberal and not a revolutionary project; to explain to them why they should accept the compromises it called for with the propertied and privileged classes; and to show how, even with such compromises, they would still derive greater benefits under the new order. Aristide must have known that he was walking a tightrope without a safety net and that the slightest error might send him tumbling down. Nonetheless, his behavior during the next seven months raises doubts about how clearly he understood this.

President Aristide, Prime Minister Préval, and other ministers spoke often to various constituencies to explain the government's actions and policies. The president granted many interviews, gave press conferences, spoke at organized rallies and official ceremonies, and made radio and television addresses. The government, in short, tried to honor its commitment to openness. But when they spoke, Aristide and his ministers did not always do so with one voice, and they did not explain clearly their objectives or their actions. The government ministers typically explained their programs in technical terms and spoke mainly to the press, the intelligentsia, and the bourgeoisie; President Aristide took most of the responsibility for speaking to the masses. Yet he himself often gave contradictory messages—sometimes to the same audiences. On some occasions, he sought to reassure the bourgeoisie and the middle classes, but at other times, he chastised and threatened them. He sometimes appeared to mollify the masses, and at other times, he energized them by adopting a defiant and even revolutionary posture against his opponents. This dual strategy gave the impression that the government was proceeding on an ad hoc basis: improvising, unsure of itself, and contradictory. This inconsistency could not help but create confusion among both supporters and detractors of the government, and ultimately, it played into the hands of the government's enemies. Confusion can be tolerated from a government in power when the stakes are not high and when the government has enough confidence in its policies and enough resources at its disposal to preserve its base of support and fend off the opposition. But in a highly charged atmosphere, such as the one confronted by the Aristide government, where the stakes were high and where enemies were waiting for the slightest mistake to attack, Aristide simply could not afford to confuse the various sectors of the population about his intentions.

In many ways, it was inevitable that Aristide and his government would give the impression of being uncertain and unprepared. The government leaders promised much, and they were beleaguered from the outset by a dilapidated public treasury, an economy in ruins,[3] unforeseen crises that demanded immediate attention, threats and hostility from the Duvalierists, reticence and opposition from the bourgeoisie and parliament, and increasingly militant demands from below to deliver more quickly on their promises and move faster and go deeper with the reforms. As if these problems and pressures were not enough, the Balaguer government added still more to Aristide's woes by forcefully repatriating tens of thousands of Haitians working in the Dominican Republic, thereby straining already meager resources and aggravating an abominable unemployment situation.

Everything was a priority in Haiti. The Lavalas government needed time to sort out what deserved the most urgent attention and devise strategies to deal with the chaotic and seemingly intractable conditions it inherited (Moïse and Olivier, 1992:161). Neither the impatient popular supporters of the government who wanted immediate results nor Aristide's undaunted enemies would give him that time. But if the Lavalas government did not deliver on all its promises, it was not for lack of effort or vision for the project of government. The contradictions within the Lavalas development model itself and the difficulties that the president and his subordinates had in getting out their messages coherently ultimately exacerbated the tensions between the bourgeoisie, the military, the masses, parliament, and the government. All these factors combined created the opening for the Duvalierists to strike.

The Haitian bourgeoisie as a whole, the United States, and the other foreign aid donors (which had collaborated with the most repressive and rapacious dictatorships Haiti has known) suddenly became concerned about protecting human and democratic rights after Aristide's election. Despite assurances by his transition team that their interests would be protected under his government, the private sector remained apprehensive about the direction that Aristide would take. The wealthy elite, the foreign press, and the anti-Aristide faction in the Haitian media worried that Aristide was relying too much on a close inner circle and, within it, on leftist intellectuals who were presumed to be jockeying for influence with more moderate elements. Given Aristide's previous anticapitalist ideology and his option for the poor liberation theology, the foreign governments and the Haitian bourgeoisie feared that he would raise the minimum wage, nationalize more industries, and introduce central planning. They also wondered if Aristide would tolerate opposition to and public criticisms of his policies and turn to mob violence to intimidate his opponents (Hockstader, 1991b; Bohning, 1991; French, 1991c; *HO,* 16–23 January 1991).

In an unprecedented open meeting held with members of the press at the National Palace on February 14, Aristide pledged that press freedom would be respected under his administration (*FBIS,* 15 February 1991). With few exceptions, this largely proved to be the case.[4] Yet the press, both foreign and Haitian, engaged in a campaign of hyperbole against Aristide, which had the effect of deepening distrust of Aristide in Washington and among Haiti's elites. For example, an editorial written for the *Wall Street Journal* by one of the editors of the New York–based conservative Haitian weekly *Haiti Obser-vateur* wasted little time in warning the Haitian bourgeoisie and the United States that "if US experts expect some miraculous free-market conversion by the lifelong socialist, they likely will be disappointed. According to one source who accompanied Father Aristide as he visited the home of a wealthy Haitian family on election day, the president-elect walked out of the house with a look of astonishment. 'Wow!' Father Aristide is reported to have exclaimed. 'What a house! I'm pretty sure this could house 12 families'" (Joseph, 1990). Howard French, a longtime *New York Times* correspondent whose columns influenced opinions on Haiti among the U.S. intelligentsia and policymakers, reminded readers of Aristide's "scathing oratory" against the United States and the Haitian bourgeoisie. He told readers that one of Aristide's "most fervent backers" was the wealthy but staunchly anti-Ameri-can businessman of Palestinian descent Antoine Izméry. Although French suggested that Izméry may have been "slipping out of the President-elect's inner orbit of advisers," he pointed out that the man continued to have Aris-tide's ear in order to assure himself that Aristide was "not softening" (French, 1991d). Conservatives at the Heritage Foundation in the United States joined the chorus and urged the Bush administration not to deliver the $82 million in aid earmarked for Haiti; they warned that, as happened with the Sandinistas in Nicaragua in 1979, the aid moneys would be used to establish a "communist dictatorship in Haiti" (Wilson, 1991).

The anxiety about Aristide among the bourgeoisie was revealed not only in exaggerations about an impending communist dictatorship but also in deeds. During the two months preceding Aristide's inauguration, businesses reduced their inventories by emptying their warehouses and slowing down imports. Many exporters made plans to relocate their operations to the Dominican Republic because they anticipated unrest in Haiti (Hockstader, 1991b).

Then came the first strike by the Duvalierists. With the help of fifteen col-laborators, Roger Lafontant, who had pledged that Aristide would not take office, launched an attempted coup d'état on January 6, 1991, arrested Provisional President Pascal-Trouillot, and forced her to resign. The real target of the coup was Aristide. According to Aristide's account of the event, he escaped Lafontant's commandos who came for him at his house only because he had gone to the headquarters of the Mouvement pour l'Organisation du Pays (MOP, Movement for the Organization of the Country) that afternoon (*FBIS*, 9 Janu-ary 1991). Soon after learning of the attempted coup, thousands of Aristide's supporters took to the streets in protest. Over a span of two days, they erected barricades and blocked access to the airport; attacked Lafontant's headquarters and killed many of his supporters (in some cases, by using the infamous "Père Lebrun" practice of placing a burning tire around the victim's neck);[5] burned two supermarkets; and severely damaged businesses owned by individuals with ties to Lafontant. The mobs also ransacked the papal nunciature and burned the historic Cathedral of Port-au-Prince and the residence of the Conference of Catholic Bishops. The attacks on church properties were a response to a January 1 homily by the pro-Duvalierist archbishop of Port-au-Prince, Msgr. François Wolff Ligondé, who many people thought encouraged the Duvalierists to act. Echoing the conservative hysteria about Aristide, Monsignor Ligondé called the president-elect a "socio-Bolshevik" and warned that under his government, Haiti would become a dictatorship. But he reassured his listeners that "this too shall pass" (*FBIS,* 4 January 1991; Farmer, 1994:158).

Faced with a general uprising against Lafontant's coup, Gen. Hérard Abraham, the army's commander in chief, ordered the army to crush the coup and arrest Lafontant and his collaborators. But Abraham made his move twelve hours after the coup and only after the U.S. and Venezuelan ambassadors, among others, pressed him to do so. They made it clear to him that, unless the army intervened, the masses might turn against him and the army as well (Hockstader, 1991a; Krauss, 1991a; French, 1991a; *HM,* 15–21 January 1991).

That same month, on January 27, another rumored coup attempt to free the imprisoned Lafontant provoked a violent response by the population, and on February 3, a fire allegedly set by a macoute burned Aristide's orphanage, Lafanmi Selavi (Family Is Life), killing 4 of its young residents. In all, at least 125 people died in street violence and clashes with the army and police during the seven weeks preceding Aristide's inauguration on February 7, most of them during the January 7–8 angry popular response to Lafontant's attempted coup (*MH,* 28 January 1991; D'Adesky, 1991; Hockstader, 1991c).

In this context, one can better understand the very important speeches Aristide gave on January 9 and at his inauguration on February 7, 1991. In the first speech, Aristide told the masses who had defied the coup that he understood their disappointment at not having captured the "powerful Macoutes today so that they do not destroy you tomorrow." He warned them, however, not to be provoked by others into committing acts for which they would be blamed. He called on the masses to remain vigilant and on the officers and enlisted men of the army to join with the people to arrest the terrorist macoutes and prevent them from destroying the newly born democracy. The key part of the speech related to the attacks on church property:

> All religious authorities, democrats, diplomats, and friends of the Haitian people, please listen to the call of our dear Haiti and say no once again to impunity!
> We, the elected president of the Republic of Haiti, are protesting energetically against impunity and injustice. The fires of the nuncio and the ancient Cathedral of Port-au-Prince, the sacking of the building of the Episcopal Conference of Haiti, and other painful scenes offer a hideous show. People, the shrewd observer can recognize the explosion of popular anger in the face of impunity for the terrorists. I

share the pain of the religious authorities and the diplomatic corps. If more than one can restrain their anger, soon all will dance the dance of joy at the advent of our government, a government of justice for all, of openness and honesty, of participation (*FBIS*, 9 January 1991).

This speech and subsequent statements by Aristide made it clear that he considered the violent actions of his followers to be a legitimate defense against the macoutes, who attempted to usurp power by force and whose impunity "begets the crumbling of society, where gun-toting people do not let unarmed people exercise their rights." Until there was a system of justice that could prosecute those who hitherto committed crimes and assassinations with impunity, Aristide maintained, he would not condemn the people for taking the law into their own hands and "necklacing" the macoutes because "one must understand what is happening and what is meant by that action" (*FBIS*, 13 January 1991).

This bold stance told the masses that Aristide stood with them, but it also reinforced the suspicions of the bourgeoisie, the United States, and other foreign governments about his willingness to encourage mob violence to intimidate his opponents (French, 1991b). Those fears were heightened still further in Aristide's inaugural address on February 7, when he let it be known that his agenda in favor of the poor remained a priority. He called for unity among all Haitians and a "marriage" between the army and the people to oppose the macoutes and those who opposed democracy. He also asserted that the electoral victory of December 16, 1990, tore off "the veil of confinement skillfully draped around the isolation of the people." He made clear his intention to organize the Lavalas movement that brought him to power to implement the changes the people demanded.

From now on, this historical mobilization and avalanche organization, imbedded with the stamp of Haitian genius, will regenerate the nation. It is at this new cornerstone of history that the decisive emergence of strength asserts itself, now that the people's will is irreversible. It is at this new cornerstone of history that begins the demystifying speech of collective voices denouncing with the deep resonance of the language spoken by the whole population a language of imposture, of stolen speech, gloriously conquered indeed on the day of independence, but perfidiously conjured again later (*FBIS*, 7 February 1991; Aristide, 1992b:103).

The time had come for "the situation to really change." Echoing views he had espoused as an opposition leader, Aristide announced that this meant "the boiler must not burn only on one side"; that the poor people must "share in the country's wealth"; that those "still sitting under the table [must be] sitting around the table"; that "donkeys [must] stop working for horses (poor people [must] stop working for rich ones)"; and that "whether they like it or not, no matter what, stones in water [must] get to know the pain of stones in the sun (rich people

[must] know the struggle of the poor)" (*FBIS*, 7 February 1991; Aristide, 1992b:101–104).

To symbolize that things had changed and that henceforth the poor and excluded masses would be included and made a priority, the new president chose a peasant woman to put the presidential sash on him. The next morning, President Aristide served breakfast to hundreds of homeless people and street kids invited to the National Palace. There is little doubt that for the wealthy Haitian elite, who abhor the common Haitian people, these two gestures alone justified all their hatred of Aristide—whom many among them contemptuously called the "ugly little man from the ghetto" (*HM*, 8–14 May 1991).

In an important sense, Aristide's hardened position resulted from the events preceding his inauguration, when it became clear to him that his government would operate under a constant threat from the macoutes and without the bourgeoisie's support. Lafontant's attempted coup and the people's immediate and violent reaction placed Aristide in a quandary and brought to the surface the contradictions inherent in his views. The bourgeoisie, the United States, and the other foreign aid donors expected Aristide to reassure them that, the macoute threat notwithstanding, he would now behave as the president of all Haitians, as the prince and not the prophet, and renounce "class struggle" and mob violence. Even though Aristide did not encourage the reprisals of his supporters, the bourgeoisie, the United States, and the donors blamed him for not stopping or condemning such actions. They blamed him, rather than the macoutes whose attempted coup d'état provoked the mass reaction. U.S. officials, in their typical condescending attitude, "became increasingly disenchanted with Aristide during that period of turmoil" (Marquis, 1993g). "There can be no excuse for using the failed coup attempt as an excuse for exacting vengeance," a U.S. State Department spokesman stated bluntly after the events of January 7–8 (cited in French, 1991b). Jean-Jacques Honorat, a staunch foe of Aristide, went further and claimed that the new president was "inciting people to riot! We have all the ingredients here for a new fascism. Human rights violations have been as severe in the last month as they were under Duvalier" (cited in Farmer, 1994:166). (Honorat, the director of the human rights organization Centre Haitien de Défense des Libertés Publiques [CHADEL, Haitian Center for the Defense of Public Liberties], funded by the National Endowment for Democracy among other foreign organizations, would serve as de facto prime minister from October 1991 to June 1992 after the coup d'état of September 1991.)

Aristide knew that the bourgeoisie and the United States were not with him and that they would use the slightest mistake or provocation on his part to side with the Duvalierists against him. He understood that he could only count on the masses and that it would be suicidal for him to condemn them for defending him against the macoute threat. To keep the masses mobilized and in his camp, he continually projected a defiant attitude toward his opponents. By adopting this posture and condoning the masses' acts of violence, however, he further alienated the bourgeoisie and the United States, who both feared Aristide and the masses more than they did the macoutes.

Aristide's option for the masses, coupled with his distrust of the bourgeoisie and of the United States (and theirs of him), made it impossible for him to substitute the prince's clothing for the prophet's. It reinforced his inclination to "go it alone" and shun any attempt to form a broad consensus government. Aristide was now president, but the events preceding his inauguration forced him to behave as if he was still the leader of an opposition movement. He never abandoned that modus operandi during his brief seven months in power.

Feeling threatened and on the defensive, Aristide and his followers closed ranks. No single political party had won a majority in the National Assembly in the two rounds of elections held in December 1990 and January 1991.[6] That left Aristide free to choose his own prime minister in consultation with the presidents of the Senate and the Chamber of Deputies, rather than from the majority party as mandated by Article 137 of the 1987 Constitution. Aristide chose his close and trusted friend, the engineer-agronomist turned baker and militant anti-Duvalierist René Préval, as his prime minister. After winning confirmation from the Senate, Prime Minister Préval, who also held the posts of interior minister and national defense minister, then formed a cabinet comprised of Aristide's friends and allies from the progressive wing of the university-educated and professional intelligentsia (*FBIS*, 14 February 1991).[7] The formation of a cabinet that excluded representatives from other political parties and the FNCD coalition that had backed Aristide's candidacy occasioned immediate criticisms from the FNCD and other political leaders. They charged that Aristide would govern alone rather than seek broad consensus for his policies (*FBIS*, 20 February/b 1991; Hockstader, 1991c). That decision to exclude others from upper echelons of government would prove to be one of the several damaging yet easily avoidable errors of Aristide's presidency.

Emboldened by the spontaneous reaction of the masses to Lafontant's attempted coup and feeling confident that Lafontant's defeat had dealt a mortal blow to the macoutes,[8] Aristide pushed ahead with his agenda. He and his prime minister understood clearly that creating a government of laws and implementing the reforms envisioned by the Lavalas Project represented a formidable challenge. They knew that they had inherited a "country ruined by corruption and ravaged by the storm of dictatorship, [and that] the economy [was] in rags and tatters" (Aristide, cited in Caroit, 1991). In essence, everything had to be done, and everything required time and careful planning. In addition, Aristide and his prime minister expected that, at every turn, the forces opposed to change would seek to block their initiatives and destabilize and overthrow the government. Their fears in that regard would soon be realized.

Notes

1. Many of the arguments advanced in *La Chance qui passe* (OL 1990a) were originally developed by Anglade, especially in his *Espace et liberté en Haiti* (Anglade, 1982).

2. This argument is not original to the Lavalas intellectuals. Long before them, Andre Gunder Frank advanced similar hypotheses in his *Capitalism and Underdevelopment in Latin America.* He argued that once integrated into the "metropolitan/satellite" or "core/peripheral" relationship of the capitalist world economy, the resources of the satellite/peripheral regions/countries were transferred to the metropolitan/core regions/countries, thereby causing the underdevelopment of the hinterland/peripheral regions/countries and the development of the center/metropolitan/core regions/countries (Frank, 1969).

3. The account balance of the government in 1989, after official transfers, was −US$63 million. It had US$20 million in gross international reserves and a total external debt of US$802 million. The economy's average annual growth rate between 1980 and 1989 was −0.5 percent (World Bank, 1991a).

4. President Aristide had a confrontation with a reporter from the staunchly anti-Aristide, New York–based Haitian weekly *Haiti Observateur* during that press conference; the confrontation was widely reported and criticized by that paper and others. Unlike previous regimes, the Aristide government never suppressed that journal or any other from circulating freely in Haiti, despite *Haiti Observateur's* unrelenting and sometime vitriolic attacks against Aristide and his government during its seven months in office. One need only compare the state of terror under which the media existed in Haiti during the three years of the coup d'état to appreciate the difference that Aristide made. This fact, of course, is characteristically overlooked by Aristide's detractors.

5. The name *"Père Lebrun"* is a euphemism for "necklacing" and originates from the well-known tire salesman in Port-au-Prince who used to advertise his tires by sticking his head through them.

6. The FNCD, under whose banner Aristide ran for the presidency, captured 40 seats (13 senators and 27 deputies) and constituted the largest bloc in parliament. Bazin's ANDP came in second with 23 seats (6 senators and 17 deputies). Though eight other parties and some independent candidates split the remaining 63 seats for a total of 108 seats in both chambers (27 senators and 81 deputies), none won more than 8 seats alone (*FBIS,* 28 January/a 1991).

7. Prime Minister Préval's cabinet comprised the following: René Préval, interior and national defense minister; François Sevrain, minister of agriculture, natural resources, and rural development; Marie Michèle Rey, economic and finance minister; Renaud Bernardin, minister of planning, foreign cooperation, and state service; Marie-Laurence Jocelyn Lassègue, minister of information and coordination; Marie-Denise Fabien Jean-Louis, minister of foreign affairs and worship; Frantz Vérella, minister of public works, transportation, and communications; Ernst Verdieu, minister of social affairs; Smarck Michel, minister of commerce and industry; Daniel Henrys, minister of public health and population; Lesly Voltaire, minister of education, youth, and sports; and Bayard Vincent, minister of justice (*FBIS,* 20 February/a 1991; *HM,* 27 February–1 March 1991). Later, under popular pressure for actions they either took or failed to take, Commerce Minister Michel would be replaced by Jean-François Chamblain; Social Affairs Minister Ernst Verdieu would be replaced by Myrtho Celestin; and Carl Auguste would be replaced by

Justice Minister Bayard Vincent, whose appointment drew controversy because of his past political ties with the Duvalier regime (*MH,* 15 June 1991; *FBIS,* 20 May 1991).

8. Reflecting the views of the Lavalas camp in general, Evans Paul, mayor of Port-au-Prince, argued that the "coup gate is closed for two reasons. First, after what was revealed on 7 January and last night [27 January], I do not see how a military man or a few macoutes can imagine that they can take by force the power from the people. I do not see how. Therefore, the coup gate is closed. There is another consideration. We must be vigilant because even if they cannot effect another coup to take power, they can create a tense situation. Therefore, we have launched a watchword so that the people can be alerted through order and discipline so that they follow the watchword of the leaders they believe in" (*FBIS,* 28 January/b 1991).

6

THE LAVALAS GOVERNMENT
AND ITS OVERTHROW:
FEBRUARY TO SEPTEMBER 1991

Prelude to a Coup d'État

Two weeks after Aristide's inauguration, Prime Minister Préval outlined the immediate priorities of his government to the National Assembly, on February 17, 1991. They were numerous and included: feeding the population and providing a minimum of health and preventive medical services, attenuating the high cost of living for the impoverished masses, restricting public spending, curbing corruption, controlling the collection of taxes to prevent tax evasion, launching infrastructure projects to increase employment and facilitate private sector investments, decentralizing Port-au-Prince to encourage investments in the provinces, providing subsidies and technical assistance to the peasants to increase self-sufficiency in food production, and regulating and streamlining the public enterprises. The government also contemplated bringing to justice those accused of crimes against the people (e.g., assassinations, massacres, and theft) since 1986 and conducting a three-year literacy campaign to reach approximately 3 million people between 15 and 40 years of age (*HO*, 20–27 February 1991).

The Préval government planned to form an interdepartmental council that would work with the various ministries to study and recommend policies to achieve the government's administrative, political, economic, and cultural objectives. The Institut National de la Réforme Agraire (INRA, National Institute of Agrarian Reform) would also be created to implement the intended agrarian reform and establish a system of credits to the peasant farmers and new peasant organizations that would represent their interests within the INRA (*HO*, 20–27 February 1991).

The general policies announced by the prime minister were in keeping with the objectives of the Lavalas Project. Préval made it clear that the newly installed government would not seek a radical transformation of the existing economic system but would modernize it by reforming the corrupt state institutions. This would enable the government to perform its class-mediating role and absorb many of the costs of capital accumulation and economic development.

In late February 1991, the National Assembly approved a bill based on several articles of the 1987 Constitution (especially Article 295) that gave the first elected president the power to implement, within six months, all necessary reforms in the public administration and the magistracy (*FBIS*, 28 February 1991). Aristide and his prime minister were well aware that the announced measures would not stand a chance of implementation unless Aristide first neutralized the traditional power bases of the prebendary state system. This meant reforming the military institution and dismantling its paramilitary organization.[1] Without this, Aristide argued, there would be no justice and no security, and without security, there would be no investment of capital or economic development (Caroit, 1991). This explains why Aristide decided, starting with his inaugural address, to "strike at the head" of the army by (1) requesting the retirement (or reassignment to obscure posts) of several top-ranking officers who had controlled the armed forces under past regimes, and (2) promoting or commissioning new officers thought to be more supportive of democratization (Aristide, 1992a:160; *FBIS*, 7 February 1991; AW/NCHR/CR, 1991:4; Slavin, 1991). Among the presumed reform-minded officers was Col. Raoul Cédras (the leader of the coup d'état that eventually ousted Aristide in September 1991). Cédras was promoted in July 1991 to the rank of brigadier general and named interim commander in chief of the army to replace General Abraham, who was pressured to resign (*HM*, 10–16 July 1991).

In addition to the reshuffling at the top, the reforms contemplated for the army included three essential measures: separating the army from the police, disarming the paramilitary organization, and dismantling the chèfs seksyon system. Historically, the police force in Haiti was a division of the army, and the section chiefs, who reported to the local subdistrict army commanders, functioned as a rural police force. They recruited their own deputies, collected taxes, and charged peasants to settle land and personal disputes. They also had the power to arrest and sentence people in their localities and to suppress civic or peasant organizations they considered subversive. In short, they exercised authoritarian control over their respective local populations and often ruled through extortion and terror. There is no doubt that abolishing the section chief system was one of the most important steps that the Aristide government could have taken to establish the rule of law in Haiti (AW/NCHR/CR, 1991:9; O'Neill, 1993:106).

Separating the police and the section chiefs from the army and placing them under the jurisdiction of the Ministry of Justice, as mandated by the 1987 Constitution, would reduce the army's role to one of protecting the nation against foreign threats. Yet the modern Haitian Army (which was created during the

U.S. occupation of 1915–1934) had never fought a foreign war, and Haiti did not face any external threats. Historically, the army's primary function was to preserve the status quo and suppress domestic opposition. The restructuring envisioned by Aristide's government, therefore, would disempower it. The army and its extended apparatuses stood to lose more than they would gain under the new order, and as expected, many within the army and the police, as well as the section chiefs, opposed the intended reforms.

There was a debate within the National Assembly over the structure of the new police force and the extension of civilian control beyond the Ministry of Justice to elected officials. This debate prevented the military reform bill introduced in the National Assembly by the minister of justice in August 1991 from being enacted before the September coup. The 555-strong section chiefs force was placed under the control of the Ministry of Justice in April 1991, and members of that force were ordered to turn in their weapons. Those found guilty of corruption or other violations were to be discharged; others would be retired. These measures were not all successfully implemented. The section chiefs were renamed "communal police agents" and henceforth were supposed to report to local prosecutors. Although some section chiefs were forced out, others managed to remain in the new positions and continued to operate as before. No new laws had been passed to specify their powers or the authority of the local prosecutors over them. Thus, peasants' demands for a thorough break with the old system and for the training of a new rural police force remained largely unfulfilled (AW/NCHR/CR, 1991:9, 16; Gaillard, 1991:48).

In addition to separating the police and the section chiefs from the army, the reforms called for the creation of a small but highly trained presidential security service. The U.S. State Department and the CIA offered to train a personal security force to protect Aristide shortly after the December 1990 elections; the goal was to prevent Aristide from being "dangerously exposed" to a "restive military." The security team was to comprise three aides and fifteen soldiers. After accepting the offer, however, Aristide apparently became suspicious of the team and changed his mind. He turned instead to the French and Swiss governments to train the presidential security team (Marquis, 1993g). The suggestion of forming this Service de Sécurité du Président (SSP)[2] immediately gave rise to speculations in the pages of the anti-Aristide weekly *Haiti Observateur* and other media sources that the president intended to pattern the SSP after Duvalier's tontons macoutes and, like Duvalier, use that force to establish his lifetime dictatorship (*HO*, 17–24 July 1991, 24–31 July 1991). These rumors persisted despite evidence that the SSP would not be larger than thirty men and that it would be placed under the command of an army officer. The chief of the Swiss police team who was sent to Haiti along with French police officers to train the presidential security force also gave assurances that the SSP was to serve only as a personal security guard for the president, not as his private militia. Obviously, the rumors were aimed at fomenting discord between the army and President Aristide in order to block the desired reforms (AW/NCHR/CR, 1991:18) and to create the "tonton macoute syndrome," putting Aristide on the defensive and preventing him from taking any measures to assure his own security. Whatever the real reasons for creating the SSP, the army leadership interpreted the move as yet another indication that Aristide did not trust them and that he intended to dilute their power and influence as much as possible.

If Aristide's government did not succeed in fully implementing the military reforms, it made significant headway in combating corruption, contraband activities, drug trafficking, and human rights abuses within the military. The government established an interministerial commission in February and a second independent commission in August to investigate and bring to justice those accused of crimes and massacres between 1986 and 1990, such as those that occurred at Jean-Rabel, Piatte, Danty, Labadie, and Saint Jean Bosco. Several former officers and government officials were arrested, and arrest warrants were issued for others. Aristide also replaced several "compromised" Supreme Court justices—that is, justices who had collaborated with the previous military regimes or served under Jean-Claude Duvalier—along with many other judges in the countryside. Soldiers conducted raids against the *zenglendos* (a pejorative term for the macoutes) and disarmed and arrested scores of them. With the exception of five young men killed in July 1991, human rights abuses committed by soldiers and the police no longer occurred with impunity and actually declined significantly during the seven months of the Lavalas government. With the reestablishment of a climate of relative security, citizens no longer feared resuming nightly activities, and corpses would no longer be found on sidewalks at dawn (AW/NCHR/CR, 1991; D'Adesky, 1991; Wilentz, 1991; Gaillard, 1991; *FBIS*, 20 March 1991, 19 April 1991).

Rather than cementing the "marriage" announced by President Aristide in his inaugural address, the measures pursued by his government worsened relations between the army and the president during his short term in office. Unrest within the army occurred throughout the first six months; some actions were directed against Duvalierist officers whom soldiers wanted removed, but others were directed against the government. They included several government-preempted plots by both civilians and soldiers to assassinate or overthrow Aristide (Ives, 1991; *FBIS*, 23 April 1991). On at least two occasions, U.S. Ambassador Alvin Adams, acting on CIA intelligence reports, warned Aristide of assassination and coup attempts (Marquis, 1993g). Macoutes also engaged in many actions designed to spread panic and destabilize the government. The most dramatic event occurred on April 16–17, when zenglendos carried out their threat to burn the landmark Hyppolite Public Market in Port-au-Prince, which housed over 2,000 mostly independent petty merchants and crafts workers (*FBIS*, 18 April 1991). Thus, by the time of the September coup, the macoute camp and the rank-and-file soldiers "had been whipped into an anti-Aristide frenzy" (Constable, 1992–1993:178).

The Aristide government also came under fire from several quarters for not doing enough to reduce the high cost of living and not moving fast enough to uproot the macoute functionaries from the public enterprises, ministries, and agencies. Aristide and his ministers responded that the government was determined to implement the reforms during its allotted six-month period. They warned the impatient activists that reforming a state system in complete disarray and ridden with corruption necessarily required time and care; only then could they avoid arbitrary dismissals and retain those individuals who were not implicated in criminal activities and whose competence and skills were needed to keep the public sector functioning (Caroit, 1991; *HP,* 15–21 May 1991, 19–25 June 1991). Nonetheless, the manner in which the government carried out its dismissals gave the impression that it was engaged in a witch-hunt, leading some of its ever-watchful critics to charge that the government "confuses dismissals with reform" (*FBIS,* 6 August 1991).

In addition to removing the old guard who ran the public sector as their private prebend, the government sought to curb waste and corruption by closing some offices and agencies completely and by reducing the budgets of the targeted public agencies or enterprises, the salaries of functionaries, and the size of the public sector. To set an example, in his inaugural address Aristide asked the National Assembly to cut his US$10,000 monthly salary, and he often donated his paycheck to nongovernmental organizations, such as the United Nations International Children's Emergency Fund (UNICEF) or citizens' groups, to help them prepare for the literacy campaign (*FBIS,* 15 May 1991, 10 June 1991). The government also took steps to reduce the size of the public sector. A report from the Ministère de l'Économie et des Finances issued in May 1991 estimated that at least 5,000 employees had lost their jobs in public administration and public enterprises between February and May 1991. By early September 1991, the number rose to over 8,000, thereby reducing the total number of public sector employees to 37,000 (*HM,* 7–13 August 1991; *HO,* 11–18 September 1991; Ives, 1991).

These measures began to pay off. The government took steps to collect the arrears owed to it and to prevent tax evasion by the wealthy and fraud in the ministries and public enterprises. As a result, the Direction Générale des Impôts (Internal Revenue Administration) registered a historic increase in total revenues, thereby reversing the tendency of previous governments. Furthermore, two public monopolies that had once served primarily as sources of graft and corruption for government officials showed dramatic improvements in their performance under Aristide. The Minoterie d'Haiti (the government's flour mill), hitherto always in the red, showed a profit in April, and the Ciment d'Haiti (another bankrupt public enterprise) reduced its deficit by 60 percent between February and April 1991. Meanwhile, total monthly government expenditures were reduced from US$32.9 million in November 1990 to US$17 million in June 1991, and for the first time in many years, a budgetary surplus of US$8.2 million was recorded (*HP,* 12–18 June 1991; Ives, 1991). The government also prevented importers from hoarding foodstuffs and inflating food prices by fixing the price of certain basic food items. It proposed to raise the daily minimum wage from 15 to 25 gourdes (from US$3 to US$5), primarily for urban workers who made up a relatively small proportion of the labor force. But after heavy opposition and lobbying by the private sector, the National Assembly set the minimum wage at 24 gourdes (US$4.80) in March (*HM,* 27 March–2 April 1991; *HO,* 11–18 September 1991).[3] In its seven months in office, then, the government increased internal revenues and customs receipts; transformed hitherto inefficient and unprofitable state enterprises into efficient and profitable operations; brought government spending under control and reduced the internal financing of public sector deficit; increased the foreign exchange reserve by US$20 million; and reduced the public debt by US$127 million, from US$874 to US$747 million (Haiti, 1994a).

The Lavalas government went on the offensive on many fronts. Though it achieved mixed results with its attempted reforms in the military, public administration, magistracy, and public enterprises, there is no question that the measures it took struck at the heart of the old regime's power base and intensified the antagonism between the promacoute camp and the Aristide government. The macoute camp and the prebendary military and public sector officialdom would be the biggest losers with the advent of democracy and a government bent on implementing sweeping reforms in these institutions. They therefore had an interest in subverting the democratization process, and this could only be done by reverting to dictatorship. To avoid a collision between the macoute or neo-Duvalierist forces and the Aristide government, the latter would have had to respect the status quo and do nothing. But to do so would have earned Aristide the enmity of the popular democratic movement and of the 67 percent of all voters who elected him to carry out the *déchoukaj* (uprooting) of the Duvalierist and prebendary state system. Moreover, to capitulate to the macoute camp would have meant abandoning all hopes for a democratic alternative, of whatever kind, since this would grant the forces in control of the army and the state apparatuses veto power over any reforms.

If the animosity between the Aristide government and the neo-Duvalierist forces was expected and inevitable, the friction with the bourgeoisie, as well as the altercations with the National Assembly that paralyzed the government and prompted popular violence, could have been minimized. Aristide needed the cooperation of the bourgeoisie and the National Assembly if his reforms and his government were to have any chance of survival. Therefore, it was imperative for him to woo the bourgeoisie and both his supporters and his opponents in the National Assembly by forming a broad coalition government that included representatives from these sectors. Aristide failed to do so not only because he was predisposed to pursue a go-it-alone strategy but also because the events of January 1991, which he did not provoke, reinforced his conviction that he could not trust those who were not proven Lavalassiens.

Aristide's contradictory messages and actions as president helped sour relations with the bourgeoisie and the National Assembly. The Lavalas Project, Préval's general policies, and the *Cadre de politique économique* made it clear that the government intended to pursue an economic policy ostensibly acceptable to the IMF–World Bank, international aid donors, and the Haitian bourgeoisie. After nearly four months of negotiation, the Préval government and the IMF signed a standby arrangement in September 1991 (*HM*, 18–24 September 1991; *HO*, 18–25 September 1991). President Aristide, who had once denounced the IMF as the Front de Misère Internationale (International Misery Front), tried to put the best face on the agreement. Addressing the mass organizations that had criticized him and his government for negotiating with the IMF, he argued:

> The rules of the game have changed. The situation with the IMF is almost identical. The difference is that they are not here to give orders. They cannot give us orders. They can come to hold discussions with us and we will be willing to speak with them. They have recognized the good job we have been doing, and have said so. We are happy that they said so. They did not order us to do a good job. We are simply doing a good job. They recognize that, and will capitalize on it. In our negotiations with them, we continue doing a good job for best results (*FBIS*, 16 September 1991).

Aristide could have sounded less defensive about his government's negotiations and thereby deflected criticisms by pointing out that structural adjustment in Haiti would not mean the same thing as in other Third World countries—for example, Jamaica under Manley or Nicaragua under the Sandinistas. In those countries, the governments were being asked to cut social spending and social services that targeted the working classes and the poorest sectors of society. He could have explained that in Haiti, by contrast, the government never provided social services or subsidies to the poor or the working and peasant classes and that any reforms in the public sector would affect primarily the prebendary state officials, the clientalistic civil servants, and the extended macoute network that siphoned off public resources for its own benefit. Aristide could have argued that the structural and other adjustments his government intended to implement were necessary if it were to reach the goal of dismantling the prebendary state system and establishing a modern liberal state that would, for the first time, provide essential services and subsidies to the poor majority.

As things stood, Aristide tried to dismiss the misguided reflexive criticisms of the government's structural adjustment agreements by taking an equally misleading and defensive nationalist stance. The "good job" that Aristide referred to simply meant that his government had adopted an economic program sufficiently compatible with the goals of the IMF and the World Bank and that, as a result, those institutions and other donor governments had pledged about US$500 million in loans and foreign aid to Haiti (*HM,* 14–20 August 1991). Though the much-promised foreign aid had not materialized by the time of the September coup, Washington, which had established cordial relations with and approved several aid packages for the Aristide government, agreed to cancel Haiti's US$107 million debt to the United States as a result of the IMF agreement (Tarr, 1991a; French, 1991e; *FBIS,* 12 August 1991).

Despite the government's moderate economic policies, members of the Haitian bourgeoisie, especially the few powerful families that dominated the private sector, withheld their support from the government. If the Lavalas Project had been implemented, the bourgeoisie would have benefited, and its influence as a class would have been strengthened. However, this would have been a long-term consequence, and the Haitian bourgeoisie usually pursued its interests in the short term. For most of its history, the Haitian bourgeoisie has been a visionless, retrograde social class concerned primarily with safeguarding its immediate wealth and privileges. The monopolist faction of the bourgeoisie had collaborated closely with the Duvalier dictatorships and their successors. It has been said that "if the Duvaliers did not exist, [the wealthy elite] would have invented them" (*HM,* 8–14 May 1991). Aristide understood this, and it was imperative for him to try to persuade the bourgeoisie that it ultimately had more to gain under the new regime, even if in the short term it had to make some concessions. Unfortunately for Aristide, he attempted to persuade the bourgeoisie by threatening it, thereby dashing any hope for a rapprochement, improbable as the latter may have been.

As expected, the business elite opposed the social democratic and redistributive thrust of the Aristide government, particularly the reforms that targeted the loopholes and other prerogatives the elite enjoyed under the old regimes. The business elite considered the law that raised the minimum daily wage by a mere US$1.80 (from US$3 to US$4.80) to be "antieconomic and antinational." In a meeting with Aristide, representatives of this group argued that implementation of the law would negatively impact Haiti's competitiveness vis-à-vis its Caribbean neighbors, increase unemployment, and compel many investors to relocate in countries where labor was cheaper (Daniel, 1991; *FBIS,* 2 April 1991, 29 August 1991). The USAID also opposed the planned increase in the minimum daily wage on grounds similar to those offered by the Haitian business elite. The agency knew, however, that an increase as high as US$.75 an hour (or US$6.00 a day), well above the wage level proposed by the Aristide government, would still make Haitian labor cheaper than that of its Caribbean and Central American competitors, except for the Dominican Republic. Essentially, the Haitian business elite and the USAID wanted nothing other than the oppressive but highly profitable labor conditions that existed prior to February 1991 (NLC, 1994:144–145).

Above all, members of the bourgeoisie felt threatened by the fortification of civil society and especially by what they saw as Aristide's encouragement of the increasing militancy of the grassroots organizations, student organizations, TKL community-based organizations, trade unions, peasant organizations, and vigilante groups. The bourgeoisie, in other words, feared the empowerment of the social classes whose abject exploitation and suppression the dictatorships had guaranteed.

The momentum created by the election of Aristide and the reformist thrust of his government opened a Pandora's box of pent-up grievances and demands. Hardly a month went by without demonstrations or other actions—some violent—by one or another group or mass organization in Port-au-Prince and other cities, towns, and villages throughout Haiti. Both organized and unorganized groups made various demands on the government: Workers sought higher wages, better working conditions, and management changes in enterprises; public sector employees wanted to uproot the administrative personnel from the old regime in the provinces as well as in Port-au-Prince; students asked for university reforms; peasants sought land reform; citizens wanted to lower the high cost of living and end the food stockpiling by merchants that inflated retail prices, as well as more jobs, health care, education, and a literacy campaign; others hoped to reverse deforestation and the degradation of the environment; popular organizations sought the removal of several Préval government ministers accused of protecting the bourgeoisie's interests in their ministries, an end to negotiations with the IMF, and a halt to U.S. interference in Haiti's internal affairs (*FBIS,* 25 March 1991, 27 March 1991, 24 April 1991, 29 April/b 1991a, 6 May 1991, 23 May/b 1991, 20 June 1991, 11 July 1991, 23 August 1991, 13 September 1991).

Besieged by these multiple and conflicting demands, the government devoted considerable time and energy responding to them. Aristide, Préval, and other ministers met with various groups to discuss their grievances, and where they could, they took prompt action to satisfy the complaints. Aristide held unprecedented and open meetings at the National Palace with the press, trade union representatives, peasant delegations, thousands of unemployed people, youths, and leaders of popular organizations. When he spoke to them, Aristide tried to reassure and encourage them in their struggle. For example, he told the trade union representatives to organize themselves more effectively and thereby become a stronger force. He told the peasant delegations that his government intended to take state-owned lands from landowners and redistribute them to peasants in accordance with the constitution. To the unemployed, he said that "militants who worked in the field, who worked hard so the avalanche could overflow, should not have to go and ask for favors to get work, as if they do not have the right to work" (*FBIS,* 27 March 1991, 29 April/a 1991, 19 June 1991, 16 September 1991).

Yet when he spoke to the private sector bourgeoisie or to other groups about the bourgeoisie, Aristide often employed a more severe and even threatening tone. Although he told the bourgeoisie that "without them it would be difficult to promote a productive society and reach a balanced economy," he also reminded them that "all private property has a social mortgage, and [that] to mortgage the sovereignty [of the state and of the president's power] is to reject dignity" (*FBIS*, 18 March 1991, 25 March 1991). He went even further, making a distinction between the "good" and "bad" bourgeois. The "patriotic" bourgeois was willing to make concessions, and the "selfish" bourgeois—the *bourgeoisie patripoche*—did not identify with the national interest, having collaborated with the dictatorship to safeguard its privileges. Basically, Aristide advanced a voluntaristic argument with a compulsory dimension. According to him, the bourgeoisie had to learn new human values, respect the society as a whole, and behave differently. It had to learn that it was in its own interest to make concessions, to accept the hand offered by the lower classes, and to form an alliance between its capital and the "revolutionary capital of Lavalas" to create the new economic order. Should the bourgeoisie remain passive and selfish and refuse to cooperate with the new movement, the starving masses could be pushed to demand more radical measures. In his words, "The people who are sleeping like a log today could be roaring tomorrow" (Aristide, 1992a:162–164; *FBIS*, 2 April 1991).

Aristide's argument was premised on the threat of force as a determinant in the last instance. As he saw it, the bourgeoisie was left with a choice: Either it cooperated with the "Lavalas revolution" or it risked pushing the Haitian masses to revolution (Aristide, 1992a:164). It is difficult to see why the bourgeoisie would accept such a proposition and why, under such a threat, it would believe Aristide when he said that he would respect its rights and property.

The provocative and threatening actions of some of the groups and organizations that supported Aristide, as well as his encouragement of their behavior in several instances, further damaged his credibility with the bourgeoisie. One instance occurred with the actions taken by Jean-Auguste Mesyeux, the leader of the Centrale Autonome des Travailleurs Haitiens (CATH, Autonomous Union of Haitian Workers) who launched the Opération Vent-Tempête (Operation Storm Wind) in June 1991 (*FBIS*, 31 May 1991). In the name of uprooting macoutes from the public administration, Mesyeux and his followers threatened to enter government offices, take employees hostage, and deliver them to the National Palace. On June 17 and 18, some 2,000 to 3,000 protesters demanded the dismissal of the prime minister, his cabinet, and even the president himself. The demonstrators also threatened Préval with "Père Lebrun." On August 13, supporters of Aristide retaliated and burned down the CATH's headquarters (*FBIS*, 14 August/c 1991). Yet later, Aristide received Mesyeux at the National Palace and offered him a job as an adviser in Préval's office, which Mesyeux refused (*HM*, 21–27 August 1991). This led some critics to charge that the government was implicated in Operation

Storm Wind (*FBIS*, 17 June 1991). The government did nothing to repudiate this allegation.

Another damaging incident for Aristide occurred with the July 1991 trial of Lafontant and his accomplices for their attempted coup d'état in January. Unable to find lawyers willing to defend them for fear of popular reprisals and refusing to accept court-appointed lawyers, Lafontant and fifteen of his accomplices were found guilty of plotting against the state. They were sentenced to life imprisonment at forced labor, even though the law for such an offense provides for sentences of only fifteen to twenty years. Only four of the defendants received ten to fifteen years at forced labor (*HM*, 31 July–6 August/b 1991).

Several days before the trial, Aristide lashed out against the alleged maneuvering designed to delay the trial, denounced the corruption in the judicial administration, asked the population to remain vigilant and to follow the trial closely, and threatened to take action if the trial did not go on as scheduled (*HM*, 31 July–6 August/a 1991). Speaking at a youth rally a few days after the trial, he praised the people for their vigilance and their wise use of the threat of "Père Lebrun":

> Was there Père Lebrun inside the courthouse? [audience yells no] Was there Père Lebrun in front of the courthouse? [audience yells yes] Did the people use Père Lebrun? [audience yells no] Did the people forget it? [audience yells no] Did they have a right to forget it? [audience yells no] Do not say that I said it. [laughter]
>
> In front of the courthouse, for 24 hours, Père Lebrun became a good firm bed. The people slept on it. Its springs bounced back. The Justice Ministry inside the courthouse had the law in its hands, the people had their cushion outside. The people had their little matches in their hands. They had gas nearby. Did they use it? [audience yells no] That means that the people respect [audience yells the Constitution] Does the Constitution tell the people to forget little Père Lebrun? [audience yells no]
>
> Therefore when those inside know what is going on outside, those inside had to tread carefully [literally, walk on 13 so as not to break 14]. [The audience answers: 14 is the masses of the people] The masses have their own tool, their own secret way, their own wisdom.
>
> When they spoke of 15 years inside the courthouse, according to the law, outside the people began to clamor for Père Lebrun. . . . That's why the verdict came out as a life sentence. The people, who respect the law, who uphold the Constitution, when the people heard "life in prison," they forgot their little matches, little gasoline, and little Père Lebrun. Did the people use Père Lebrun that day? [audience yells no] But if it had not gone well, wouldn't the people have used Père Lebrun? [audience yells yes] That means that when you are in your literacy class you are learning to write "Père Lebrun," you are learning to think about "Père Lebrun," it's because you have to know when to use it, and where to use it. And you may never use it again in a state where law prevails (that's what I hope!) as long as they stop using deception and corruption. So, that's what they call real literacy

(cited in AW/NCHR/CR, 1991:26–27; *FBIS*, 5 August 1991; bracketed comments appear as such in source).

Aristide's motives may well have been to rally, educate, and shape the people into a credible force "capable of exerting legitimate pressure on the judicial system, but without threatening it, so that when the judge knows that the people are there, the judge can feel strengthened to render justice and not succumb to the weight of money or the pressures that will come upon him" (cited in Danner, 1993:51). As with many of his other speeches, however, this speech sent contradictory messages to different audiences. As Danner observed, Aristide may have wanted his followers to hear that he still believed that only they could constitute the revolutionary force that would change things in Haiti. At the same time, that speech frightened the moneyed and privileged classes; for them, the threat of deadly violence to change the system "did not seem at all reassuring coming from an elected President of the Republic, the man who was supposed to have responsibility to govern his people through the constitution and the established mechanisms of power" (Danner, 1993:51–52).

Aristide committed a major blunder here. He had chosen the electoral path to reform over the revolutionary or armed takeover of the state. Therefore, alluding to the use of deadly violence to change the status quo was an irresponsible act. The trial posed no danger to his government. And furthermore, he had everything to gain by using the opportunity offered by the trial to set an example and show that his administration would respect the principle of separation of powers outlined in the 1987 Constitution, allowing the courts to function without interference from the executive. The masses who assembled in front of the courthouse during the trial had the right to demand a life sentence for Lafontant and his collaborators, but they did not have the right to threaten the justices for imposing a sentence in accordance with the law. Aristide overstepped his powers by encouraging them in that direction. As Moïse and Olivier observed, instead of using the trial to indict Duvalierism as a whole, the government preferred a

> botched job that left the troublesome impression that the courts were being used as an instrument to settle accounts with the *macoutes*. The general offensive of the Executive against a wanting judicial system, the indiscriminate accusations of corruption against the judges encouraged the popular pressure groups to intimidate judges in several regions (Moïse and Olivier, 1992:167).

Another costly error on Aristide's part came when he failed to condemn his supporters for threatening to use "Père Lebrun" on members of the National Assembly who opposed the government. In addition, the government became embroiled in ceaseless conflict with the National Assembly over numerous issues: the interpretation of the "transitional" Article 295 of the constitution, the delays in approving government appointments, voting on the budget presented by the government, the separation of the police from the army, the law to create a permanent electoral council, and a series of other government initiatives. It may be that, at bottom, the conflict between the executive and the legislative was about which of the two branches would exercise greater control over the government. Ironically, the unfolding power struggle pitted Aristide against the FNCD, the very coalition that made his candidacy and his election possible.

Leaders of the FNCD began to feud openly with Aristide. They accused him of having betrayed them when he referred to the FNCD as "just a legal hat that enabled him to run in the elections" and when he opted to form a cabinet that excluded representatives from their group and other political organizations that offered to form a broad left-of-center parliamentary majority in support of the government. Some of Aristide's supporters contended that the FNCD wanted Aristide to choose one of their members as prime minister. When Aristide refused, the FNCD began to oppose him, signaling that the newly formed National Assembly would become the locus of opposition to the Lavalas government. The president and prime minister deepened the rift by bypassing members of the FNCD and other parliamentary parties for administrative posts, reserving those spots for close Lavalas supporters instead. Aristide considered the political parties to be mere "talk shops" and believed that he and Lavalas alone truly represented the people. With the people behind him, he thought, he could govern without the National Assembly and the give-and-take of democratic politics. He thus rejected the hand offered him (*HM,* 29 May–4 June 1991, 14–20 August 1991, 21–27 August 1991; French, 1991g; *FBIS,* 23 May/a 1991; Tarr, 1991b).

The conflict between the legislature and the executive reached the boiling point when the National Assembly summoned Préval to appear before it and account for his government's performance during the preceding six months. When he failed to appear, the assembly called for his resignation and threatened a vote of no confidence against him that could have brought down his government. Reacting to these parliamentary maneuvers against the prime minister and seeing them as attacks against Aristide himself, the ever-vigilant popular groups, who had burned the headquarters of the CATH, soon attacked the home of an FNCD senator, ransacked the offices of the KID (a faction within the FNCD), and stoned the office of Evans Paul, KID leader and mayor of Port-au-Prince. Between 2,000 and 4,000 demonstrators descended on the National Assembly, threatened legislators with "Père Lebrun," beat two of them, and trapped the legislators along with the prime minister inside the Legislative Palace. The police finally intervened with tear gas to disperse the protesters and allow the legislators and prime minister to leave the premises (*FBIS,* 13 August 1991, 14 August/a,b 1991).

The government condemned and distanced itself from the actions of the demonstrators, called on the people to respect the rights of others, and expressed sympathy for the legislators and the victims of the violence. This response was too little and too late, however. The National Assembly, bowing to popular threats, postponed the censuring debate but subjected Préval to a six-hour public interrogation and criticism of his government's behavior. The Senate also unanimously denounced the popular acts of intimidation against members of the National Assembly, interpreting them as a threat to the burgeoning democracy. There is little doubt that the four major political blocs in the Chamber of Deputies, including the FNCD, would have voted in favor of the censure motion if it had been taken (*FBIS*, 14 August/c 1991, 15 August 1991, 17 August 1991; Tarr, 1991b; French, 1991f). By the time the coup d'état got under way in September, Aristide and the government of his prime minister had clearly lost the support of their major allies in the National Assembly.

The Coup d'État of September 1991

It is in the context of the preceding events that one must consider Aristide's (in)famous September 27, 1991, speech, the last impassioned address he made before his overthrow three days later by the military. Aristide had just returned to Haiti from New York, where he had addressed the United Nations on September 25, and the defiant tone of his September 27 speech was a reaction to the information that he received in New York about the impending coup d'état against him (AW/NCHR/CR, 1991:24; Danner, 1993:52). Aristide launched a direct attack against the macoutes and especially the bourgeoisie patripoche. Speaking to the bourgeoisie, he said:

> That money which you have is not really yours. You earned it in thievery, through bad choices you've made, under an evil regime and system and in all other unsavory ways. Today, seven months after February 7, in this day ending with the numeral 7, I give you a chance, because you won't have two, nor three chances. It's only one chance that you'll have. Otherwise, things won't be so good for you!
> If I speak to you in that way, it's because I've given you seven months to conform, and the seven months are up—to the day.

Turning to the masses, he said:

> Now whenever you are hungry, turn your eyes in the direction of those people who aren't hungry. Whenever you are out of work, turn your eyes in the direction of those who can put people to work. Ask them why not? What are you waiting for?
> Whenever you feel the heat of unemployment, whenever the heat of the pavement gets to you, whenever you feel revolt inside you, turn your eyes in the direction of those with the means. . . .
> And if you catch a cat (the slang in the Creole language for thief), if you catch a sticky finger slob, if you catch a false *Lavalassien*, if you catch . . . (he stopped in the

middle of the word), if you catch one who shouldn't be there, don't-he-si-tate-to-give-him-what-he-de-serves (staccato for effect and repeated twice).

Your tool in hand, your instrument in hand, your constitution in hand. Don't-he-si-tate-to-give-him-what-he-de-serves.

Your equipment in hand, your trowel in hand, your pencil in hand, your constitution in hand, don't-he-si-tate-to-give-him-what-he-de-serves.

The 291 . . . says: Macoute isn't in the game. Don't-he-si-tate-to-give-him-what-he-de-serves (repeated twice).

Everywhere, in the four corners, we are watching, we are praying . . . when you catch one, don't-he-si-tate-to-give-him-what-he-de-serves.

What a beautiful tool! What a beautiful instrument! What a beautiful device! It's beautiful, yes it's beautiful, it's cute, it's pretty, it has a good smell, wherever you go you want to inhale it. Since the law of the country says Macoute isn't in the game, whatever happens to him he deserves, he came looking for trouble.

Again, under this flag of pride, under this flag of solidarity, hand in hand, one encouraging the other, one holding the other's hand, so that from this day forward, each one will pick up this message of respect that I share with you, this message of justice that I share with you, so that the word ceases to be the word and becomes action. With other actions in the economic field, I throw the ball to you, you dribble it, you shoot . . . on the goal adroitly, because if the people don't find this ball to hold it in the net, well, as I told you, it's not my fault, it's you who will find what-you-de-serve, according to what the Mother Law of the country declares.

Alone, we are weak! Together we are strong! Altogether we are *Lavalas*! (*HO*, 9–16 October 1991).

The September 27 speech was inflammatory insofar as it condoned popular violence against the recalcitrant bourgeoisie and the macoutes. But this speech was defensive and preemptive rather than provocative. Aristide knew of the impending coup, and he probably believed that, with the events of January 7 and 8 fresh on everyone's mind, he could preempt the coup plotters by "brandishing what had always been his greatest strength and his most feared weapon—the Flood, the avalanche represented by the poor multitudes who were now cheering before him" (Danner, 1993:52). Aristide acknowledged this himself later in an interview when he said, in response to a question about his speech, that his words should be put in context. As he put it, "The coup had started. I was using words to answer the bullets," in a vain effort to forestall the coup (Attinger and Kramer, 1993:28; also cited in Danner, 1993:52n). This time, however, the army high command and the macoute camp, with the support of the bourgeoisie and especially its wealthiest faction, were prepared to unleash the most brutal wave of repression, terror, and assassination against Aristide's supporters and the entire spectrum of the prodemocratic forces.

Three days after this speech, a unit of the army under the command of Chief of Police Michel François, then a major, launched the coup that toppled Aristide and his government (Danner, 1993:52; Moïse and Olivier, 1992:177).

Thanks only to the intervention of the French, U.S., and Venezuelan ambassadors, the putschists spared Aristide's life and allowed him to flee into exile (Goshko, 1991).

There are times in history when a leader is justified in calling on the people to rise up against their enemies and to use whatever means are necessary to repel them. Such a situation existed in Saint-Domingue in 1802 during the revolution when Napoléon Bonaparte sent an expedition to recapture the colony from Toussaint Louverture and restore the slave regime. As C.L.R. James argued, Louverture should have acted decisively once he learned of the expedition. He should have called the population to arms and given the French colonialists a clear choice: Either leave the colony or accept the new order and defend it. The properties of all those who refused to side with the new regime, James maintained, should have been seized, and those French who showed any sign of treason should have been summarily executed. Moreover, rather than reassuring the whites that they and their properties were safe, Louverture should have spoken to the masses to explain to them what was happening and what had to be done. For it was what they thought that mattered then, not what the imperialists thought. James added, "If to make matters clear to them [the masses] Toussaint had to condone a massacre of the whites, so much the worse for the whites. He had done everything possible for them" (James, 1963:286–287).

Haiti under Aristide, however, was not in a revolutionary situation. And his government was not seeking to expropriate the dominant classes and establish a new social order. Quite the contrary, his government preached class conciliation and proposed an economic program that depended on the collaboration of the bourgeoisie. This does not mean that Aristide should have remained passive against threats to his government. He may have been justified, for example, in not condemning the violent reaction of his supporters to the stillborn coup d'état of Lafontant in January 1991 and in placing the blame for the violence squarely on the shoulders of the would-be coup-makers. He certainly had a right to call on his supporters to be vigilant and to defend his government on September 27 if a coup was launched against him. But just as he was wrong to praise his popular supporters on August 4 for their "wise" reference to "Père Lebrun" during the trial of Lafontant and his accomplices, he was wrong to threaten popular violence against the bourgeoisie for the latter's recalcitrance and exercise of its property rights. Aristide himself, after all, had promised to respect the bourgeoisie's property and interests. In politics, it is always dangerous to threaten to use force against one's opponent unless one is willing and able to carry out the threat. In a fragile transitional period, as was the case in Haiti in 1991, empty threats against opponents who were by class instincts predisposed to subvert the democratization process were disastrous. Aristide had never armed or formed a disciplined organization among his supporters, and he therefore relied only on veiled threats and an unpredictable populace. These two combinations are always deadly. The army, by contrast, had all the weapons, was organized (at least against Aristide's defenseless supporters), and was anxious to strike against the defiant priest.

As president, it was Aristide's ultimate responsibility to uphold the law and human rights, "to refrain from any statement that could be understood to support *Père Lebrun*, and to speak out firmly and consistently against this barbaric practice" (AW/NCHR/CR, 1991:28). Aristide failed to do so because he became deluded by his own charismatic powers and believed that, with the masses behind him, he was invincible and could rule without winning over the bourgeoisie, the parliament, or the army. This was his greatest mistake. The error that Aristide made in all those instances when popular violence was used or threatened with his explicit or implicit encouragement was political, not moral. It stemmed from his failure to distinguish between democratic rights and violent and illegal threats to democracy (and his presidency).

Aristide's erratic behavior and errors of judgment divided and confused his defenders and ultimately weakened them. But they also reinforced the worst fears of the bourgeoisie, who came to believe that their future lay in joining with the neo-Duvalierists to topple the Lavalas government and get rid of Aristide once and for all. By the time of the coup, the bourgeoisie, who had wanted to topple Aristide from the start, had found an excuse to act. Aided by Aristide's blunders, members of the bourgeoisie convinced themselves that he was determined to carry out his "social revolution" and that there was no alternative but to overthrow him (Danner, 1993:52). The macoute forces in control of the armed forces, for their part, needed no justification to act, only the right moment. For them, the right moment came with Aristide's departure for New York to address the United Nations. The president's standing with the National Assembly had reached a low point, even among his own parliamentary supporters. He was under attack by many popular organizations for his government's agreement with the IMF. He had completely alienated the bourgeoisie after the events of July and August. The military hierarchy was angered by Aristide's attacks against corruption and drug trafficking and worried that the warming of relations between the Aristide government and the U.S. Embassy in Haiti would lead to greater drug enforcement activities in the country. They were also restive about the formation of a presidential security force that would be loyal to Aristide, his intentions to disband the infamous Leopard Battalion, and Cédras's "interim" status as commander in chief of the army. In sum, the political climate seemed propitious. If the macoute forces did not act, they might well lose their chance to do so later, especially if Aristide returned from his intended visit with President Bush with hundreds of millions of foreign aid dollars starting to flow into the country (Danner, 1993:52; COHA, 2 October 1991). Neither the macoutes nor the bourgeoisie, however, understood that this was 1991 and not 1986 and that Washington, under the guise of the so-called new world order, was reassessing its long-standing Cold War policy of instinctively supporting military or right-wing dictatorships in the hemisphere in the name of anticommunism.

It is quite wrong to say, as Aristide's detractors did, that his September 27 speech was "the straw that broke the camel's back . . . about the military rebellion that forced the Haitian president out of power" (*HO*, 2–9 October 1991). The coup had been plotted well before the speech, which itself was a desperate attempt on Aristide's part to forestall his overthrow. If the September 27 speech was not the immediate cause of the coup, neither was Aristide's allegedly poor human rights record or his violation of the constitution. Such arguments were used as post facto justifications by the putschists and their supporters in the U.S. government and media in an attempt to discredit Aristide and convince the Bush and Clinton administrations to find a solution to the Haitian crisis that did not involve returning Aristide to power.

For all his political errors and even his abuse of powers as president, Aristide's human rights record showed dramatic improvements, compared favorably with the record of any of his predecessors, and certainly paled in comparison with the reign of terror that followed his overthrow.[4] Whatever the human rights failings of the Aristide government, as an Americas Watch report concluded, they could not "be used to justify committing yet a further, serious human rights violation by depriving the Haitian people of the right to elect their government" (AW/NCHR/CR, 1991). As Mark Danner aptly put it, "In the end human rights did not bring Aristide down, politics did" (Danner, 1993:52). The September 30 coup d'état resulted from a classic power struggle between a reformist and populist (but unpredictable) president who lacked a well-organized and disciplined political base, a parliamentary majority, and control over the military, on the one hand, and economic and prebendary political-military elites who feared democracy and the masses, as well as the loss of their power and their privileges, on the other hand.

Aristide himself understood his overthrow in political terms and referred to the social forces lined up against him as the "gang of four": the army, the political class and the bourgeoisie, the church hierarchy, and the United States. First, he argued, the army could not tolerate any reform that would affect it directly and weaken its powers and prerogatives. The creation of a constitutional order would take away from that institution its true vocation, that is, its expertise in coups d'état and ruling by terror. The army also feared losing control over its lucrative and illicit activities, particularly its participation in drug trafficking, an activity it shared with the macoutes and the continental mafias. Second, the bourgeoisie and the political class allied to the army also had an aversion to democracy and the creation of a government of laws. For the political class (that is, the functionaries of the public bureaucracy and public enterprises), total control over the state apparatuses and the prebendary practices that this made possible constituted the source of their power, wealth, and privileges. For the bourgeoisie, who held the uneducated popular classes in contempt, nothing was more frightening than the masses attaining the status of citizens. "Seven months of the 'Lavalassian nightmare,'" Aristide wrote, "excused and justified the reinforcement of the walls of class, their watchtowers lined with armed watchmen"(Aristide, 1994b:31–33). Third, the church hierarchy, which vehemently opposed the emergence and influence of the Ti Légliz liberation theology movement, sided openly with the putschists and legitimated the coup d'état by appointing a new papal nuncio to Port-au-Prince. In fact, the Vatican was the only foreign state to have recognized the new regime diplomatically (Aristide, 1994b:34–35). Fourth, there was the United States, which, after the fall of communism, sought to change its ugly image as the defender of dictatorship by promoting an "ersatz of democracy" in the poor countries. In Haiti, the problem for Washington was how to compel its traditional allies—the bourgeoisie and the military establishment—to accept a minimal democracy, sever their ties with the system of corruption, and abandon their age-old practice of treating the masses like slaves, while at the same time preserving Haiti as a source of cheap labor for the assembly industries and the multinational agribusinesses. The solution lay in electing a candidate who accepted the new game plan and who was supported by the local oligarchies and the United States. Unfortunately, the Haitian masses, who had been excluded from this new schema, spoiled it (in the opinion of the U.S. strategists) by voting for their own unexpected and unpredictable candidate (Aristide, 1994b:35–37).

Aristide succinctly summarized the underlying fears of his protagonists and the reasons why they ousted him or supported his ouster from power. His musings, however, do not go far enough in weighing the role that his own behavior as president played in these actions. The creation of a liberal social democratic state threatened the most fundamental interests of the prebendary Duvalierist state and military, and short of capitulating to those sectors, there is little that Aristide could have done to win their support for democracy. They had vowed to oppose and topple him, and for them, it was a matter of when, not whether, they would act.

Although the marriage that Aristide called for between the army and the people may not have been possible, he could have done much more to reassure the bourgeoisie and win it over to his side, difficult as that task was. But in fact, the entire postelection conjuncture worked against this rapprochement. Even if Aristide had succeeded in wooing the bourgeoisie, it may still not have been sufficient to prevent the military from toppling him. The class imperatives of the military leadership, not those of the bourgeoisie, compelled it to act. But the army would have acted alone and been left completely isolated and without influential and wealthy supporters within Haiti. As things stood, Aristide's contradictory behavior reinforced the bourgeoisie's distrust of him and encouraged it to side with the army and the macoute camp arrayed against him.

On one hand, Aristide preached class conciliation, and the entire social democratic project of his government was based on forming a broad consensus and a class alliance between the bourgeoisie, the working class, and the peasants. On the other hand, he threatened to unleash popular violence against and expropriate the bourgeoisie when the latter refused to go along with his program. He preached respect for the constitution and the rule of law but sanctioned the use of force if necessary to achieve his vision of justice, even when that contravened the law. And though he declared his adherence to the democratic process and the separation of powers, he disdained all established political parties, sought to bypass the National Assembly, and even encouraged his popular supporters to harass and intimidate parliamentarians who opposed him.

Aristide, therefore, sent quite contradictory messages to his supporters and opponents alike, and the confusion that this caused among all sectors of the population eroded confidence in him and weakened his defenders while emboldening his enemies to act. In short, though the demise of Aristide's presidency stemmed from the unwillingness of the antidemocratic forces to accept any changes in the status quo, Aristide's confrontational and sometimes threatening behavior added fuel to the fire of the class conflicts that were exacerbated by his election to the presidency. Aristide, in other words, failed to make the change from prophet to prince. He proved unable to abandon the radical rhetoric he employed as a charismatic opposition leader and adopt the compromising discourse and conciliatory behavior of a democratically elected president. Doing so was all the more important because he lacked a parliamentary majority and had no control over the army and its extended apparatuses and instruments of power. Under such conditions, the chances that his reformist program would succeed were slim at best. Given the configuration of class interests and the balance of class forces in Haiti and globally after Aristide took office, the antidemocratic forces would have sought to overthrow him even if he had adopted a conciliatory and princely approach. By eschewing that approach, Aristide played into the hands of his zealous enemies and gave them the excuses they needed to topple him. In the end, only a power bigger than the Haitian Army could veto the army's veto of the democratic process. And that power did not reside with Aristide or his Lavalas movement but with the "cold country to the North."

Notes

1. The members of the armed paramilitary organization were variously known as macoutes, zenglendos, or attachés.

2. This special force was also called the Groupement de Sécurité du Président (GSPR, Presidential Security Group).

3. Given the market exchange rate of 8.5 gourdes to US$1 in 1991, the minimum daily wage would have been worth only US$2.82.

4. For a thorough discussion of the human rights situation under Aristide's government, see AW/NCHR/CR 1991. For comparisons with the records of preceding governments, see AW/NCHR 1990 and AW/NCHR 1989. For comparisons with the postcoup military regime, see Amnesty International 1992; CCOH 1993; AW/NCHR 1993; and A/HRW/NCHR 1994.

7

The Prophet Tamed: The Coup d'État and the Moderation of Aristide

The Bush Administration and the September Coup d'État

If Aristide's inconsistent behavior did not cause the September coup, it played into the hands of his enemies by providing them with a ready-made justification for his overthrow. Aristide was overthrown, his detractors assert, because he disregarded the constitution, preached class warfare, and encouraged violence and mob rule. In other words, his opponents blame him for his overthrow and not the neo-Duvalierists, the military, and the bourgeoisie who wanted to preserve their power and privileges and who felt threatened by Aristide's agenda.

At the same time, Aristide's opponents in Haiti and abroad portrayed the Haitian Army as acting to save the nation from "mob rule," rather than being the principal obstacle to a democratic transition. Echoing the views of the Haitian Right, Lally Weymouth wrote in the *Washington Post* that the Haitian Army staged the coup to protect opposition leaders who feared for their lives (Weymouth, 1992). John Goshko, a *Washington Post* staff writer, also opined that Aristide's "strident populism led the Haitian armed forces to seize power" (Goshko, 1992). Howard French of the *New York Times* asserted that, his immense popularity notwithstanding, "Father Aristide was overthrown in part because of concerns among politically active people over his commitment to the Constitution, and growing fears of political and class-based violence, which many believe the President endorsed" (French, 1992).

Bush administration officials also shared these sentiments. They blamed the coup in part on Aristide's "condoning and even encouragement of vigilante justice by mobs" and used what they referred to as a "thick notebook detailing accounts of human rights abuses that took place during Father Aristide's rule" to distance themselves from him shortly after his overthrow. "Father Aristide," these officials maintained, "must publicly disavow mob violence and work toward sharing power with the Parliament. Such acts . . . are necessary if he is to gain the Haitian and international support he needs to return to office" (cited in Krauss, 1991b). This attitude underscored the dual strategy that the Bush and Clinton administrations pursued vis-à-vis Aristide: condemning the coup publicly while pressuring him to make concessions to his domestic ene-mies as the price for his return to office. These concessions included: granti-ng a general amnesty for the coup leaders and reigning in the popular move-ment through a politics of "reconciliation" with the antidemocratic camp; forming a broader-based government that included representatives from the bourgeoisie who opposed Aristide and supported the coup against him; accepting the U.S. neoliberal agenda developed by the USAID and the multi-lateral lending and regulatory institutions; and agreeing to hold new presi-dential elections in 1995 and not to reclaim the years Aristide lost from his five-year term due to the coup.

Aristide understood the underlying objectives of U.S. policies toward the military leaders. The United States, Aristide argued, pushed the OAS and later the UN to adopt a series of embargoes against the putschists in Haiti.[1] But those embargoes remained largely unenforced until May 1994, and it soon became evident that Aristide, not the putschists and their de facto govern-ments, was the real target of U.S. pressure. Washington's objective in not enforcing the embargoes, Aristide maintained, was to wrench more and more concessions from him, to compel him to enter into a power-sharing agreement with the enemies of change, and to "apply in Haiti its hemispheric definition of democracy: the return of a maimed and encircled Aristide" (Aristide, 1994b:38–39).

To understand the responses of the Bush and Clinton administrations to the coup in Haiti, they must be analyzed in the context of the post–Cold War new world order ideology. The end of the Cold War, the June 1991 OAS resolution making representative democracy the sine qua non of membership in the hemi-spheric organization, and the OAS pledge to suspend the membership of any state whose democratically elected government was overthrown by a coup d'état all made it difficult for the United States to support the coup against Aristide and obtain the consent of the rest of the OAS members in the name of containing communism. Moreover, the Bush administration and the conser-vative Right in Congress were seeking to isolate and squeeze the Castro gov-ernment further—under the guise that it was the only nonelected and hence nondemocratic government in the hemisphere. So, appearing to support the coup in Haiti would make the case against Cuba that much more difficult to sell to Congress.[2]

At the same time, the United States could not simply abandon its tradition-al allies in the Haitian military and the bourgeoisie and return Aristide to power without weakening him and forcing him to compromise with both the army leadership and the bourgeoisie. To ensure that Aristide would be unable to rekindle the popular mobilization that brought him to power, the popular organizations and Aristide's base of support had to be severely weakened, if not destroyed, and the ties between them and Aristide had to be broken. As an Americas Watch and National Coalition for Haitian Refugees report put it, "The military forces that overthrew Haiti's first freely elected president . . . have consolidated their rule by ruthlessly suppressing Haiti's once diverse and vibrant civil society—the range of civic, popular and professional organizations that had blossomed since the downfall of the Duvalier dictatorship seven years ago." The primary aim of the repression, the report continued, was "to return Haiti to the atomized and fearful society of the Duvalier-era so that even if international pressure secures the return of President Aristide, he would have difficulty transforming his personal popularity into the organized support needed to exert civilian authority over a violent and recalcitrant army" (AW/NCHR, 1993:1).

Many analysts observed that both the Bush and Clinton administrations pursued a dual policy. On the one hand, they publicly condemned the coup d'état and refused to accept any of the governments installed by the military leaders between October 1991 and September 1994.[3] On the other hand, both administrations pressured Aristide to make more and more concessions to his enemies, and they allowed the military to consolidate its power and pursue a campaign of terror against the popular democratic movement and Aristide's supporters. By the time the U.S.-led forces ended the junta's rule in September 1994, the human toll for their three-year reign was staggering: An estimated 4,000 people were killed, around 300,000 became internal refugees, thousands more fled across the border to the Dominican Republic, and more than 60,000 took to the high seas to seek asylum in the United States (Constable, 1992–1993; Doyle, 1994; Ives, 1995a, 1995b; I. Martin, 1994).[4]

It is necessary to distinguish between the objectives of the two administrations. The Bush administration supported the interests of the Haitian military and bourgeoisie and was more responsive to the Right within the U.S. Congress, the CIA, and the State Department, all of which opposed Aristide's return.[5] Thus, even though the coup d'état challenged Washington's post–Cold War doctrine of supporting democracy and human rights, the Bush administration was working to find a solution to the crisis in Haiti that involved a return to civilian rule but without Aristide and with the military as a dominant institution. Since the Haitian Constitution of 1987 prohibited the reelection of an incumbent president, the Bush administration thought it could simply stall Aristide's return until his term of office expired in 1996. To achieve this goal, it was necessary to appear to be encouraging a negotiated settlement of the crisis while allowing the Haitian military junta—Lt. Gen. Raoul Cédras, Brig. Gen. Philippe Biamby, and Lt. Col. Michel François—to reject any deals that involved Aristide's return.[6] The administration justified its position by recalling Aristide's allegedly poor human rights record, and it participated in a campaign of misinformation and character assassination designed to portray Aristide as unstable and unfit to hold office.

The strategy followed by the Bush administration consisted of weakening the embargo, downplaying the human rights violations committed by the military, accusing Aristide (but not the military) of intransigence when the Haitian president rejected certain demands, and always pressuring him instead of the military to make more concessions. The signals the administration sent to the Haitian military leaders were clear: The United States was not going to force them out of power, even if they continued to defy the international community and refuse to negotiate seriously for Aristide's return (Doyle, 1994:51). Moreover, the Bush administration defined the Haitian refugees who sought asylum in the United States as economic and not political refugees and forcefully repatriated those intercepted at sea without asylum hearings. This policy may well have been adopted for two reasons: because the administration exaggerated the threat of an "invasion" of unskilled and illiterate "boat people" to the United States and because it feared alienating conservative and anti-immigrant voters, especially in Florida (Constable, 1992–1993:184–187). But by defining the "boat people" as economic rather than political refugees and returning them to Haiti, the Bush administration implicitly endorsed the coup, disregarded the military's human rights violations, and encouraged its further repression of Aristide's supporters. It also sent a clear message to Aristide: If he wanted an end to the repression and the killings of his supporters, as well as a solution to the refugee crisis, it was incumbent upon him to reach a political settlement with the de facto authorities (see the chronology at the end of this volume). As Kate Doyle concluded, by the end of the Bush presidency, the "administration's mistrust of Aristide was an open secret. As one senior U.N. official put it, 'Two lines about Haiti co-existed at the time. There was the line about the return to democracy, which was for public consumption. And then there was a second line, spoken privately within the administration. And the Haitian military knew it perfectly well'" (Doyle, 1994:52).

The Clinton Administration Takes Over

Not until the advent of the Clinton administration would the United States reassess and shift its policy toward the Haitian junta and its de facto governments. But this would not come until 1994. As a presidential candidate, Clinton had vowed to end Bush's "inhumane" policy of repatriating Haitian refugees. But he reversed himself after assuming office when confronted with the possibility of having tens of thousands of Haitians reaching U.S. shores. While he continued the same practice as his predecessor, Clinton claimed that he would resolve the crisis that caused the outflow of refugees by returning Aristide to office (Doyle, 1994:52; I. Martin, 1994:74). Clinton warned Aristide, however, that his return to power would occur "under conditions of national reconciliation and mutual respect for human rights" (cited in COHA, 30 March 1993). This phrase conveyed the fears of the White House, the Haitian military, and the bourgeoisie about the possibility of popular vengeance if Aristide returned. Clinton also expected Aristide to make concessions to the dominant classes and to contain the masses when he returned. Aristide's endorsement of the concept of "reconciliation" was an important factor in the decision to return him to Haiti in October 1994. Translated, "reconciliation" meant an amnesty for and no popular reprisals against the coup leaders and those who killed, tortured, raped, and mutilated Haitian citizens during the three years of the junta.

To stem the flow of refugees, Clinton enlisted Aristide's cooperation in urging Haitians to stay in their homeland in return for the U.S. government taking a tougher stance against the Haitian military (Doyle, 1994:52; COHA, 8 January 1993). As Aristide himself put it: "A deal . . . could be struck between [President Clinton] and me. I would discourage the boat people, and he would work for a return to democracy. The Haitian refugees would stay in the country and, in cooperation with the UN, the American president would put all his weight in the balance to oust the de facto government" (Aristide, 1994b:133–134). Aristide wrote a letter to the UN and OAS secretaries-general in early January 1993 to request that multinational observers be sent to Haiti to monitor the human rights situation. In that letter and in a subsequent address to Haiti on the Voice of America, Aristide also agreed that once the multinational observers were in place, he would name a new prime minister, form a consensus government, and grant amnesty to the army. In return, the sanctions against Haiti would be lifted, international aid resumed, and international assistance provided to "professionalize" the army, separate the police from the army, and reform the judicial system. Once the new prime minister was chosen and a new government was formed, a date would be set for Aristide's return. The Haitian Army's high command agreed to this plan after a visit by Maj. Gen. John Sheehan of the U.S. Marines, who presumably told them that things would get tougher for them if they did not cooperate. The general also made offers of "nonlethal" aid to help "professionalize" the army, as a "carrot for cooperation" (Farah, 1993a; I. Martin, 1994:76–77).

Between January and June 1993, a struggle ensued between the de facto military government, Aristide, the UN-OAS, and the United States over several issues: the deployment of human rights observers, armed international police monitors, the future size and role of the army, the separation of the police from the army, and the fate of the army high command and those responsible for the coup and ensuing repression. In April 1993, Clinton first raised the issue of installing a multinational peacekeeping force to maintain order and prevent widespread violence if Aristide returned to Haiti (Marquis, 1993a).

The Haitian junta agreed to the presence of civilian human rights monitors, whom they knew would be ineffective in curbing the repression. But playing the nationalist card, they remained steadfast in their opposition to the deployment of armed police monitors. The junta, trusting Washington more than the UN (which they believed was more supportive of Aristide), played on the fears and the divisions within the Clinton administration, the State Department, and the Pentagon over Aristide's return. They looked to the United States to ensure a future for the Haitian Army and prevent it from being pared down to a minimum size—from 7,000 to about 1,000—as Aristide proposed (I. Martin, 1994:74–75; Aristide, 1994b:192). Though generally opposed to Aristide's return, the putschists rejected the proposition that they quit the army in exchange for amnesty—a condition upon which Aristide insisted.

Although he was reluctant to endorse an armed international force in Haiti, Aristide clearly understood that without such a force, it would be difficult to ensure a peaceful transition to constitutional rule, carry out the intended reforms in the armed forces and other institutions, and prevent another coup d'état. Aristide also mistrusted Washington's ties to the Haitian military and would have preferred it if the UN had taken a much stronger lead in handling the crisis, in the deployment of the international police and peacekeeping forces, and in overseeing the postrestoration transition. Aristide understood, of course, that the United States would not allow the UN to usurp its leadership role and send into Haiti a multinational force that did not have a predominant U.S. component and was not under U.S. command.

Aristide pursued a strategy that would maximize his maneuverability within the limits imposed by his dependence on the United States to return him to power. Knowing that the Haitian military leaders had no intention of abiding by any agreement that would lead to his return, Aristide moved on two fronts simultaneously. On the one hand, he set out to negotiate in good faith, make concessions to the Haitian bourgeoisie to win their support and break their ties with the military, and induce the military leaders to expose their own perfidy. On the other hand, he hoped to convince Washington that, without his return, the crisis in Haiti and its consequences for the United States, especially the refugee dilemma, would not be resolved. Aristide's implicit message was this: Without him, it would be impossible to create a climate of stability that would help end the refugee crisis and further Washington's neoliberal economic agenda for Haiti.

Aristide, in short, understood that the price of defeating the Haitian military would be high in terms of the concessions that he would have to make. He also realized that this was perhaps the only chance that Haiti had to revive the democratic process, albeit within the limits imposed by the hegemony of the United States. As Aristide put it,

We have already paid a high price for democracy; today it is costing us an exorbitant price. And for this prohibitive price, they would want to give us less democracy. The more we wait, the more we pay, and the less we have of this commodity. Unless one thinks that after two centuries of deprivation and more than two years of equivocation, we should settle for a few rotten fish or for some spoiled vegetables. . . . I recalled it for the third anniversary of the victory of Lavalas: the people don't buy democracy in a market (Aristide, 1994b:180).

For Aristide, the priority was not "the return of citizen-president Aristide, but that of the constitutional order. And of the right to have rights. The vast majority of Haitians wish that and say so . . . when the risk to speak is not too high" (Aristide, 1994b:182). He knew, of course, that the resumption of constitutional rule depended on his return but that it was not reducible to him. In the process, deals and concessions would be required, and he was prepared to make them. The coup and its aftermath, it seemed, had produced a change in Aristide. He was being transformed into a politician who reconciled himself to the give-and-take of politics. At last, he was ready to substitute the prince's clothing for the prophet's.

The major difference between 1991 and 1993 was that Aristide was now dealing from a position of weakness. Exiled and severed from his mass base, he could no longer call on his supporters to pressure and intimidate his opponents. Without a following, his charismatic powers lacked their contextual and material bases and simply could not be used to mobilize the masses. Consequently, he had to adopt the language of conciliation. The prophet, in other words, had been tamed and silenced.

The central problem of the Clinton administration in its original approach to the Haitian crisis stemmed from (1) splits between the liberal and conservative forces within the various U.S. state apparatuses (i.e., the White House, State Department, Defense Department, CIA, and Congress), and (2) the initial decision to retain the key personnel in the State Department who had been responsible for Haiti policy under Bush and who had worked to prevent Aristide's reinstatement (COHA, 11 February 1993). Despite the Haitian military's brutal history of repression, its known corruption and involvement in drug trafficking, and its aversion to democracy, these officials still believed that they could "professionalize" that institution and convert the high command into ardent democrats. The real reason for insisting on a future role for the Haitian military, of course, was that many U.S. officials in the White House, State Department, Pentagon, CIA, and Congress simply could not conceive of Aristide returning to Haiti without a counterbalancing force to check his and the popular movement's power. The balance of class forces had to be maintained at all cost in favor of the propertied elite and the military. Thus, while Clinton and other administration officials declared their support for Aristide and sought concessions from him, others within the administration worked behind the scenes to undermine that eventuality and protect the Haitian Army. As Ian Martin observed, "U.S. officials, who had been in direct discussion with the military, concluded that the army needed further reassurance of its future. That was a key moment: For the first time, the military learned that the Clinton administration was not prepared to have tough talk followed by tough action" (I. Martin, 1994:77).

Haitian military leaders received this sort of reassurance all along from U.S. officials. That led them to dismiss the tough talk coming from Washington and to reject the plan proposed to them in May 1993 by Lawrence Pezzullo, President Clinton's special envoy to Haiti, and Dante Caputo, Pezzullo's counterpart at the UN-OAS. (Pezzullo, a former U.S. ambassador to Nicaragua, had replaced Bernard Aronson, Bush's special envoy to Haiti, in March 1993.) The plan, endorsed by Aristide, reiterated proposals made earlier. It called for deploying a multinational police force of 500 to 1,000 members in Haiti, obtaining the resignation of the army high command and issuing a broad amnesty for the military, retraining the army and police, creating a consensus government acceptable to both Aristide and his opponents, and returning Aristide to power (Bohning, 1993a; Farah, 1993b; French, 1993a, 1993c).

Aristide tried to reassure the putschists that he "would not put them in jail or pursue them" and that they might even be free to remain in Haiti after his return (cited in French, 1993a). He never promised, however, that they would not be subject to criminal indictments by citizens pursuing justice through the courts or that he would allow them to remain in the armed forces. Indeed, he remained consistent on this point throughout the negotiating process. On October 4, 1994, shortly before he returned to Haiti, Aristide addressed the UN and repeated his pledge of "Yes to reconciliation, No to violence, No to vengeance, No to impunity, Yes to justice!" (Aristide, 1994c). The Haitian junta, certain that Washington would not force it to accept the terms of the plan and Aristide's return, not only rebuffed the United States and the UN but also showed its flagrant disregard for the presence of human rights monitors by stepping up its repression during March and April (Tarr, 1993; French, 1993b).

Clinton and members of his administration, who had believed that the junta wanted a deal, felt double-crossed and angered by its defiance. They ordered tougher sanctions against the military high command, the de facto government, and other officials and pushed for a stronger trade embargo against Haiti at the UN Security Council (Marquis, 1993a). The sanctions included targeting and freezing the assets of state-owned enterprises and those Haitians who supported the coup, as well as barring entry to the United States for those who impeded negotiations toward a settlement and a return to constitutional rule (Marquis, 1993b; Farah, 1993c). On June 15, 1993, the UN Security Council voted unanimously to adopt sweeping new sanctions against the Haitian junta (now without the semblance of a government since the resignation of de facto Prime Minister

Bazin on June 8). The UN sanctions included those adopted earlier by the Clinton administration, plus a worldwide ban on the sale to Haiti of petroleum and petroleum products, arms, ammunition, and military vehicles and equipment (Marquis, 1993c).

The new sanctions, combined with the threat of a naval blockade of Haiti, sent General Cédras to the negotiating table. For the first time, it appeared that the Haitian junta was serious about reaching a settlement. Negotiations arranged by the UN between Cédras and Aristide began in late June on Governors Island in New York and ended on July 3, 1993, with the signing of the ten-point Agreement of Governors Island. The agreement, essentially crafted by Caputo and U.S. officials with the endorsement of the other "friends of Haiti"—Canada, France, and Venezuela—called for the departure of the junta and Aristide's return to power. In fact, the pact contained all the loopholes that would allow the junta to violate the agreement and prolong its own hold on power for another year. Under heavy pressure from UN and U.S. mediators, Aristide, who had serious reservations about many of the clauses of the agreement and who warned against trusting Cédras's words, agreed to sign it on July 3; Cédras had done so the day before. Essentially, UN and U.S. officials told Aristide that this was a take-it-or-leave-it deal and threatened that, even without his approval of the agreement, Washington would push the UN Security Council to lift the embargo against Haiti (COHA, 18 October 1993; "The Challenges Ahead," 1993). UN Secretary-General Boutros Boutros-Ghali reportedly told Aristide, "Don't think any more, Mr. President, just sign." Caputo, reacting to Aristide's hesitation, told a reporter in an indignant tone, "He [Aristide] will have to answer to history. I am fed up" (cited in Marquis, 1993d, 1993e; French, 1993d).

Aristide's reservations were well founded. The Agreement of Governors Island included the following: nomination of a new prime minister by Aristide and his or her confirmation by the legally reconstituted National Assembly; suspension of the UN sanctions of June 1993; assistance for economic development, administrative and judicial reforms, and modernizing the Armed Forces of Haiti; the creation of a new police force and appointment of a new commander in chief of the police force by the president; amnesty for the military; the retirement of Cédras and the appointment of a new commander in chief of the Armed Forces of Haiti; the return of Aristide on October 30, 1993 (i.e., in four months); and UN-OAS verification of the fulfillment of the agreement (Aristide, 1994b:195–197).

The Agreement of Governors Island was profoundly flawed, Doyle observed, on many levels: It made "dangerous concessions" to the Haitian military leaders, contained no mechanisms of enforcement or penalties for noncompliance, granted amnesty to those responsible for the mass killings and the repression, allowed the military leaders to stay in power until Aristide's return, and lifted the embargo after Aristide's newly chosen prime minister was confirmed and before Aristide returned to Haiti (Doyle, 1994:53–54). Doyle concluded that "behind the terms of the accord, lay a fundamental miscalculation about the Haitian military, which led Pezzullo and Caputo to stake the transition on the word of Raoul Cédras. Their faith in him as an honest broker and in his role as the ultimate guarantor for the agreement was based only in part on the belief that Cédras had no alternative" (Doyle, 1994:54).

When one places the agreement in the broader context of U.S. relations with the Haitian military since the coup d'état (if not since 1986), it becomes apparent that the "fundamental miscalculation" Doyle mentioned was not a miscalculation at all. The UN and U.S. mediators obtained precisely what they wanted, namely, an agreement from Cédras that he and possibly some of the other henchmen of the military high command—such as the chief of police, Lt. Col. Michel François—would resign but that the Armed Forces of Haiti would be preserved as an institution, albeit "professionalized" and reformed, with Aristide forced into a power-sharing arrangement with the military and the bourgeoisie. This would be done by forming a new consensus government—a new power bloc—that would be approved by them and that would leave Aristide powerless. That this was the real objective of Pezzullo would be revealed in the months ahead, after the Haitian junta disregarded the agreement and stepped up its repression.

The New Partnership

For his part, Aristide knew that the military rulers could not be trusted and that they would not implement the agreement. Hence, he would gain the high ground by calling their bluff. He set out to implement the provisions of the accord that pertained to him—nominating a new prime minister and later issuing an amnesty that was never voted on by parliament because the junta prevented it. Aristide also started to do what he should have done when he was in power in 1991: wooing the Haitian bourgeoisie and getting it to rescind its support for the putschists. On July 22, 1993, Aristide's government in exile organized the Haiti Government/Business Partnership Conference in Miami; most of the participants were members of the Haitian haute bourgeoisie (some 200 attended), foreign businesspeople involved in Haiti, U.S. officials and members of the U.S. Congress, representatives from the international aid and regulatory organizations, and members of Aristide's cabinet. At that conference, Aristide pledged that his next government would "create the mechanisms of consultation, call on the resources and the exercise of the private sector and of the 'tenth Department,' promote capital investment from local and foreign investors, and establish an industrial and tourist development plan." Raymond Roy, the elder spokesman for the Haitian bourgeoisie, replied that, for its part, the business sector wants to be a party to the solution and believes that it is in everyone's interest that a real climate of trust and harmony be established in this country where economic growth and human development become the central focus. In this sense we are convinced that the essential prerequisite for growth and development is the reestablishment of a climate of confidence by putting in place a state of laws where private property and civil liberties are guaranteed, and where all relations are regulated by laws and contracts and by clear and fair rules (cited in Ethéart, 1993:8).

By "climate of confidence," the bourgeoisie always means a government that understands, respects, and responds to the interests of business. A government that fails to do so quickly loses the confidence of business, and when this loss of confidence is based on outright fear, business goes on strike by disinvesting. The climate of confidence is restored when government changes its policies to conform to business interests. Aristide learned the meaning of the term "climate of confidence" the hard way between February and September 1991, and he was now ready to apply what he had learned. To "reassure the property owners," Aristide chose Robert Malval as his prime minister designate (Aristide, 1994b:162). Malval was a prominent businessman and member of the haute bourgeoisie who was said to be "preoccupied by social issues" and a "liberal democrat without partisan affiliation" (cited in *HM*, 28 July–3 August 1993).

This was not the first time that Aristide, as president, had met with members of the haute bourgeoisie and pledged allegiance to private property and private sector-led economic development. But the situation had changed significantly since Aristide's first seven months in power. Now he was completely dependent on the goodwill of the United States to return him to Haiti, and he was dealing with the Haitian bourgeoisie and the foreign investors from a weakened position. He, not they, had to make all the concessions. Aristide's promises to the bourgeoisie in Miami, therefore, were not rhetoric. They signaled a decisive shift in the balance of class forces: The Haitian bourgeoisie, under Washington's hegemony and with the full weight of the U.S. government and the international financial institutions behind it, had regained the upper hand. Aristide understood that he would have to conform to the dictates of the bourgeoisie and foreign capital in their current neoliberal manifestation, and he modified his discourse and behavior accordingly. As Prime Minister Malval put it shortly before Aristide was scheduled to return to Haiti on October 30, 1993, "The president has learned that this is not a Manichean world—the good on one side, the ugly on the other, the bourgeoisie on one side, the masses on the other. He has grown up a lot" (cited in Reiss, 1993). By "growing up a lot," of course, Malval meant that Aristide had finally learned who was in charge and that he would have to include representatives of the Haitian haute bourgeoisie in the new government he would form upon his return to Haiti.

The turnaround of Aristide and his government in exile was evident not just in the promises made at the Miami conference and in the choice of his new prime minister but also in the "Strategy of Social and Economic Reconstruction" (issued by the Aristide government in exile in August 1994 [Haiti, 1994b]) and in a letter written in November 1994 by Marie-Michèle Rey, economic and finance minister, to the president of the International Development Association (IDA) (Rey, 1994). These two documents were based largely on the Emergency Economic Recovery Program developed by a multiagency task force (the Joint Mission) of the IDA, the Inter-American Development Bank (IDB), and other bilateral and multilateral organizations (i.e., the IMF, World Bank, and USAID). They made it clear that the Aristide government had abandoned its moderate social democratic objectives and its dirigiste conception of the role of the state in economic development in favor of the "market-friendly" or neoliberal model (Rey, 1994:1).[7] The objective of the latter was to create a state of laws, with the checks and balances of independent branches of government and the subordination of the military to civilian rule. In contrast to the goals of the Lavalas Project, the new economic objectives were to "limit the scope of state activity, and concentrate it on the mission of defining the enabling milieu for private initiative and productive investments; reduce the involvement of the central government in the commercial production of goods and services; and improve the quality of public administration" (Haiti, 1994b:1).

This new economic orientation shared much with the Lavalas Project, including such goals as: downsizing and modernizing the public sector and the civil service administration; curbing corruption; reforming the tax system to make it more progressive and enforcing tax collection to reduce tax evasion by the wealthy; allowing the exchange system to operate freely according to the market rate; reducing public spending while targeting and improving the delivery of services to the social sectors in greatest need, including the delivery of health, nutrition, and educational services; and giving priority to infrastructural investments. Insofar as the new strategy corresponded to the recommendations of the Joint Mission, it did not differ much from the project. It advanced a similar view of the urban and industrial sectors, and it stressed the need to assist the handicraft and small-scale industries and promote industrial decentralization and investments in the provinces (IDB, 1994:2–27).

But the new strategy broke decisively with the social democratic, basic-needs-oriented Lavalas Project in several respects. The major difference lay in its overall emphasis on wealth and resource redistribution and the dirigiste role of the state. The new strategy did not begin by conceptualizing the centrality of the peasantry within the Haitian economy, and it rejected the logic of the majority perspective developed by the project. Hence, the strategy did not start from the premise that a reconstructed, equal, just, and democratic Haiti must give priority to the interests, needs, and participation of the peasantry and the rural and urban informal, handicraft, and small industrial sectors. As such, the strategy avoided the issues of land reform and the promotion of peasant organizations, peasant cooperatives, and small- and medium-size agro-industrial enterprises. It emphasized trade liberalization, except for a few products—such as rice, corn, beans, and sorghum—whose subsidies would be phased out over several years.

The strategy, advanced via the Joint Mission, emphasized the accumulation of capital and specified numerous functions for the state: providing basic services, creating labor-intensive projects to generate employment, rebuilding the rural infrastructure (e.g., irrigation systems, tertiary roads and footpaths, and water cisterns), controlling erosion and encouraging reforestation, providing production inputs (such as fertilizers, pesticides, and hand tools), offering veterinary services, and facilitating access to credit for "selected small-scale farmers and marketing groups" to increase agricultural production and boost the income of small farmers (IDB, 1994:20). To be sure, these measures were necessary and important. But they were not sufficient. The state also had to take a strong role in organizing and regulating markets, directing investments to the strategic sectors of the economy (e.g., agriculture), encouraging technological innovation, and giving priority to meeting the basic needs of the population in health care, food, housing, education, and public transportation.

Concerning the privatization of public enterprises, the recommendations of the strategy differed only in emphasis from the objectives of the Lavalas Project. Whereas the project emphasized streamlining and/or privatizing the management of the enterprises still owned by the state to make them more efficient and responsive to the market, the strategy called for the immediate sale (partial or whole) of several public enterprises (such as the flour mill, the cement factory, the electric and telephone companies, and the central bank). Mindful of the politically sensitive nature of this proposition, government officials stated that they were "democratizing" the sale of these public assets by targeting foreign investors, domestic savers, and members of the Haitian diaspora. The government leaders also considered including the "traditionally excluded segments of the society," especially the victims of the repression, in the transfer of public assets to private individuals. Though they admitted that the "practical modalities of such transfers [were] not yet specified," they said they were exploring several alternatives (Haiti, 1994b:6).

If implemented, however, the free and open market policies advocated by the Joint Mission and the new strategy would actually have effects opposite to those that were originally anticipated. Without sustained state intervention to guarantee the basic needs of the population, the laissez-faire strategy would affect the most vulnerable sectors of the Haitian economy—the agricultural, informal, and handicraft sectors—most directly because they could not compete with cheaper foreign imports. Though unstated, the objective of the neoliberal economic model adopted by the strategy was to maintain Haiti's main comparative advantage, namely, its cheap labor. The dislocations caused by the cheap labor strategy were already well known, and they would inevitably lead to still greater unemployment and rural-to-urban migration. The main beneficiaries undoubtedly would be the private local and foreign investors, foreign exporters, and the small wealthy faction of the bourgeoisie that controls the import sector.

Be that as it may, the aspects of the strategy and the Joint Mission that called for providing basic health, education, nutrition, and other services to the population, as well as investments to rebuild Haiti's rural and urban infrastructure, were positive steps. These measures, if adopted and implemented as public policies rather than being delegated to the private sector, would benefit the impoverished majority and improve their standards of living. Haiti, it must be remembered, has never had a state that provided such services to its citizens. Thus, the creation of a liberal state, even one that pursued neoliberal economic policies and implemented the stipulated reforms, would constitute a major improvement in the lives of average Haitians, especially those of the poor majority who have only known abject poverty and the most brutal and avaricious of dictatorships. But would the government be able to generate sufficient revenues to pay for these services, especially if, as might be expected, the free market policies should fail to stimulate sustained growth and reverse Haiti's trade imbalances?

What was clear in late 1994 was that the restored Aristide government would depend on the international institutions, under USAID leadership, to clear the arrears Haiti owed to foreign governments and financial institutions and to fund and oversee the implementation of the "Strategy of Social and Economic Reconstruction." These bilateral and multilateral agencies intended to be involved in all aspects of the "nation-building" activities (not just those that pertained to reforming the state apparatuses) and in implementing the neoliberal, "market friendly" economic development strategy. Haiti, in effect, would be placed under the trusteeship of the international regulatory and aid organizations and would depend on them to provide the hundreds of millions of dollars needed to rejuvenate its bankrupt and stagnant economy (Goshko, 1994b).

The international aid agencies pledged their full support for Aristide's government because they were confident that he would now implement the government reforms and economic policies they devised. Henceforth, Aristide would no longer speak of the Lavalas Revolution to which the bourgeoisie had to accommodate itself. Rather, one would hear Aristide and members of his government in exile talk about the need to return to a government of laws and the necessity for "reconciliation," "stability," "sound macroeconomic policies," and "a vibrant, private sector with an open foreign investment policy" (Haiti, 1994b:1).

The Haitian bourgeoisie, particularly the sector that had financed the coup, also began to realize that the junta's desperation and defiance of the international community no longer served its class interests. The bourgeoisie began to reconsider its reliance on and alliance with the neo-Duvalierist junta and now viewed Aristide's return as the best hope for the future (Farah, 1993e). Being assured that the Lavalas Revolution was over (actually, it had never really begun) and that Aristide would respect their interests while pacifying the masses, influential members of the bourgeoisie (whose only principle was to safeguard their property rights and their privileges) abandoned the putschists and denounced them as bloody and greedy rogues bent on holding on to power at all cost. "I frankly was quite happy with the coup," a businessman who supplied food to the military said to a *Washington Post* reporter. "I do not like Aristide, and thought maybe Cédras would be another Pinochet. But he is not. He is a failure, and now we have to accept the fact that Aristide is president. All we can do is hope the international community keeps him from his own worst instincts." Another wealthy businessman said he was now "absolutely sure that François controls everything. He is the center of the mafia. We did not understand this at first. And Cédras is a willing partner." "It is not the traditional bourgeoisie that are actively opposing Aristide now," said yet another. "It is the young guys who made a lot of money fast after the coup, who have a certain lifestyle and are not about to give it up. They have no money outside the country, nothing to fall back on, so it is all or nothing" (cited in Farah, 1993e).

Aristide, once a hated symbol to the bourgeoisie, had become its symbol of salvation from a voracious and barbaric military. Members of the bourgeoisie may still not have liked Aristide, but they needed him because they knew no one else could compromise with them as he did and still remain revered by the popular classes. For them, this was the best of both worlds. They could now embrace Aristide and sing the Haitian national anthem along with him.[8] But this was an opportunistic marriage, one of convenience, not affinity or compatibility of interests.

The recalcitrance of the Haitian junta and their misunderstanding that a new deal had been reached stood in the way of this new partnership between Aristide and his government, the Haitian bourgeoisie, foreign investors, and the bilateral and multilateral aid agencies. Aristide took the Governors Island Agreement seriously, but Cédras and the putschists, who personally stood to lose much if the agreement was implemented, had no intention of abiding by its provisions. Soon after Prime Minister Malval was sworn into office and he and his new cabinet began their functions, the putschists went on a killing spree and a terror campaign against Aristide's supporters. On September 11, 1993, armed attachés, ostensibly under the orders of Lt. Col. Michel François, pulled Antoine Izméry (Aristide's close personal friend and financial backer during the 1990 electoral campaign) from the church where he was attending mass and murdered him. Afterward, bands of attachés terrorized street vendors in downtown Port-au-Prince. Earlier in the week, attachés had also killed several people as they tried to stop Evans Paul, the mayor of Port-au-Prince and an Aristide supporter who had gone into hiding after the coup, from returning to his office. In July and August, scores of grassroots and neighborhood organization members "disappeared," often turning up dead on sidewalks at dawn. In all, it was estimated that attachés and the police killed more than 100 people between July and October 1993 (Marquis, 1993f; Bohning, 1993b; French, 1993e; Farah, 1993d).

Then came the USS *Harlan County* incident. The Clinton administration sent the *Harlan County* to Haiti to transport the first contingent of U.S. and Canadian soldiers (about 200 in all) to "professionalize" the Haitian army and oversee the return to democracy, as mandated by the Governors Island Agreement. When the *Harlan County* reached the Port-au-Prince harbor, however, the White House ordered it to retreat after foreign diplomats who had assembled to welcome the troops were threatened by about 100 armed attachés, organized by the recently formed neo-Duvalierist death squad Front pour l'Avancement et le Progrès d'Haiti (FRAPH, Front for the Advancement and Progress of Haiti). This was yet another demonstration of the divisions within the Clinton administration over Haiti policy. The *Harlan County* was ordered to return to the U.S. naval base at Guantanamo Bay in Cuba, and future troop deployments to Haiti were canceled primarily because the Defense Department and conservative members of Congress opposed efforts to restore Aristide to power; fears of becoming embroiled in a Somalia-like situation in Haiti played only a secondary part in this decision. Ultimately, it was Pentagon and congressional pressure that led Clinton to order the ship's retreat (Sciolino, 1993; Holmes, 1993; Doyle, 1994:55–56).[9]

The opposition to Aristide's return was not confined to Washington. As Allen Nairn has shown, the CIA and U.S. Defense Intelligence Agency (DIA) have long been involved in building, supervising, and training the brutal Haitian military "security system," and the CIA itself was instrumental in helping Emmannuel "Toto" Constant, who was on the its payroll, to launch FRAPH in 1993. Originally known as the Haitian Resistance League, FRAPH was formed specifically to counterbalance and spy on Aristide's Lavalas movement and the grassroots Ti Légliz movement (Nairn, 1994b: 458–461, 1994c:481–482). Moreover, U.S. intelligence sources in Haiti knew of Constant's planned portside demonstrations at least one day before the *Harlan County* arrived at the Port-au-Prince harbor and yet did nothing to halt them (Nairn, 1994b:461; Ives, 1995a:85).

Haiti's military leaders had no intention of honoring the Governors Island Agreement and stepping down on October 15. Their defiance was encouraged by the factions within the Clinton administration and the various agencies of the U.S. government that opposed Aristide's return, despite his compromises and willingness to enter into a power-sharing arrangement in which the bourgeoisie would be clearly dominant. To drive their point home, attachés—

allegedly under Lieutenant Colonel François's orders—assassinated the newly appointed minister of justice, Guy Malary, whose duties were to reform the police and the judiciary.

The End Game

As the violence escalated in Haiti and tensions mounted between the Clinton administration and the Haitian military leaders, the UN pulled out its human rights monitors. President Clinton urged the UN to renew the sanctions against the junta, and, along with Canada, France, and Argentina, he dispatched warships to blockade Haiti. The administration also talked openly about the possible use of force to oust the military junta (Apple, 1993; Friedman, 1993b). It was then that conservatives in Congress and the U.S. special envoy to Haiti, Lawrence Pezzullo, tried to mount their own "coup" against Aristide and Clinton's efforts to reinstate him.

Republican senator Robert Dole, then Senate minority leader, launched the attack against Clinton's talk of using military force to reinstate Aristide by stating that "he [Dole] wouldn't risk any American lives to put Aristide back in power" because Aristide's human rights "shortcomings" would not "win [him] any blue ribbons in most places" (cited in Friedman, 1993a). The CIA's thirty-year veteran and national intelligence officer for Latin America, Brian Latell, followed suit by holding a "secret briefing" for members of Congress at the request of Republican senator Jesse Helms; the content of the meeting was leaked to the press (Danner, 1993:44). In this briefing, Latell presented a psychological profile of Aristide that portrayed him as mentally unstable, allegedly suffering from manic depression; he also was said to have organized ruthless gangs who routinely used violence. Even though that report was based on unsubstantiated allegations made by Aristide's enemies in Haiti (see Danner, 1993:44–45n; Marquis, 1993h), Senator Helms maintained that the CIA had "confirmed every jot and tittle" of what he had said about Aristide and that "Aristide is a killer. He is a demonstrable killer" (cited in Danner, 1993:44). Echoing Senator Dole, the North Carolina senator went on to say that he did not "want the life of one soldier or sailor from the United States of America to die in the interest of that man" (cited in Danner, 1993:44).

By contrast, Latell praised the Haitian military leaders and their de facto government in a 1992 memo he wrote for the CIA. He considered de facto Prime Minister Marc Bazin and his supporters one of the "most promising group[s] of Haitian leaders to emerge since the Duvalier family dictatorship was deposed in 1986." He further claimed that the Haitian military did not engage in "systematic or frequent lethal violence aimed at civilians" and that General Cédras was a "conscientious military leader who genuinely wishes to minimize his role in politics, professionalize the armed services, and develop a separate and competent civilian police force" (cited in Marquis, 1993h).[10]

While the conservative members of Congress and the CIA were propagating misinformation about Aristide, Pezzullo, the State Department, and the U.S. Embassy in Haiti were pushing Aristide for still more dialogue with and concessions to the military. Aristide and nine of Malval's ten ministers rejected Malval's call for a "national reconciliation conference" between the prodemocratic sector, the de facto military government, and the procoup camp until Aristide was back in power. Shortly after, on December 15, Malval resigned and openly accused Aristide of "stabbing him in the back" and blocking efforts to resolve the crisis (EPICA, 1994:44; Williams, 1993; Marquis, 1993j).

Officials of the Clinton administration, still trying to force Aristide to accommodate the junta and concerned about a renewed flow of refugees, also accused Aristide of being "intransigent" and wondered if "their get-tough strategy toward the Haitian military [was] backfiring—punishing the wrong people while failing to induce a negotiated solution." They and even Clinton, with his characteristic flip-flopping, suggested that the administration might reassess its support for Aristide (Greenhouse, 1994a; Marquis, 1993i, 1993j). Feeling betrayed by the Clinton administration, Aristide played one of the few cards he had at his disposal to pressure the United States in return. Raising the sensitive issue of the Haitian refugees, he criticized the administration's repatriation policy. He stated that it was the "coup leaders—and not the innocent victims of the coup—[who] should be forced to leave Haiti" and that "Constitutional order and democracy— not Haitians desperately fleeing state-sponsored violence—should be returned to Haiti." Moreover, Aristide asserted, "having given the international community close to one year to resolve the crisis, and having faced the weapons in their country for over two years, the voice of the refugees must now be heard" (cited in Marquis, 1993j).

At a subsequent conference that Aristide organized in Miami, Haitian activists and members of the congressional Black Caucus, as well as Jesse Jackson, criticized the Clinton administration's refugee policy as racist and chastised the administration for pushing Aristide to negotiate with a "fascist military." They also called for U.S. military action to oust the putschists (Marquis, 1994). Adding weight to these criticisms, Ian Martin, a co-leader of a joint UN-OAS human rights monitoring force in Haiti in 1993, and other human rights observers denounced the State Department for understating the death toll in Haiti and for doubting that many of the killings were politically motivated in order to justify the Clinton policy of repatriating Haitian refugees (Nusser and Maass, 1994).

Pezzullo then played his last card. The United States refused to impose stronger measures on the Haitian military leaders as the latest deadline imposed on them to step down from power—January 15, 1994—passed. Instead, the Clinton administration and the UN prodded Aristide to accept a new plan to resolve the crisis, and they again accused him of intransigence when he refused to do so (French, 1994). Others in the U.S. media also blamed Aristide for the impasse. Aristide's refusal to accept the new plan, John Goshko and Julia Preston wrote in the *Washington Post*, "posed another obstacle in the long struggle to find a way to end the military dictatorship in Haiti and allow his return to the presidency" (Goshko and Preston, 1994).

The Clinton administration presented the so-called miniplan as having been proposed by a Haitian parliamentary delegation invited to Washington by the Center for Democracy (a right-wing think tank funded by the USAID) at the request of Pezzullo and the U.S. Embassy in Haiti. Secretary of State Warren Christopher said that the delegation consisted of a "centrist group who are committed to constitutional government and who believe in the ultimate return of President Aristide" and contained a "number of people who are basically pro-Aristide" (cited in Goshko and Preston, 1994). The miniplan called on Aristide to name a new prime minister and form a "national unity government" that would ask parliament to pass an amnesty law to induce the military leaders to step down. Once this was done, Aristide's return would be negotiated, but no date for this was specified (Goshko and Preston, 1994; French, 1994).

Aristide saw the plan for what it was and flatly rejected it. Contradicting Secretary of State Christopher, Fritz Longchamp, Aristide's UN ambassador in exile, wrote in February 1994 to the UN secretary-general, "The one thing [the legislators] have in common despite differences in political affiliation" is that "they are all opponents of Aristide" (cited in Goshko and Preston, 1994). The only pro-Aristide member of that delegation, in fact, resigned from it when he "realized that he had been lured to Washington not to discuss the embargo (the ostensible purpose of the trip), but to be used to denigrate Aristide" (COHA, 4 March 1994).

Aristide was right. The whole affair was a hoax designed by Pezzullo and the State Department to dupe Aristide into accepting a deal that neutralized him but protected the coup leaders (COHA, 4 March 1994, 7 March 1994). In testimony given to a Senate Foreign Relations Subcommittee in March 1994, Pezzullo admitted that the State Department had actually drafted the miniplan (as a memo) in December 1993 and that he and U.S. Ambassador William Swing handpicked the parliamentary delegation that went to Washington (COHA, 7 March 1994; EPICA, 1994:44; Haitian Information Bureau, 1994:236). Allan Nairn further revealed that during the meetings in Washington, Pezzullo and the State Department used the buildup of the FRAPH and its terrorist activities against Aristide supporters to pressure him into making the concessions the United States demanded of him (Nairn, 1996:15).

Aristide responded to the miniplan with his own counterplan. In contrast to the miniplan, Aristide called for Cédras, François, and other leaders of the coup to step down first and, simultaneously, for the UN Security Council to order a global trade embargo against Haiti. The Haitian National Assembly would then pass a general amnesty law and other acts to separate the police from the army.

The UN would resume its technical assistance program. Once these steps were taken, Aristide would name a new prime minister and return to Haiti within ten days after that nomination, and only then would the UN lift its sanctions against Haiti (Goshko and Preston, 1994).

Aristide knew that his plan would be rejected, but it served an important political purpose. It showed that he was willing to negotiate seriously for an end to the crisis and that he had drawn important lessons from the Governors Island debacle. By contrast, the United States continued to side with the Haitian military leaders despite the evidence of their untrustworthiness. To strong-arm Aristide into accepting a miniplan that was worse than the Governors Island Agreement and that sought to "fleece him of his legitimate powers" (COHA, 7 March 1994), the United States proposed a UN draft resolution in February that called for new sanctions against the Haitian junta only if Aristide pursued a political compromise with the military rulers. The draft also asked him to name a new prime minister without any guarantee for his own return, and it gave the UN secretary-general the authority to lift the sanctions altogether if he deemed that the military rulers showed signs of cooperation and Aristide did not (Spiegelman, 1994; COHA, 7 March 1994). Treachery is a given in politics, but it served Aristide well to expose how far the United States and the UN were willing to go to accommodate the junta in Haiti.

By March 1994, the tide began to shift in favor of Aristide and against the putschists. Amid increasing repression and more killings in Haiti, liberal members of Congress, whose support Clinton needed for his broad social agenda, began to mobilize and pressure him to change his policies toward the Haitian junta and the refugees. Approximately 100 people (including prominent entertainers; Hollywood actors; civil rights, labor, and religious leaders; and members of Congress) signed a letter to Clinton accusing his administration of pursuing a racist policy toward the Haitian refugees and demanding the return of President Aristide. The congressional Black Caucus, supported by other liberal Democratic members of Congress, introduced legislation calling for the resignation of Lawrence Pezzullo and for tougher measures against Haiti's junta. To palliate these critics, the administration, in a seeming about-face, admitted that it had tacitly encouraged the Haitian military's intransigence by asking for concessions only from Aristide. Henceforth, it pledged to push for the ouster of the junta (Merida, 1994a, 1994b; Greenhouse, 1994b, 1994c).

Still, nothing changed. In fact, the administration not only was reluctant to take action against Haiti's junta but also appeared to be defending them while engaging in its usual double-talk. Even as the administration in Washington was adopting a tougher language against the Haitian junta, the U.S. Embassy in Port-au-Prince was downplaying the junta's human rights violations and terror campaign. In a cablegram sent to Secretary Christopher, the embassy's human rights officer accused the Haitian Left, Aristide, and his supporters in Washington, as well as nongovernmental organizations and the human rights monitors of the UN-OAS in Haiti, of "consistently manipulat[ing] and even fabricat[ing] human rights abuses as a propaganda tool" (cited in Sciolino, 1994).

In April, Aristide went on the offensive. Characterizing the Clinton policy toward Haitian refugees as a "cruel joke" and "racist," he informed the administration that, in six months, he would rescind the 1981 agreement between the Duvalier government and the United States that allowed Washington to intercept Haitians at sea and repatriate them. At the same time, liberal Democratic senators began calling for the use of military force against the junta, and they introduced a bill in the Senate that replicated the one introduced earlier by the congressional Black Caucus to force a shift in the administration's policy toward Haiti. Among other provisions, the Senate bill asked for a complete commercial embargo against Haiti, the suspension of air traffic between Haiti and the United States, the denial of visas to members of the Haitian armed forces and their civilian supporters, the freezing of the assets of Haitian Army members and their backers, the cutting of funds used for the repatriation of any refugee who was denied a proper asylum hearing, and the cessation of U.S. aid to those countries that violated the embargo. Pressure on Clinton came from other quarters as well. Randall Robinson, director of TransAfrica (a lobbying organization on African and Caribbean issues), wrote a biting letter to the *New York Times* in which he accused Clinton of not understanding "America's new role in the world" and having "neither an aptitude for foreign policy nor an interest in it." He also asserted that by "standing by while men like Lieut. Gen. Raoul Cédras and Lieut. Col. Michel François strangle Haiti," Clinton was sending "a clear and awful message spelling out the superiority of the bullet over the ballot" (Robinson, 1994). Robinson then announced that he would go on a hunger strike until the administration fired Pezzullo and changed its policies toward the Haitian military and the refugees (Greenhouse, 1994d, 1994e; Goshko, 1994a; Merida, 1994c).

As Daniel Williams observed, Aristide's offensive and his U.S. supporters "won a tactical duel with Washington, beating the Clinton administration at its practice of claiming the moral high ground" (Williams, 1994). Clinton could not cover up the duplicitous maneuverings of the State Department and his special envoy. He was also aware that the refugee interception and repatriation policy was not working and that the refugee crisis was about to get worse. He could not answer the charge that he was pursuing a double-standard policy vis-à-vis Cuban and Haitian refugees and that his policy toward Haitians was racist "in outcome if not intentionally" (Ifill, 1994; Williams, 1994). Finally, he caved in to the pressure, fired Pezzullo in late April, and, in a conciliatory gesture toward the Black Caucus, named William Gray III, a former congressman and president of the United Negro College Fund, as his new special envoy to Haiti. The administration immediately announced a shift in its refugee policy and declared that all Haitians picked up at sea would be granted proper asylum hearings aboard U.S. ships or in third countries. That action led Robinson to end his hunger strike; it also quieted the Black Caucus and bought Clinton more time. At the urging of the United States, the UN Security Council adopted sweeping new worldwide sanctions against Haiti's military junta on May 6 that included many of the provisions of the House and Senate bills mentioned earlier. It also explicitly stipulated that Generals Cédras and Biamby and Lt. Col. Michel François had to step down (P. Lewis, 1994; Williams, 1994; Preston, 1994).

The United States, Canada, France, the Netherlands, and the Dominican Republic subsequently suspended their commercial flights to Haiti. The United States froze the bank accounts of the coup leaders and their supporters and ordered a ban on their international transactions. In a clear shift in tone, turned against the junta, that signaled a determination to end the crisis, Clinton stated that the junta leaders had "visited abject misery on their people," that "they're now once again killing and mutilating . . . innocent civilians," and that "it's time for them to go" (cited in Gellman and Marcus, 1994).

By June 1994, it had become clear to the Clinton administration that its critics were correct. As long as the military junta stayed in power, the crisis in Haiti would remain unresolved, as would be the refugee problem for the United States. The renewed flow of refugees, which in June alone surpassed the total for all of 1993, threatened to overwhelm the U.S. Coast Guard, even though the U.S. naval base at Guantanamo Bay in Cuba was reopened to house the refugees (Colon, Alvarez, and Marquis, 1994). Lastly, it seemed that the Haitian junta had no intention of relinquishing power, despite the tougher stance taken by the United States and the UN. The junta responded to the new sanctions adopted in May by installing the eighty-one-year-old, military-appointed head of Haiti's Supreme Court, Emile Jonassaint, as provisional president (Jehl, 1994a). On July 11, offering yet other signs of defiance and an impending crackdown, the junta ordered the expulsion from Haiti of all UN and OAS human rights monitors. That act led Caputo to exclaim that the "reasons [for the expulsion] are quite obvious. They kill people. They torture people. They rape people. And they don't want any witnesses in their country" (cited in Meisler, 1994). On July 31, the UN Security Council adopted Resolution 940, which determined that "the situation in Haiti continues to constitute a threat to peace and security in the region" and that "the illegal de facto regime in Haiti has failed to comply with the Governors Island Agreement and is in breach of its obligations under the relevant resolutions of the Security Council." Acting under Chapter VII of the UN Charter, the Security Council authorized "Member States [i.e., the United States] to form a multinational force under unified command and control and, in this framework, to use all necessary means to facilitate the departure from Haiti of the military leadership . . . the prompt return of the legitimately elected President and the restoration of the legitimate authorities of the Government of Haiti" (NYT, 1994).

The Haitian junta still refused to budge and became even more daring. On August 28, 1994, attachés assassinated Father Jean-Marie Vincent. The first priest to be killed by the regime, Vincent was a close friend of Aristide and a leader of the grassroots movement. This was to be the junta's final act of defiance (Bragg, 1994; Farah, 1994a). In a public address on September 15, 1994, Clinton outlined the reasons why the United States was organizing and leading the "international effort to restore democratic government in Haiti." "Haiti's dictators, led by General Raoul Cédras," Clinton exclaimed, "control the most violent regime in our hemisphere. For three years, they have rejected every peaceful solution that the international community has proposed." He continued: "They have broken an agreement that they made to give up power. They have brutalized their people and destroyed their economy. And for three years, we and other nations have worked exhaustively to find a diplomatic solution, only to have the dictators reject each one." He then offered additional reasons why the United States would intervene militarily in Haiti: to "protect our interests, to stop the brutal atrocities that threaten tens of thousands of Haitians, to secure our borders, and to preserve stability and promote democracy in our hemisphere, and to uphold the reliability of the commitments we make and the commitments others make to us" (Clinton, 1994).

Four days after that speech, about 20,000 U.S. troops entered Haiti peacefully after a U.S. delegation—composed of former President Jimmy Carter, former chairman of the Joint Chiefs of Staff Gen. Colin L. Powell, retired , and Sen. Sam Nunn of Georgia—reached an agreement with the Haitian junta that would let the latter step down "with dignity" in return for an amnesty for them and the Haitian military (Harris and Farah, 1994; Jehl, 1994b; Farah, 1994b). Aristide, who had endorsed the use of military force to oust the Haitian junta in a letter to the UN Security Council on July 29, 1994, initially disliked the agreement that allowed the junta to remain in power until October 15. But pressured by the Clinton administration and subjected to patronizing criticisms from members of Congress for being ungrateful to his liberators, Aristide gave his approval to the accord and thanked Clinton for the U.S. intervention after he received reassurances that the junta would leave and that he would be returned to power (Dowd, 1994; Goshko, 1994c; Lee, 1994; Wilentz, 1994).

On September 29, at the urging of the United States, the UN voted to end all sanctions against Haiti as soon as Aristide returned to his country. The Haitian parliament voted for a limited amnesty law that granted immunity to the coup leaders for "political crimes" only, not the general amnesty that Cédras had wanted. The junta's henchman, Lieutenant Colonel François, brave and defiant when facing the unarmed Haitian people and foreign diplomats, fled to the Dominican Republic on October 4. Cédras, finding the limited amnesty voted by the parliament unacceptable, hinted that he might not step down as agreed by October 15. The ranking U.S. Army general in Haiti, however, reminded Cédras of who was now in charge and made it clear to him that he would be removed forcefully if he did not leave voluntarily. Humiliated and defeated, Generals Cédras and Biamby left Haiti for exile in Panama on October 12 amid jeers from the rejoicing masses.

Their exile did not come without its rewards. To entice the people Clinton denounced as "dictators" and "thugs" to step down from power and leave Haiti, the White House announced that it had agreed to rent Cédras's homes in Haiti for US$5,000 per month. The United States also unfroze the bank accounts of the other 600 officers of the Haitian Army (estimated at US$79 million) and planned to provide US$5 million to pay off and retrain those Haitian soldiers who would not be recruited into the "new" Haitian police because of their past record of repression. Cédras's own fortune, amassed during his time in power, is estimated at around US$100 million. Gen. Manuel Antonio Noriega of Panama, who once enjoyed the status of "most favored U.S. dictator" but is now wasting away in a U.S. jail after having been captured by U.S. soldiers in 1989 and tried and convicted by a U.S. court for drug trafficking, might well be wondering what Cédras had done for his patrons that he himself had not!

On October 15, 1994, jubilant crowds welcomed Aristide back to Haiti to the total dismay of the neo-Duvalierist forces and the ardent supporters of the coup among the bourgeoisie, who undoubtedly felt betrayed by Clinton. This was the first time the United States had intervened militarily in the hemisphere to restore a popular president to power—a man who was once branded by the U.S. Embassy in Haiti as a radical firebrand and who was intensely disliked and distrusted by the allies of the United States in Haiti, as well as by many in the Clinton administration, the State and Defense Departments, the CIA, and Congress. As Wilentz put it so aptly, it was Cédras, not Aristide, who had been blindsided, and it was Clinton, not Carter, who was running the show. U.S. troops seized the Haitian Army's heavy weaponry after they secured control of the country, and soon after his return, Aristide dissolved what remained of the power structure of the military institution that dominated Haitian politics since the U.S. occupation of 1915–1934. These events were a watershed and marked a turning point in Haiti's post-1915 history (Rupert, 1994; Booth and Farah, 1994; Rohter, 1994; Benesch, 1994; Kelley and Squitieri, 1994; Sims, 1994; Farah, 1994c, 1994d; Robberson, 1994; Jehl, 1994c; Wilentz, 1994).

The question still remains: Why did Clinton, with UN Security Council approval, make the unpopular decision to intervene in Haiti and risk further damage to his already embattled presidency? The answer is contained in his speech of September 15: "to protect our interests, to stop the brutal atrocities that threaten tens of thousands of Haitians, to secure our borders, and to preserve stability and promote democracy in our hemisphere" (Clinton, 1994).

Of all the reasons Clinton offered to justify a military intervention, the human rights argument is the most compelling. But stopping the brutal atrocities of the

Haitian military against Haitians was not the main reason why Clinton sent in the troops. For decades, the United States had intervened in the hemisphere and supported brutal and murderous right-wing military regimes, including the thirty-year Duvalier dictatorship, the subsequent neo-Duvalierist military-led governments (1986–1990), and, indirectly, the junta that overthrew Aristide and killed thousands of Haitians between September 1991 and September 1994. Clinton would have been more forthright had he acknowledged that the policies of both his administration and his predecessor's—which allowed the putschists to remain in power in Haiti and forced Aristide to make concessions to them—encouraged their intransigence and atrocities against Haitian citizens. As Martin correctly observed, it was the "failure to view the human rights situation as central [that] contributed to the failure of the political process" (I. Martin, 1994:87). And that made the recourse to military force to remove the junta from power inevitable in the end. Still, the human rights argument, even if it came belatedly and was insincere, was sufficient ground for an intervention. It represented an instance where the international community (the UN) sanctioned the use of a greater force (organized and led by the United States) to end the violence of a tyrannical dictatorship against a defenseless people who dared to exercise their democratic rights.

The other claims Clinton made are less convincing, and the issues they involved could have been resolved diplomatically. The United States has a long-standing and legitimate concern about the influx of tens of thousands of illegal immigrants from the pan-Caribbean region in general and Haiti in particular. But the refugee situation became a "crisis" only after the September coup against Aristide. Had the Bush administration supported Aristide (and not the junta) and negotiated the terms of the junta's departure immediately after the coup, the junta might have been persuaded to step down from power much earlier. Had this happened, the refugee crisis could have been averted. Clinton, who at first criticized the Bush policy toward the Haitian refugees as "immoral," later adopted the same repatriation policy, cajoled the junta, and thereby aggravated the refugee crisis. When the Clinton administration reached the conclusion that the refugee crisis would be resolved only by removing the junta from power, a military solution was again seen as the only viable alternative.

"Stability" is another reason used to justify U.S. interventions abroad, and it has historically been linked with the notion of national security. The real but unarticulated assumptions behind the U.S. security strategy since the Cold War have always been "to foster a world environment in which the American system can survive and flourish," according to the famous passage in the 1950 National Security Council document (NSC 68) that outlined Washington's Cold War strategy (cited in Layne and Schwartz, 1993:5). But stability and security were simply two components of an ideological arsenal articulated along with other principles ("upholding democracy" and "world order," defending the "vital interests" of the United States) to justify U.S. interventions in the Third World. By "stability," the United States has historically meant the existence of governments that promote the free enterprise system, accept the rules of the international capitalist system and their place in the international division of labor, and acknowledge the global dominance of the United States. Washington has never equated stability or security with legitimate government; the only concern is whether, elected or not, the government in power maintains the status quo. For many countries in the Western Hemisphere in the twentieth century, the status quo could be maintained and "stability" achieved only with strong and repressive military governments. The United States intervened repeatedly in the hemisphere (and elsewhere) throughout the century to overthrow governments or to support brutal dictatorships in the name of stability, freedom, and security.

Since the Cold War, propping up right-wing dictatorships in the name of freedom and containment of communism lost its persuasiveness, and stability and security came to be equated with democratic government. The United States understood the term "democratic government" to mean any government that did not challenge the rule of property and did not tamper with the fundamental tenets of capitalism. Fearing that the democratically elected Aristide government would not play by the rules of the game and would cause instability in Haiti— that is, a change in the status quo—the Bush and, at first, the Clinton administrations tried to find a solution to the crisis generated by the coup that excluded Aristide. Again, when the Clinton administration realized that there would be no stability and no democratic government in Haiti without the return of Aristide, diplomacy no longer sufficed to remove the intransigent junta.

It could be said that, beginning in 1915, the United States created a monster in Haiti (the Haitian Army), which it armed, protected, nurtured, and in the end could no longer control except by destroying it. The second direct U.S. intervention in Haiti, therefore, resulted from the failure of Washington's own policies toward that country's dictatorships, without ever achieving the long-term stability Washington desired. Stability can only be achieved when those who govern do so with the consent of the governed, and the elections of Aristide and the National Assembly in 1990 represented the first time that the majority of Haitians directly chose who would govern them. Had the tiny antidemocratic minority that tried to override the will of the majority succeeded in consolidating its power, Haiti would have reverted once again to an ungovernable and unstable condition.

Implications of the Intervention

Clinton may be thought of as the first post–Cold War U.S president to carry out one of the tenets of the new world order in the Western Hemisphere, even if he did so unwittingly. The intervention may not yet prove Laennec Hurbon's claim that "the Kantian idea of a human universal has begun to emerge as a concrete reality in the geopolitical sphere" (Hurbon, 1994:38). But the intervention does indicate that—given the change in the global balance of power, the victory of Western capitalism over the bankrupt Leninist model of socialism, and the rupture with the Cold War containment ideology—right-wing or would-be right-wing (military) dictators in the hemisphere can no longer count on unwavering support from Washington. The U.S. intervention in Haiti, then, signaled a radical break with the past and represented a major defeat for the forces of tyranny and for the prebendary state system that had evolved into its "gangsterized" form between September 1991 and September 1994.[11]

The intervention was a double-edged sword. If the intervention made possible a reopening of the democratic process and thus corresponded to the interests of the majority of the Haitian people,[12] it also brought with it the direct occupation of Haiti by U.S.-UN forces, albeit for the limited duration stipulated in UN Security Council Resolution 940—that is, until the end of Aristide's term and the transfer of power to the newly elected government in February 1996. The military intervention needs to be considered as part of a contradictory process that has both short- and long-term direct and indirect consequences for Haiti and the democratic process.

The contradictions engendered by the intervention and occupation may be summarized as follows. Aristide could not have returned to Haiti without the protection of U.S. or UN troops. If the leaders of the coup had been compelled to leave Haiti before the U.S. troops entered, the rest of the army, the police, and the paramilitary death squads would have gone on a killing spree against the population, and Aristide would have been targeted for assassination. The return of Aristide was the necessary but not sufficient condition for the resumption of legitimate government in Haiti. Without Aristide, the population would not have participated in the parliamentary, municipal, and local elections of June (and September) 1995 or the presidential election of December 1995 because those elections would have been considered illegitimate. Without those elections, there would have been no democratic renewal, and the state would have remained pitted against civil society since those who governed would be doing so without the consent of the people.

The dissolution of the Armed Forces of Haiti was also essential for the renewal of the democratic process.[13] As long as the FADH remained a powerful and autonomous institution, those who controlled it would have sought to subvert the democratization process and revert to dictatorship to preserve their power and privileges. Furthermore, the need for order in general was as crucial as the need to dismantle the armed forces. This meant that the popular movement had to be prevented from engaging in acts of retribution against the members of the military and the attaché death squads, thereby avoiding a potential descent into a bloody civil war. No doubt, the need to seek justice for those who tortured, maimed, and killed thousands of Haitians with impunity during recent years remains urgent. But for democracy and the rule of law to take hold, justice must be sought through the courts and not in the streets. Protecting the members of the armed forces, the death squads, and the bourgeoisie that supported the coup was a necessary step toward democratization. This was yet another reason for deploying such a large military force. As a U.S. Army psychological operations official put it, the objective was to make sure that Haitians "don't get the idea that they can do whatever they want" (cited in Nairn, 1994a:344).

One must not confuse maintaining order with preventing dissent and political activism. The intervening forces did not crack down on popular protests or the reemergent popular movement, as many who opposed the intervention had predicted. Whether or not the United States intended it, Hurbon has correctly argued, the military intervention has "begun to unblock Haitian society; it has created a space for free speech and for public demonstrations. But its effects still fall far short of installing a democratic regime in the full sense of the word" (Hurbon, 1994:39). For this to happen, Hurbon continued, Haitians will have to transform the deep-seated cultural traditions that have nurtured dictatorial power. Concretely, this means placing the general interest above personal interests, pursuing individual interests through dialogue and consensus, abandoning the traditional method of resolving conflicts by murdering or terrorizing one's adversary, establishing public forums for debate according to rules understood by all, and creating a new system of justice in which the rule of law is substituted for private vengeance (Hurbon, 1994:39). For these cultural changes to solidify, the structures of power must also be changed. They necessitate a dismantling of the prebendary state system, its institutions, apparatuses, and means of violence. Much of the latter has already happened with the dissolution of the FADH and the paramilitary death squads. Political power must be decentralized, and new political structures that maximize participation at all levels must be built. Resources must be redistributed to make such participation possible. The right of all to participate openly in the political process must be guaranteed, and a new police force must be created, placed under civilian control, and made to operate in accordance with the law. In short, the rule of law, to which all groups are subordinated, must replace rule by the few.

These goals were integral components of Aristide's agenda. But the intransigence of the Duvalierist and neo-Duvalierist forces and the bourgeoisie in regard to any change in the status quo, combined with Aristide's erratic rule during the first seven months of his presidency, undermined the project of transforming Haiti into a modern society from the start. By intervening as it did in Haiti, by dismantling the old apparatuses and instruments of power (i.e., the Haitian Army, the police, the rural section chiefs system, and the auxiliary death squads), the United States has radically altered the terrain of politics and political conflicts in Haiti.[14] For the first time, it may be possible to strengthen the institutions of civil society in relation to the state and thus consolidate the transition to democracy.

However, what the intervention offers with one hand it seeks to take away with the other. The democratic opening created by the intervention is contravened by the direct and indirect occupation of Haiti. The direct occupation of Haiti by U.S. and UN troops, albeit temporary and authorized by UN Security Council resolutions and Aristide, raises legitimate questions about the meaning of democracy or democratic transition under such conditions. Franck Laraque captured the essence of this paradox when he stated:

> If the concept of democratic transition means the absence of dictatorship and the exercise of national sovereignty, it follows that a democratic transition excludes a fortiori the occupation of a country by another, as the occupier holds the supreme authority over the occupied. National sovereignty implies the exclusive right of a nation to exercise executive, legislative, and judicial power, directly or indirectly (Laraque, 1995:2).[15]

The return of the duly elected president and the election of a new parliament and president notwithstanding, exogenous actors who are not accountable to the Haitian people, in collaboration with the exiled leaders of Haiti who are, had already drafted an agenda for Haiti.

That agenda is intended for the long term. As such, it could constitute the continued but indirect control of future governments in Haiti by these exogenous interests—if it remains unchallenged by the Haitian people or their elected governments. Although that agenda had been developed long before the military intervention and occupation, the latter give the United States an unparalleled opportunity to push for its implementation. Put differently, the Aristide government in exile negotiated and accepted an economic program without subjecting that program to popular debate and parliamentary approval. Foreign multilateral and bilateral aid organizations that have no accountability to the Haitian electorate but control the aid moneys needed by the government are tying the release of the funds to the implementation of the institutional reforms. The U.S. and multinational aid institutions, in short, have great leverage against the Aristide government and that of its successor, and the Haitian government will consequently be more constrained by and responsive to these foreign interests than to the needs and interests of the Haitian people. As Farmer put it, Aristide, who once considered capitalism to be a mortal sin,

> now meets regularly with representatives of the World Bank, the International Monetary Fund (IMF) and AID. He was once the priest of the poor; now he's the president of a beleaguered nation, run into the ground by a vicious military and business elite and by their friends abroad. Aristide finds himself most indebted to the very people and institutions he once denounced from the pulpit (Farmer, 1995:227).

Farmer further observed that the indirect control by the international regulatory agencies may be more insidious than the short-term U.S.-UN military occupation (Farmer, 1995:227). Both are part of a process of subordinating Haiti to exogenous and unaccountable interests and intentionally or unintentionally undermining its people's democratic sovereignty. Democracy, however, is unpredictable. As Adam Przeworski put it so succinctly: "The essential feature of democracy is that nothing is decided definitively. If sovereignty resides with the people, the people can decide to undermine all the guarantees reached by politicians around the negotiating table. Even the most institutionalized guarantees give at best a high degree of assurance, never certainty" (Przeworski, 1991:79).

Insofar as the liberal model of democracy will exist in a sharply divided society with a vastly unequal distribution of wealth, property, and resources, the interests of the dispossessed majority are bound to clash with those of the propertied and wealthy minority, and this will lead the former to contest the powers of the latter. This was evident in Haiti from 1986 to 1990. The movement that led to the election of Aristide in 1990 and the popular demands that underlay his overthrow by the military in 1991—for more and better jobs, housing, sanitation, health care, education, land reform, a more equal distribution of resources and wealth, and a new system of justice—cannot be silenced and excluded from the political agenda. The struggle for democracy and development (and to determine who will benefit most from them) is engaged once again.

Notes

1. The resolutions included those of the OAS in October 1991 and the UN in June 1993 and May 1994.

2. The Bush administration's efforts to make life more difficult for the Castro government, which was now deprived of valuable Soviet aid, came in the form of the Cuban Democracy Act, also know as the Torricelli Bill (named after its sponsor, Rep. Robert Torricelli [D–N.J.]). This act, signed into law by President Bush on October 23, 1992, prohibits "foreign-based U.S. subsidiaries from trading with Cuba, threatens U.S. trading partners with commercial sanctions if they conduct business with the island, and bans any ship which has been in a Cuban port from docking in the U.S. for at least six months" (COHA, 16 December 1992).

3. The de facto governments were those of Prime Ministers Jean-Jacques Honorat (October 1991 to June 1992) and Marc Bazin (June 1992 to June 1993) and Presidents Joseph Nerette (October 1991 to May 1994) and Emile Jonassaint (May 1994 to October 1994).

4. These figures are from Aristide (1994b:40), EPICA (1994:20), and Coalition for Civilian Observers in Haiti (1993).

5. The choice for Aristide was never between negotiation or revolution, as Ives maintained. He argued that Aristide betrayed the masses by choosing the former course and a rapprochement with the Lavalas bourgeoisie, who sought accommodation with the traditional bourgeoisie and the United States (Ives, 1995a). Ives offered no evidence to support his claim that the Haitian masses were willing or capable of launching and sustaining an armed revolution against the military. There is, however, much evidence to the contrary. The majority of poor Haitians who were the victims of the Haitian military's repression after the coup welcomed the U.S. military intervention that brought an end to

the military's rule and the return of their beloved president (Farmer, 1995, 223–227; EPICA, 1994:3).

The "revolutionary" option, if there ever was one, would have been calamitous, not only in terms of further bloodshed and the loss of life but also in terms of further damaging an already crippled economy. Advocating such a course of action is irresponsible. Ives himself was well aware that "should popular insurrection or guerrilla war break out and threaten the Duvalierists' grip on power, U.S. or UN intervention would be quickly mounted" (Ives, 1995a:86). Despite this awareness, Ives still argued that Aristide should have chosen that course of action. Assuming that the Haitian masses could fight against the Haitian army and its attachés, did Ives really believe that they could win against a U.S.-led invasion? Imagine for a moment that the Haitian masses won; what then? Where would they turn for international support? Could the Haitian masses succeed where the Nicaraguans, Salvadorans, and Cubans have not? Lastly, just as one can fantasize a revolutionary victory against the Haitian military and/or U.S. forces, one must also consider the more likely outcome: a massive defeat. What would Ives then advocate for them?

Maingot took the self-determination argument a step further. Unlike Ives, who called on Haitians to rise up on their own against the military, Maingot suggested that Aristide should have trained his own army, taken over the islands that are off Haiti's shores (Île de la Tortue in the north and the larger, more strategically located Île de la Gonave in the Bay of Port-au-Prince), and, with U.S. protection, launched an invasion of the mainland to topple the junta (Maingot, 1994). If Ives's argument is adventurist and irresponsible, Maingot's is naive. He simply failed to understand the real objectives of the United States in regard to Haiti and Aristide. These were either to prevent Aristide's return or, failing that, to weaken, control, and force him to compromise with his enemies. Under no circumstances would Washington have allowed Aristide to return to Haiti in charge of his own armed forces, thus being more powerful than before his ouster.

6. The scenario for stalling negotiations and blocking Aristide's return was laid out in detail in a so-called secret memo purportedly written by an adviser to the U.S. Embassy in Port-au-Prince at the behest of de facto Haitian government officials. The following were among the recommendations of the memo: The United States and the OAS should insist on the return of Aristide. But the "return of A could be for only a brief (symbolic) period of time, he could be returned to be impeached, or he could simply be returned as a figurehead. Mr. A does not necessarily need to return for some period of time until all guarantees are in place. If the guarantees were not met, then a constitutional process could remove A while he was still out of the country. If A were allowed to return, he would not need to return right away and he would hold no power. If A refuses to deal or refuses what OAS considers a reasonable deal, he is finished. US and other countries now believe that A was a very bad guy and no one wants to see him back with any real power, but because of other problems in the hemisphere, they want him returned, even if only for one day to resign and leave. U.S. and others believe that negotiation must begin with the Parliament Group's visit to Washington. The Group must look like it is ready to bargain in good faith, otherwise, if the U.S. feels the talks are going nowhere they will impose sanctions. The Group must put forth its position regarding OAS interference, etc., but it must focus on a resolution and keeping negotiations going. It should compare A to the Ayatollah (and) what would happen if he is allowed to return (but do not dwell on his return). If the Group looks like it is bargaining in good faith, the sanctions will be held in reserve, and some solution will be worked out, probably excluding A's return" ("The 'Embassy' Memo,"

1994:104–105). The Council on Hemispheric Affairs (COHA), which "had at first raised questions about the authenticity of the document," concluded that "later research has now validated [it] as being completely reliable, in spite of State Department denial." Significantly, the strategy pursued by the Bush administration conformed closely to many of the memo's recommendations (COHA, 10 January 1992).

7. The propositions contained in the "Strategy of Social and Economic Reconstruction" are largely based on the recommendations of the Joint Mission of the USAID (1993), the Inter-American Development Bank (IDB, 1994), and the United Nations Development Program (UNDP, 1993a, 1993b).

8. At the end of Roy's speech, he and Aristide embraced each other. Aristide then whispered to him, "I love you," and the audience sang the Haitian national anthem (Fields, 1993; Ethéart, 1993).

9. Two weeks before the *Harlan County* went to Haiti, 18 U.S. soldiers were killed in Somalia where U.S. troops had been sent to restore order.

10. Bush administration officials, as well as the State and Defense Departments, made wide use of Latell's 1992 report to justify their opposition to Aristide's return and, hence, their tacit support for the Haitian military regime (Marquis, 1993h).

11. This term is borrowed from Hurbon (1994:39).

12. To the chagrin of radical Left newspapers like *Haiti Progrès*, some Haitian and leftist U.S. intellectuals and organizations, and a few leaders of grassroots organizations like Chavannes Jean-Baptiste (who heads one of the most influential and most persecuted peasant organizations, the Mouvman Peyizan Papaye [MPP, Papaye Peasant Movement]), the vast majority of Haitians welcomed the U.S. troops who came to remove their oppressors from power and return Aristide (see Farmer, 1995:223–226, and Note 4).

13. Many observers deplored the fact that the U.S. troops did not pursue a vigorous campaign of disarming the attaché death squads and that, as such, they could resurface after the U.S.-UN troops left. Armed gangsters are always dangerous, but they are even more dangerous when they are protected by an organized military institution bent on maintaining its power. Insofar as the Haitian Army has been dismantled and replaced by a new civilian-controlled police force, civil society will be strengthened. As a government of laws gradually supplants the prebendary state system, the conditions for the existence of paramilitary organizations will also disappear. At least, that is the challenge ahead.

14. Soon after Aristide's return, what was left of the Haitian Army and the police crumbled. The United States and the Haitian government are in the process of reconstituting a new police force under the supervision of the International Criminal Investigations Training and Assistance Program (ICITAP). This would be done by "vetting out" the worse human rights abusers of the old army and police, not by doing away with the vast network of U.S. Army trainees and CIA and DIA informants (Nairn, 1994a:346; Wilentz, 1994–1995:100). Created in 1968 to train security forces in El Salvador and Guatemala, ICITAP is staffed by former and current members of the Federal Bureau of Investigation (FBI), Drug Enforcement Administration (DEA), Secret Service, and U.S. police departments (Nairn, 1994a:345–346; Ives, 1995b:116).

15. Progressives might want to link the concept of democratic sovereignty with that of national sovereignty. Beyond the geopolitical and geographical boundedness of the concept of the nation-state, it is difficult to understand where it could derive its sovereignty if not from its citizens. If one equates the concept of sovereignty with the right of a people to determine their government's agenda, then one could defend more easily the prin-

ciple of external intervention to restore the right of a people to self-determination and self-government. By contrast, such external intervention becomes difficult to defend if the nation-state, qua nation-state, is said to be sovereign. The putschists and their supporters in Haiti, viscerally opposed to any notion of democratic rights, were the first to cover themselves under the mantle of national sovereignty in order to deny the right of the international community (the UN-OAS) to interfere in the internal affairs of Haiti (i.e., their right to oppress, murder, maim, and exploit Haitians with impunity).

8

EPILOGUE

The events of 1995 proved that the popular demands for a restructuring of Haitian society remain at center stage politically. The renewed waves of popular protests throughout the year coalesced around the demands enumerated at the end of Chapter 7 and in opposition to Prime Minister Smarck Michel's proposed neoliberal and privatization measures (i.e., trade and price liberalization and the sale of public enterprises, banks, the national port authority, and so forth). Michel, who had formed his cabinet in November 1994, resigned in October 1995 when Aristide publicly distanced himself from the prime minister's unpopular policies. Aristide's disavowal of his own prime minister seemed all the more remarkable since it was he who had authorized his advisers—albeit under pressure from the Clinton administration—to negotiate the neoliberal economic program with the foreign aid agencies while he was still in exile in Washington. But this was not the first time that Aristide had deserted Michel when faced with mounting public criticisms of the latter's policies. In 1991, Michel, then serving as commerce minister, was forced to resign when the public blamed his policies for a rise in the cost of living and Aristide did not defend him. These incidents point once again to Aristide's unpredictability. Compelled by powerful domestic and foreign interests to adopt economic policies he distrusted, Aristide quickly abandoned them when confronted with popular opposition, even if that meant sacrificing members of his government in the process.

Other than stalling the further implementation of the neoliberal reforms, Aristide did not offer concrete counterpolicies. He appointed Claudette Werleigh, who was serving as minister of foreign affairs in the Michel government, to replace Michel as prime minister. Werleigh belongs to the faction of the Plateforme Politique Lavalas (PPL, Lavalas Political Platform)—a newly formed coalition within the Lavalas movement that is resistant to the neoliberal policy reforms. Werleigh immediately suspended further implementation of the reforms, especially those concerning the sale of the major public enterprises. The international aid agencies responded by halting the delivery of aid moneys to Haiti until the government resumes the reforms.

Aristide pursued a deliberate strategy in abandoning Michel, appointing Werleigh, and halting the implementation of the neoliberal policies. He was faced with mounting popular discontent in regard to his government's policies, and he anticipated that his former prime minister (and close friend and ally) René Préval would likely win the December 1995 presidential election. Aristide, perhaps thinking ahead to the presidential elections five years down the road, sought to preserve his image as the defender of the people's interests and indirectly buy time for his successor to negotiate new terms with the foreign aid organizations.

One of Aristide's last consequential political acts consisted of sowing discord in the population, especially the political parties and candidates aspiring to the presidency. He did this by once again raising the vexing issue of the three years he spent in exile and lost from his five-year presidential term. Responding to widespread calls by his supporters to reclaim his three years, Aristide hinted that he might indeed reconsider his agreement with the United States to leave office in February 1996. A swift visit to Haiti by Anthony Lake, President Clinton's national security adviser, got Aristide to back off and put the issue to rest definitively. But the damage had been done: Large numbers of Aristide's followers lost interest in the December 1995 election, and he took no action to mobilize them behind the Lavalas candidate. The result was a relatively low voter turnout for the December polling, with only about 30 percent of eligible voters casting ballots.

The low participation in the December presidential election (and also the parliamentary elections of June and September 1995) highlighted at least three important points. First, Aristide's careful cultivation of a cult of personality among his followers led him and his Lavalas organization to avoid engaging the population in a public debate about the meaning and responsibilities of democracy. Aristide, awash in his image as the spokesman for the voiceless, actively reinforced the tradition of "one-manism" and the personalization of politics. Consequently, the paternalistic relations he nurtured with his followers and their devotion to him led his supporters to be indifferent toward the formal political process and the exercise of their franchise.

Second, the low voter turnout notwithstanding, the elections completely discredited the so-called traditional political parties—especially those that collaborated with the military regime between 1991 and 1994—and rendered them inconsequential in Haitian politics. By the same token, the elections confirmed that, even with Aristide out of the picture, the Lavalas Political Platform had become the major and only viable political organization in Haiti. Lavalas candidates for the legislature won 80 percent of the seats in both houses of the National Assembly in the June–September 1995 elections, and as expected, former Prime Minister Préval, the PPL candidate for president, captured 88 percent of the popular vote in the December polling.

By mid-1996, Lavalas was the uncontested dominant political organization, but governing alone may prove to be an obstacle to building a more substantive democracy. For a democratic culture to take hold in Haiti, it is vital that minority voices and interests be considered and represented and that the system not be seen as rewarding only the winners. Without minority representation and the belief that those in the minority today may become tomorrow's majority and vice versa, the excluded may seek to subvert or withdraw from the democratic process, thereby undermining its legitimacy.

Third, the voters sent a clear message to those they elected. They threw their support to the PPL because they believed it was the only movement that could still represent their interests. Their continued support is contingent on the ability of the PPL-dominated legislature and the Préval administration to deliver on their promises of change and make a real difference in the lives of the majority of the people.

President Préval and the new government formed by Prime Minister Rony Smarth face a formidable challenge as this century comes to a close. They have obtained a fresh popular mandate and face a parliament dominated by Lavalas legislators. The political opposition is weak and discredited. The macoute Haitian Army, the rural section chiefs system, and auxiliary terrorist organizations like FRAPH are dissolved. The Préval government ostensibly will be in a stronger position than the preceding government was in 1991 to establish its priorities and negotiate the conditions and direction of economic development for Haiti through the end of the century. Though their organizations have been dismantled, members of the former Haitian Army and police and FRAPH are still armed and capable of carrying out terrorist activities against the government and its supporters. Without an organized and heavily armed military institution, it is unlikely that these antidemocratic forces could mount and sustain another coup d'état as they did in September 1991. Nonetheless, Préval and Smarth will have to make security a priority of their administration, either with the newly trained National Police alone or with the continued presence of international peacekeepers.

Without the threat of a hostile military institution supported by the antidemocratic elites that Aristide faced in 1991, the political conjuncture of mid-1996 favors the new Lavalas legislature and presidency. Ironically, this raises the stakes for Préval and Smarth. They will govern under much more propitious conditions than Aristide and former Prime Minister Préval ever enjoyed. But they will govern practically alone, and without a viable parliamentary opposition, they will be more accountable for their failures and successes.

If the political conjuncture seems to favor the new government, the domestic and international balance of class forces weighs against the possibility of progressive reforms. The Haitian bourgeoisie can no longer rely on the Haitian Army to suppress the population and their troublesome demands. Yet it actually enjoys a much stronger economic position since the demise of Duvalierism because it is no longer encumbered by a rapacious prebendary state with which it must share the spoils of the class system. The bourgeoisie stands to benefit even more from the creation of a modern state and the neoliberal policies that the USAID, IMF, and World Bank are determined to impose on Haiti.

Préval has made it clear that he wants to come to terms with the Haitian bourgeoisie and the foreign sector, whose interests diverge fundamentally from those of the coalition that elected him president. Préval, who, as Aristide's prime minister, boasted that his government had begun to turn the inefficient and unprofitable public monopolies into efficient and profitable operations in a mere seven months in office, is now firmly committed to carrying out the neoliberal policies endorsed by Aristide in 1994 in the name of efficiency and profitability.

The popular movement unleashed in 1986 equated democracy with fundamental social change in favor of the majority. Aristide symbolized those aspirations, and the vast majority of Haitians supported him because they believed he could and would deliver on his promises. He did not succeed in making Haiti into a more equal and just society, but his and his supporters' undaunted opposition to Duvalierism and dictatorship led to some historic accomplishments. Duvalierism has been defeated, and its repressive institutions—the army and police, the auxiliary death squads, the rural section chiefs system—have been dismantled; furthermore, a formal democracy is slowly replacing the hitherto dominant prebendary state system.

Nevertheless, Aristide's overthrow and exile led him to submit to the dictates of the overlords of the international system and to embrace the haute bourgeoisie of Haiti that had financed the coup against him. His successor is following in his footsteps. In 1990, Aristide warned his followers that unless a candidate "from the people" entered the presidential race, an "acceptable" candidate opposed to changing the status quo and supported "by the privileged [classes] and Uncle Sam" would surely be elected. Such an outcome, he went on to say, would make it possible for the bourgeoisie to establish a formal democracy "that would exclude the lower classes . . . and rule without any social outlook, without transparency, without fairness" (Aristide, 1992a:138–139). Aristide probably never thought then that these prophetic words might come back to haunt him.

CHRONOLOGY

The United States and the Coup d'État at a Glance, September 1991–October 1994

September 1991   The Haitian military overthrows President Aristide on September 30. He leaves Haiti for exile in Venezuela. He leaves Venezuela in early 1992 for Washington, D.C., where he remains until his return to Haiti in October 1994.

October 1991   After hesitating to implement the trade embargo adopted by the OAS shortly after the coup d'état, the Bush administration orders a halt to all exports to and imports from Haiti, except for the delivery of humanitarian aid to Haiti (COHA, 30 October 1991; EPICA, 1994:42; Haitian Information Bureau, 1994:208). Responding to this pressure, the de facto military government invites the OAS to Haiti to discuss ending the economic sanctions and normalizing relations but without indicating if Aristide's return is a prerequisite for such negotiations.

November 1991   U.S. Ambassador Alvin Adams calls on Aristide to nominate a new prime minister to replace Prime Minister Préval and for Aristide's return to be delayed at least six months (EPICA, 1994:42). Aristide refuses to accept a proposition made by a delegation of procoup Haitian parliamentarians to lift the embargo without setting a date for his return to Haiti. The United States labels Aristide as "intransigent" for refusing (EPICA, 1994:42; Ives, 1995a:71; Haitian Information Bureau, 1994:210).

December 1991   Arguing that Haitians fleeing Haiti by boats to seek asylum in the United States are economic and not political refugees, the Bush administration appeals the decision by U.S. District Judge C. Clyde Atkins to issue a stay in the repatriation of Haitian refugees to Haiti under the 1981 interdiction agreement hammered out by the Reagan and Duvalier governments (COHA, 18 December 1991).

After procoup parliamentarians block the nomination of Victor Benoit (leader of KONAKOM) as Aristide's first choice for a new prime minister, the United States again labels Aristide "intransigent." Bowing to pressure from the State Department, he reluctantly accepts the nomination of (anti-Aristide) Haitian Communist Party leader and former presidential candidate René Théodore.

January 1992   Théodore writes to Aristide that he would accept the post of prime minister only after the embargo is lifted and international aid resumed. Armed attachés and members of the police force under the command of Col. Michel François attack a meeting held by Théodore and kill his bodyguard. The State Department recalls Ambassador Adams to Washington and hints that it may revert to military action to oust the Haitian junta. Worrying about what Aristide's grassroots movement would do if he returns to Haiti, the United States hints that it may explore a solution to the crisis that does not involve Aristide's return (COHA, 30 January 1992).

February 1992   Théodore says that, though he is ready to accept Aristide's "political return," he is not yet ready to accept his "physical return" (EPICA, 1994:42; COHA, 10 January 1992; Ives, 1995a:71–72).

In a context of increasing violence in Haiti and relentless pressure from Washington, Aristide accepts the terms of the Protocole d'Accord à Washington (Protocol of Accord). The accord calls for an amnesty for the army and the putschists, respecting all postcoup parliamentary legislation (including the appointment of General Cédras as head of the army through 1994), and lifting the embargo after Théodore is ratified as prime minister and forms a government of "national consensus." Though the accord recognizes Aristide as president, it does not stipulate a date for his return to Haiti. A few days later, Aristide insists that the amnesty clause in the accord means amnesty only for "political" crimes, not for "common law" crimes that he accuses Cédras of having committed. The United States angrily charges that Aristide is backing out of the accord (Ives, 1995a:74–75; COHA, 25 February 1992; EPICA, 1994:42).

Agreeing with the State Department's claims that the returned Haitian refugees are not persecuted because of their political beliefs, the U.S. Supreme Court votes in favor of the Bush administration's repatriation policy (COHA, 11 March 1992).

The Bush administration, under pressure from U.S.-owned assembly industries in Haiti, permits those industries to continue their export and import activities. Despite its tough talk, the administration does not enforce the embargo. This nonaction allows the junta to receive oil deliveries and other supplies. The cross-border trade between Haiti and the Dominican Republic flourishes. The administration also fails to carry out its threat to freeze the assets and cancel the visas to the United States of those known to have participated in the coup. (EPICA, 1994:42; COHA, 5 February 1992).

March–April 1992 In Haiti, procoup parliamentarians, under the watchful eye of the army, violently interrupt the ratification session in March and force senators who had signed the accord in Washington to disavow it. The projunta Cour de Cassation also rules the accord unconstitutional (Ives, 1995a:74–75; COHA, 11 March 1992, 3 April 1992, 8 April 1992; EPICA, 1994:42).

May 1992 President Bush signs an executive order (the so-called Kennebunkport Order) declaring that all Haitians intercepted at sea will be forcefully returned to Haiti without first being screened for political asylum in the United States (COHA, 28 May 1992).

June 1992 Washington continues to send mixed signals to the Haitian authorities about its resolve to oust them from power. The de facto Haitian Senate and Chamber of Deputies ratify pro-U.S. and ex-presidential candidate Marc Bazin as acting prime minister. These actions follow the so-called Villa d'Accueil agreement forged by the military, the de facto government, and National Assembly. No representative of Aristide participates at the meeting. The State Department, which first denounced Bazin for holding his post illegally, later reverses its position and calls on Aristide to negotiate with the new prime minister (COHA, 17 June 1992, 26 June 1992; EPICA, 1994:43).

July 1992   Aristide responds to the schemes of the de facto gov-
                       ernment by forming his own "presidential commission"
                       headed by Father Antoine Adrien. Composed of mem-
                       bers of parliament and the business and professional
                       communities, the commission's charge is to represent
                       Aristide's government in Haiti and to dialogue with
                       the army and all other sectors of Haitian society (such
                       as the church, businesses, unions, political parties,
                       peasants, and human rights organizations) (COHA, 10
                       July 1992).
                           The U.S. Second Court of Appeals rules that Bush's
                       (May) executive order is illegal because it violates the
                       Refugee Act of 1980. The U.S. Supreme Court lifts the
                       lower court's finding and rules that the United States
                       can continue to intercept and repatriate Haitians at sea
                       without first granting them asylum hearings (COHA, 9
                       October 1992; EPICA, 1994:43).

September 1992   In his address to the UN, Aristide criticizes the Vatican
                       for recognizing the government of Prime Minister
                       Bazin and sending a representative to Haiti. He calls on
                       the United States and OAS to tighten the embargo
                       against the de facto military government (COHA, 9
                       October 1992).

January 1993   President Clinton declares that he will continue the
                       Bush administration's policy of repatriating Haitian
                       refugees and succeeds in enlisting Aristide's support by
                       promising a tougher stance against the military junta in
                       return. In a radio broadcast to Haiti, Aristide urges
                       Haitians not to flee by boat.
                           In the meantime, the de facto government holds par-
                       liamentary elections, which the United States considers
                       illegal, and fourteen new promilitary senators and
                       deputies take their seats in the legislature (COHA, 8
                       January 1993; EPICA, 1994:43).

March 1993   Lawrence Pezzullo, former U.S. ambassador to
                       Nicaragua, replaces Bernard Aronson as President
                       Clinton's special envoy to Haiti. Pezzullo and Dante
                       Caputo, the UN-OAS's special envoy, propose a plan,
                       endorsed by Aristide, that calls for sending a multina-
                       tional force to Haiti, the resignation of the army high
                       command, a broad amnesty for the army, and the for-
                       mation of a new consensus government. Albeit reluc-
                       tantly, Aristide accepts the principle of an armed multi-

	national peacekeeping force in Haiti (EPICA, 1994:43; COHA, 30 March 1993).

June 1993
The Haitian junta rejects the plan, and de facto Prime Minister Bazin resigns. President Clinton urges the UN to adopt tougher sanctions against Haiti, including a worldwide fuel and arms embargo against the junta and targeting and freezing the assets of Haitians and of the state enterprises who supported the coup (Marquis, 1993a, 1993b, 1993c; EPICA, 1994:43).

July 1993
General Raoul Cédras and President Aristide sign the Governors Island Accord. The ten points of the accord call for: Aristide to name a new prime minister, the UN to suspend the sanctions of June 1993, parliament to be legally reconstituted, the army and police to be reformed, political amnesty to be granted to those involved in the coup, General Cédras to leave office, and Aristide to return to Haiti on October 30, 1993 (COHA, 18 October 1993; Haitian Information Bureau, 1994:224; Aristide, 1994b:195–197; EPICA, 1994:43).

Aristide's government in exile organizes the Haiti Government/Business Partnership Conference in Miami. There, Aristide embraces the Haitian bourgeoisie that had supported his overthrow and promises the business sector that his next government would work in concert with the private sector to promote capital investment and an industrial and tourist development plan (Ethéart, 1993).

August 1993
In keeping with the accord, the illegally elected members of parliament leave office, the parliament ratifies Aristide's new prime minister, Robert Malval, and the UN Security Council suspends the June embargo amid new reports of increasing murders and human rights violations by the military and its paramilitary death squads (Haitian Information Bureau, 1994:225).

September 1993
Antoine Izméry, close friend and supporter of Aristide, is assassinated by the military and its attachés while attending a memorial service for the victims of the Saint-Jean Bosco massacre (Aristide's former parish). Aristide calls for the resignation of Cédras and Police Chief Col. Michel François (Haitian Information Bureau, 1994:225).

| | Duvalierists and neo-Duvalierists form the Front pour l'Avencement et le Progrès d'Haiti, a death squad with ties to the Haitian Army and the CIA (Nairn, 1994b, 1994c; Haitian Information Bureau, 1994:226). |

October 1993 — Members of the FRAPH successfully prevent the USS *Harlan County* from docking in Port-au-Prince and unloading its contingent of about 200 U.S. and Canadian soldiers sent to begin "professionalizing" the Haitian Army as called for by the Governors Island Accord. Clinton orders the *Harlan County* to return to the Guantanamo naval base in Cuba. The UN Security Council votes to reimpose the embargo if Cédras does not resign by October 15. The military and FRAPH respond by unleashing a new wave of repression and murder, including the assassination of Guy Malary, the minister of justice. Aristide calls for a total blockade of Haiti. The U.S. ambassador to Haiti presses Malval to "broaden" his cabinet to include promilitary ministers, and the CIA holds a special briefing for U.S. lawmakers on Aristide's alleged mental instability (EPICA, 1994:43–44; Haitian Information Bureau, 1994:227; Doyle, 1994:55–56).

November 1993 — The United States continues to push Malval to broaden his government to include coup supporters. In the *New York Times,* Tim Weiner reveals that the CIA had created a so-called intelligence service, the Service d'Intelligence National (SIN, National Intelligence Service), in the 1980s that turned into "an instrument of political terror whose officers at times engaged in drug trafficking." The CIA kept the high-ranking officers involved in the coup on its payroll until shortly after Aristide was overthrown (Weiner, 1993; Haitian Information Bureau, 1994:229).

December 1993 — Prime Minister Malval resigns after he fails to convene a "national reconciliation conference" between the prodemocratic camp and coup supporters. Aristide and nine of ten ministers in Malval's cabinet criticize and reject the conference, and Aristide counters by organizing a conference on the refugee question for January 1994 in Miami. In the meantime, members of FRAPH allegedly set fire to over 1,000 homes in Cité Soleil, an Aristide stronghold, in retaliation for the discovery there of a slain FRAPH treasurer. Canada, France, the

United States, and Venezuela announce that they will strengthen the sanctions if the junta fails to resume the Governors Island process by January 15, 1994 (Haitian Information Bureau, 1994:230; EPICA, 1994:44).

January 1994   In January, at the Miami conference that Aristide organized, Aristide and his supporters, including members of the congressional Black Caucus and Jesse Jackson, criticized the Clinton administration's refugee policies and its failure to take a stronger stance toward the coup leaders in Haiti. The January 15 deadline passes without further action from the international community, but the United States cancels the visas of 500 Haitian army officers (Haitian Information Bureau, 1994:232–233; EPICA, 1994:44; Marquis, 1993).

February 1994   Pezzullo plays his last card. The Clinton administration, accusing Aristide of "intransigence," prods him to accept a new plan supposedly drafted by Haitian parliamentarians. The plan calls for a broad "coalition government," an amnesty law for the coup-makers, the retirement of Cédras and the "transfer" of François, and the lifting of the embargo, but it suggests no date for Aristide's return. Aristide flatly rejects this plan. In congressional testimony in March 1994, Pezzullo admits that the plan originated in the State Department and that he and U.S. Ambassador Swing handpicked the parliamentary delegation that was flown to Washington to present the plan to Aristide (COHA, 4 March 1994, 7 March 1994; EPICA, 1994:44).

February 1994   Aristide counters the Pezzullo plan with his own eight-point plan, which calls for the immediate departure of Cédras and the other coup leaders, for a total trade embargo against Haiti, for a parliamentary vote for a general amnesty law and a law to separate the army and the police, and for the UN to resume its technical assistance program. According to the plan, Aristide would then name a new prime minister and return to Haiti within ten days (Goshko and Preston, 1994; EPICA, 1994:44).

March 1994   The congressional Black Caucus and liberal Democratic members of Congress introduce a bill calling for tougher U.S. sanctions against the junta; they also demand Pezzullo's resignation (Greenhouse, 1994b, 1994c; EPICA, 1994:44).

April 1994   Randall Robinson, director of TransAfrica, begins a
                hunger strike and calls on President Clinton to fire
                Pezzullo and change his policies toward the Haitian
                military and the refugees (Goshko, 1994a; Greenhouse,
                1994d, 1994e).

May 1994   The UN Security Council adopts new resolutions call-
                ing for the departure of Cédras and the other coup
                leaders, imposes new sanctions against the coup leaders
                and supporters, and threatens to tighten the embargo.
                U.S. Embassy officials in Port-au-Prince leak a memo
                accusing the Haitian Left and Aristide supporters of
                manipulating and fabricating human right abuses in
                Haiti. Meanwhile, Clinton announces a change in
                refugee policy to allow the refugees to apply for politi-
                cal asylum at sea or in a third country, fires Pezzullo,
                and appoints former Congressman William Gray III as
                his new special envoy to Haiti. Robinson ends his
                hunger strike. Canada, the Dominican Republic,
                France, the Netherlands, and the United States suspend
                their commercial flights to Haiti, and Washington
                freezes the bank accounts of the coup leaders and their
                supporters and orders a ban on their international
                transactions (P. Lewis, 1994; Williams, 1994; Preston,
                1994; EPICA, 1994:45).

July 1994   As the flow of refugees increases, Washington
                announces that they will no longer be eligible for asy-
                lum in the United States but will be held in refugee
                camps at Guantanamo and in other countries. The de
                facto government in Haiti expels the UN Civilian Mis-
                sion in Haiti, and the UN Security Council adopts
                Resolution 940, authorizing a multinational force to use
                "all means necessary" to remove the coup leaders from
                power (*NYT,* 1994; EPICA, 1994:45).

August 1994   The Haitian junta replies to these tougher measures by
                increasing their repression. Attachés assassinate Father
                Jean-Marie Vincent—a close friend of Aristide's and
                the first priest to be killed by the regime (Bragg, 1994;
                Farah, 1994a; EPICA, 1994:45).
                    Aristide's government in exile adopts the "strategy of
                social and economic reconstruction," a neoliberal eco-
                nomic plan based largely on the Emergency Economic
                Recovery Program developed by a multiagency task

force of the IDA, IDB, IMF, World Bank, and USAID (Haiti, 1994b).

September 1994

President Clinton goes on national television to announce and justify the impending military intervention to oust the recalcitrant Haitian junta and return President Aristide to office. Clinton dispatches former President Jimmy Carter, retired Gen. Colin Powell, and Sen. Sam Nunn of Georgia to negotiate the terms of the junta's departure and the mode of entry of the 20,000-strong U.S.-led multinational force (Harris and Farah, 1994; Jehl, 1994b; EPICA, 1994:45).

October 1994

With the multinational force in control of the territory, Police Chief Michel François flees to the Dominican Republic. The legitimate parliament reconvenes and passes a limited amnesty law covering political crimes but not other criminal acts. Cédras hints that he might not resign as agreed, but the ranking U.S. Army general in Haiti reminds him just who is in charge. Humiliated and defeated, Cédras and General Biamby, the other high-ranking member of the junta, leave Haiti for exile in Panama. On October 15, jubilant crowds welcome President Aristide back to Haiti, to the total dismay of the neo-Duvalierist and procoup forces who undoubtedly felt betrayed by Clinton.

REFERENCES

The following acronyms are used in the references and related citations in the text:

A/HRW/NCHR	Human Rights Watch/Americas and National Coalition of Haitian Refugees
APB	Association Professionelle des Banques
AW/NCHR	Americas Watch and National Coalition for Haitian Refugees
AW/NCHR/CR	Americas Watch, National Coalition for Haitian Refugees and Caribbean Rights
CCOH	Coalition for Civilian Observers in Haiti
COHA	Council on Hemispheric Affairs
FBIS	*Foreign Broadcast Information Service*
HM	*Haiti en Marche*
HO	*Haiti Observateur*
HP	*Haiti Progrès*
IDB	Inter-American Development Bank
LAN	*Latin America Newsletter*
MH	*Miami Herald*
MIDH	Mouvement pour l'Instauration de la Démocratie en Haiti
NLC	National Labor Committee
NYT	*New York Times*
OL	Opération Lavalas
OPL	Organisation Politique Lavalas
UNDHA	United Nations Department of Humanitarian Affairs
UNDP	United Nations Development Program
USAID	United States Agency for International Development
USDOL	United States Department of Labor

Ahmad, Aijaz. 1992. *In Theory: Classes, Nations, Literatures*. London: Verso.

Allison, Graham, and Gregory F. Treverton, eds. 1992. *Rethinking America's Security*. New York: W. W. Norton.

Alterman, Eric. 1992. "Operation Pundit Storm." *World Policy Journal* 9, no. 4 (Fall-Winter):599–616.

Americas/Human Rights Watch and National Coalition of Haitian Refugees. 1994. *Terror Prevails in Haiti: Human Rights Violations and Failed Diplomacy*. New York: Human Rights Watch/Americas and National Coalition for Haitian Refugees.

Americas Watch and National Coalition for Haitian Refugees. 1989. *Human Rights in Haiti: One Year Under Prosper Avril*. New York: Americas Watch and National Coalition for Haitian Refugees.

_____. 1990. *In the Army's Hands: Human Rights in Haiti on the Eve of the Elections.* New York: Americas Watch and National Coalition for Haitian Refugees.

_____. 1993. *Silencing a People: The Destruction of Civil Society in Haiti.* New York: Human Rights Watch and National Coalition for Haitian Refugees.

Americas Watch, National Coalition for Haitian Refugees and Caribbean Rights. 1991. *The Aristide Government's Human Rights Record.* New York: Americas Watch and National Coalition for Haitian Refugees, and St. Michael, Barbados: Caribbean Rights.

Amnesty International. 1992. *Haiti: Human Rights Held Ransom.* New York: Amnesty International.

Anglade, Georges. 1982. *Espace et liberté en Haiti.* Montreal: Groupe d'Études et de Recherches Critiques d'Espace et Centre de Recherches Caraïbes.

Apple, R. W., Jr. 1993. "President Orders Six U.S. Warships for Haiti Patrol." *New York Times,* 16 October.

Aristide, Jean-Bertrand. 1990. *In the Parish of the Poor: Writings from Haiti.* Translated and edited by Amy Wilentz. Maryknoll, N.Y.: Orbis Books.

_____. 1992a. *Tout moun sé moun/Tout homme est un homme.* With Christophe Wargny. Paris: Éditions du Seuil.

_____. 1992b. *Théologie et politique.* Montreal: Les Éditions du CIDIHCA.

_____. 1994a. *Névrose vétéro-testamentaire.* Montreal: Les Éditions du CIDIHCA.

_____. 1994b. *Dignité.* With Christopher Wargny. Paris: Éditions du Sevil.

_____. 1994c. "Aristide's Talk: 'Yes to Reconciliation.'" *New York Times,* October 5.

Arrighi, Giovanni. 1991a. "World Income Inequalities and the Future of Socialism." *New Left Review,* no. 189 (September-October):39–65.

_____. 1991b. "Marxist Century, American Century," in Robin Blackburn, ed., *After the Fall: The Failure of Communism and the Future of Socialism.* London: Verso.

Association Professionelle des Banques. 1991. *Le livre blanc du secteur privé national: Propositions de politique économique.* Port-au-Prince: Association Professionelle des Banques.

Attinger, Joelle, and Michael Kramer. 1993. "It's Not If I Go Back, But When." *Time,* 1 November.

Barthélemy, Gérard, and Christian Girault, eds. 1993. *La République haitienne: État des lieux et perspectives.* Paris: Éditions KARTHALA.

Bazin, Marc. 1990. *Construire ensemble: Discours et messages.* Vol. 2. Port-au-Prince: Henri Deschamps.

Benesch, Susan. 1994. "Haitian Senators Approve Amnesty." *Miami Herald,* 8 October.

Benitez Manaut, Raul. 1993. "Identity Crisis: The Military in Changing Times." *NACLA Report on the Americas* 27, no. 2 (September-October):15–19.

Bergsten, C. Fred. 1992. "The Primacy of Economics." *Foreign Policy,* no. 87 (Summer 1992):3–24.

Blackburn, Robin, ed. 1991. *After the Fall: The Failure of Communism and the Future of Socialism.* London: Verso.

Boff, Leonardo, and Clovis Boff. 1990. *Introducing Liberation Theology.* Translated by Paul Burns. Maryknoll, N.Y.: Orbis Books.

Bohning, Don. 1991. "Aristide's Next Job: Set Course for Haiti." *Miami Herald,* 10 February.

_____. 1993a. "U.S. Backs U.N. Police for Haiti." *Miami Herald,* 9 May.

_____. 1993b. "In Haiti, Killing Revives Haunting Memories." *Miami Herald,* 13 September.

Booth, William, and Douglas Farah. 1994. "Feared Police Chief Quits, Flees Haiti." *Washington Post*, 5 October.

Borosage, Robert L. 1993. "Disinvesting in America." *The Nation* (October 4):346–347.

Boutros-Ghali, Boutros. 1992. *An Agenda for Peace: Preventive Diplomacy, Peacemaking and Peacekeeping*. Report of the Secretary General Pursuant to the Statement Adopted by the Summit Meeting of the Security Council on 31 January. New York: United Nations.

Bragg, Rick. 1994. "Haitians Bury Slain Priest as a Hero." *New York Times*, 3 September.

Bread for the World. 1990. *Hunger 1990: A Report on the State of World Hunger*. Washington, D.C.: Bread for the World Institute on Hunger and Development.

Brenner, Robert. 1991. "Why Is the United States at War with Iraq?" *New Left Review*, no. 185 (January-February):122–137.

Briggs, Barbara, and Charles Kernaghan. 1995. "The U.S. Economic Agenda: A Sweatshop Model of Development," in NACLA, ed., *Haiti: Dangerous Crossroads*. Boston: South End Press.

Broad, Robin, and John Cavanagh. 1988. "No More NICs." *Foreign Policy*, no. 72 (Fall):81–104.

Burbach, Roger. 1993. "Clinton's Latin America Policy: A Look at Things to Come." *NACLA Report on the Americas* 26, no. 5 (May):16–22.

Bush, George. 1990. "Address Before a Joint Session of the Congress on the Persian Gulf Crisis and the Federal Budget Deficit." *Weekly Compilation of Presidential Documents* 26, no. 37 (September 17):1358–1363.

Caprio, Giovanni. 1993. "Économie et société (1970–1988)," in Gérard Barthélemy and Christian Girault, eds., *La République haitienne: État des lieux et perspectives*. Paris: Éditions KARTHALA.

Caribbean Report. 1988. "Haiti: Manigat Ousted in Clash with Namphy." London: Latin American Newsletter, RC-88-06. 21 July.

Caroit, Jean-Michel. 1991. "Interview avec le Président Aristide: Bilan et perspectives." *Haiti en Marche*, 8–14 May.

Castañeda, Jorge G. 1993. *Utopia Unarmed: The Latin American Left After the Cold War*. New York: Alfred A. Knopf.

Castor, Suzy. 1991. "L'Expérience démocratique haitienne," in Suzy Castor, Micha Gaillard, Paul Laraque, and Gérard Pierre-Charles, *Haiti: À l'aube du changement*. Port-au-Prince: Centre de Recherche et de Formation Économique et Sociale pour le Développement.

Castor, Suzy, Micha Gaillard, Paul Laraque, and Gérard Pierre-Charles. 1991. *Haiti: À l'aube du changement*. Port-au-Prince: Centre de Recherche et de Formation Économique et Sociale pour le Développement.

Catanese, Anthony V. 1991. "Rural Poverty and Environmental Degradation in Haiti." Series on Environment and Development, Occasional Paper No. 5. Bloomington, Ind.: Indiana Center on Global Change and World Peace.

"The Challenges Ahead: An Analysis of the Governors Island Accord." 1993. *Haiti Reborn*. Hyattsville, Md.: Haiti Reborn.

Chamberlain, Greg. 1987. "Up by the Roots." *NACLA Report on the Americas* 21, no. 3 (May-June):15–23.

_____. 1988. "Manigat Wants to Bring Democracy." *Caribbean Contact*, March.

_____. 1990a. "The Duvalierists Return." *Caribbean Contact*, July.

_____. 1990b. "As Pascal-Trouillot Fumbles." *Caribbean Contact*, September–October.

_____. 1990c. "Aristide Likely to Be Haiti's President." *Caribbean Contact*, November–December.

Charlier, André. 1988. "Déchoukaj à Demi." *Haiti en Marche*, 5–15 October.

_____. 1990. "Titid, les yeux grands ouverts." *Haiti en Marche*, 7–13 November.

Chomsky, Noam. 1985. *Turning the Tide: U.S. Intervention in Central America and the Struggle for Peace*. Boston: South End Press.

_____. 1992. "What We Say Goes: The Middle East in the New World Order," in Cynthia Peters, ed., *Collateral Damage: The "New World Order" at Home and Abroad*. Boston: South End Press.

[Clinton, William J.] 1994. "Text of President Clinton's Address on Haiti." *Washington Post*, 16 September.

Coalition for Civilian Observers in Haiti. 1993. *Internal Exile in Haiti: A Country Held Hostage by Its Own Army*. Washington, D.C.: Washington Office on Haiti.

Coll, Alberto R. 1992. "America as Grand Facilitator." *Foreign Policy*, no. 87 (Summer):47–65.

Colon, Yves, Lizette Alvarez, and Christopher Marquis. 1994. "U.S. to Open Guantanamo for Haitians." *Miami Herald*, 29 June.

Constable, Pamela. 1992–1993. "Dateline Haiti: Caribbean Stalemate." *Foreign Policy*, no. 89 (Winter):175–190.

Council on Hemispheric Affairs. 1991. "The Coup That Is Destined to Fail." Press release no. 91.35. 2 October.

_____. 1991. "Deteriorating Haitian Situation Punctuated by Washington's Compliance with Economic Sanctions." Press release no. 91.40. 30 October.

_____. 1991. "Washington's Asylum Policy in Disarray." *Washington Report on the Hemisphere* 12, no. 4 (18 December).

_____. 1992. "Compromised Haiti Policy Produces Flawed Results." Press release no. 92.04. 10 January.

_____. 1992. "Haiti Staggers into Its Latest Crisis." Press release no. 92.07. 30 January.

_____. 1992. "Washington Torpedoes Haitian Trade Embargo and All but Undercuts Prospect for Aristide's Return with His Powers Intact." Press release no. 92.10. 5 February.

_____. 1992. "OAS Accord Marks Defeat for Aristide, Setback for Haitian Democracy." Press release no. 92.15. 25 February.

_____. 1992. "OAS Accord Brings Uneasy Still to Haitian Drama." *Washington Report on the Hemisphere* 12, no. 9 (11 March).

_____. 1992. "In Which Direction Is Haiti Policy Moving?" Press release no. 92.18. 3 April.

_____. 1992. "Storm Clouds on Haiti's Horizon." *Washington Report on the Hemisphere* 12, no. 11 (8 April).

_____. 1992. "Washington's Haitian Policy Continues in Disarray." Press release no. 92.29. 28 May.

_____. 1992. "The Struggle for Haitian Democracy." *Washington Report on the Hemisphere* 12, no. 15 (17 June).

_____. 1992. "State Department Yet Again Changes Course on Haiti." Press release no. 92.34. 26 June.

_____. 1992. "President Aristide's Latest Proposal Demonstrates Political Astuteness and a Genuine Move Towards Reconciliation." Press release no. 92.37. 10 July.

_____. 1992. "Haitian Policies Under Attack." *Washington Report on the Hemisphere* 12, no. 23 (9 October).

_____. 1992. "Havana Wins Big at the U.N." *Washington Report on the Hemisphere* 13, no. 4 (16 December).

_____. 1993. "Clinton Missing the Boat on Haiti." Press release no. 93.2. 8 January.

_____. 1993. "Haitian Solution Not Necessarily Near." Press release no. 93.8. February 11.

_____. 1993. "Aristide's Dilemma Continues." *Washington Report on the Hemisphere* 13, no. 10 (30 March).

_____. 1993. "U.S. Paints Itself into a Corner on Haiti Policy." *Washington Report on the Hemisphere*, 18 October.

_____. 1994. "COHA Policy Analysis: Haiti: Pezzullo and the Haitian Delegation Caper." Press release. 4 March.

_____. 1994. "The State Department's Haiti Parliamentary Plan: The Unmasking of a Hoax." *Washington Report on the Hemisphere* 14, no. 7 (7 March).

Cummings, Bruce. 1991. "Trilateralism and the New World Order." *World Policy Journal* 8, no. 2 (Spring):195–222.

D'Adesky, Anne-Christine. 1991. "Reform-Minded Priest Is Now Haiti's President." *San Francisco Examiner*, 7 February.

Danaher, Kevin, ed. 1994. *50 Years Is Enough: The Case Against the World Bank and the International Monetary Fund*. Boston: South End Press.

Daniel, Myrlène. 1991. "Ouvriers: Salaire minimum—Patrons: Avantages maximum?" *Haiti Progrès*, 10–16 July.

Danner, Mark. 1993. "The Fall of the Prophet." *New York Review of Books* 40, no. 20 (December):44–53.

Danroc, Gilles, ed. 1990. *Haiti, quelle démocratie: Les Élections générales de 1990*. Port-au-Prince: Solidarité Internationale.

Deblock, Christian, Cary Hector, Guy Pierre, Gérard Pierre-Charles, and Marc Romulus. 1990. "Table ronde sur l'économie haitienne." *Rencontre: Une Revue d'analyse et d'action sociale*, no. 2.

Delatour, Leslie. 1990. *Propositions pour le progrès*. Port-au-Prince: La Fondation des Industries d'Haiti.

Delince, Kern. 1993. *Les forces politiques en Haiti: Manuel d'histoire contemporaine*. Paris: Editions KARTHALA, and Plantation, Fla.: Pegasus Books.

Delva, Gladys. 1991. "Haiti et la concurrence internationale dans l'industrie de l'assemblage," in Cary Hector and Hérard Jadotte, eds., *Haiti et l'après-Duvalier: Continuités et ruptures*. Port-au-Prince: Henri Deschamps, and Montreal: CIDIHCA.

DeWind, Josh. 1990. "Elections Without Democracy? The Impact of United States Economic Assistance on Politics in Haiti." *Cimarron: New Perspectives on the Caribbean* 2, no. 3:64–83.

DeWind, Josh, and David H. Kinley III. 1988. *Aiding Migration: The Impact of International Development Assistance on Haiti*. Boulder: Westview Press, 1988.

Diamond, Larry. 1992. "Promoting Democracy." *Foreign Policy*, no. 87 (Summer):25–46.

Dietz, James L., and Emilio Pantojas-Garcia. 1994. "Neo-Liberal Policies and Caribbean Development: From CBI to the North American Free Trade Agreement," in

Hilbourne A. Watson, ed., *Human Resources and Institutional Requirements for Global Adjustments: Strategies for the Caribbean*. Special issue of *21st Century Policy Review* 2, no. 1–2 (Spring).

Dowd, Maureen. 1994. "The Mouse That Roared Squeaks Back." *New York Times*, 22 September.

Doyle, Kate. 1994. "Hollow Diplomacy in Haiti." *World Policy Journal* 11, no. 1 (Spring):50–58.

Dupuy, Alex. 1989a. *Haiti in the World Economy: Class, Race, and Underdevelopment Since 1700*. Boulder: Westview Press.

_____. 1989b. "Peasant Poverty in Haiti." *Latin American Research Review* 24, no. 3:259–271.

Dussel, Enrique. 1992. "Liberation Theology and Marxism." *Rethinking Marxism* 5, no. 3 (Fall):50–74.

Duvalier, François. 1969. *Mémoires d'un leader du Tiers Monde: Mes négociations avec le Saint-Siège ou une tranche d'histoire*. Paris: Hachette.

Ellis Marc H., and Otto Maduro, eds. 1990. *Expanding the View: Gustavo Gutiérrez and the Future of Liberation Theology*. Maryknoll, N.Y.: Orbis Books.

"The 'Embassy' Memo," in James Ridgeway, ed., *The Haiti Files: Decoding the Crisis*. 1994. Washington, D.C.: Essential Books.

EPICA. 1994. *Beyond the Mountains, More Mountains: Haiti Faces the Future*. Washington, D.C.: EPICA.

Ethéart, Elsie. 1993. "Le Business découvre le Président Aristide." *Haiti en Marche*, 28 July–3 August.

Evans, Gareth. 1994. "Cooperative Security and Intra-State Conflict." *Foreign Policy*, no. 96 (Fall):3–20.

Evans, Peter B. 1989. "Predatory, Developmental, and Other Apparatuses: A Comparative Political Economy Perspective on the Third World State." *Sociological Forum* 4, no. 4:561–587.

Farah, Douglas. 1993a. "Aristide Asks Haitians to Stay Home and Await His Return." *Washington Post*, 13 January.

_____. 1993b. "Haiti Rejects Proposal to End Crisis." *Washington Post*, 25 May.

_____. 1993c. "U.S. Tightens Sanctions on Regime in Haiti." *Washington Post*, 5 June.

_____. 1993d. "Opponents Accelerate Drive to Bar Aristide." *Washington Post*, 2 October.

_____. 1993e. "Defiant Tactics of Haitian Military Drive Off Collaborators Among Elite." *Washington Post*, 15 October.

_____. 1994a. "Haiti's Military Leaders Alienate Supporters with Hard-Line Stance." *Washington Post*, 14 September.

_____. 1994b. "U.S. Troops Find Haiti Calm, Military Cooperative." *Washington Post*, 20 September.

_____. 1994c. "Final Symbol of Old Regime Quits in Haiti." *Washington Post*, 13 October.

_____. 1994d. "U.S. Assists Dictators' Luxury Exile." *Washington Post*, 14 October.

Farmer, Paul. 1994. *The Uses of Haiti*. Monroe, Me.: Common Courage Press.

_____. 1995. "The Significance of Haiti," in NACLA, ed., *Haiti: Dangerous Crossroads*. Boston: South End Press.

Fass, Simon M. 1988. *Political Economy in Haiti: The Drama of Survival*. New Brunswick, N.J.: Transaction Books.

Ferguson, James. 1987. *Papa Doc, Baby Doc: Haiti and the Duvaliers.* Oxford and New York: Basil Blackwell.

Fields, Gregg. 1993. "There's New Hope Haitians Can Revive Island's Economy." *Miami Herald*, 25 July.

Fishlow, Albert, Catherine Gwin, Stephan Haggard, Dani Rodrik, and Robert Wade. 1994. *Miracle or Design: Lessons from the East Asian Experience.* Washington, D.C.: Overseas Development Council.

Foreign Broadcast Information Service. 1991. "Bishop Romélus Reacts to Archbishop's Statements." FL0401211591. Port-au-Prince Radio Métropole in French. 1145 GMT, 4 January.

_____. 1991. "Aristide Discourages Revenge; Urges Unity, Faith." FL10001024191. Port-au-Prince Radio Haiti-Inter in Creole. 1700 GMT, 9 January.

_____. 1991. "President-Elect Aristide Outlines Tasks, Goals." FL1401015591. Mexico City NOTIMEX in Spanish. 1329 GMT, 13 January.

_____. 1991. "Further on Results of 20 January Elections." FL2901004591. Port-au-Prince Radio Soleil Network in Creole. 1200 GMT, 28 January/a.

_____. 1991. "Port-au-Prince Mayor Discusses Recent Events." FL2801224591. Port-au-Prince Radio Soleil Network in Creole. 1200 GMT, 28 January/b.

_____. 1991. "President Aristide's Inaugural Address 7 February." FL0702224591. Port-au-Prince Radio Nationale in Creole. 1945 GMT, 7 February.

_____. 1991. "Senate Approves René Préval as Prime Minister." FL1402124091. Bonaire Trans World Radio in English. 1130 GMT, 14 February.

_____. 1991. "Aristide Assures Journalists of Freedom of Press." FL2002012091. Port-au-Prince Radio Metropole in French. 1700 GMT, 15 February.

_____. 1991. "Formal Appointment Decree Read." FL200234691. Port-au-Prince Radio Antilles Internationales in French. 1245 GMT, 20 February/a.

_____. 1991. "Political Leaders React to Cabinet Appointments." FL2102150891. Port-au-Prince Radio Haiti-Inter in Creole. 2100 GMT, 20 February/b.

_____. 1991. "Chamber Votes Aristide Six-Month Reform Limit." FL0403210391. Port-au-Prince Radio Haiti-Inter in French. 1200 GMT, 28 February.

_____. 1991. "Aristide Interview on Economy, Foreign Relations." FL1903222091. Port-au-Prince Radio Metropole in French. 1700 GMT, 18 March.

_____. 1991. "Authorities Detail Operations Against Zenglendos." FL210322091. Port-au-Prince Radio Soleil Network in Creole. 1200 GMT, 20 March.

_____. 1991. "Youth Groups Demonstrate Support for Aristide." FL2603212091. Port-au-Prince Radio Metropole in French. 1700 GMT, 25 March.

_____. 1991. "Unions Discuss Demands with President Aristide." FL2703202191. Port-au-Prince Radio Nationale in Creole. 1400 GMT, 27 March.

_____. 1991. "Aristide, Private Sector Debate Economic Solutions." FL0304225091. Port-au-Prince Radio Metropole in French. 1700 GMT, 2 April.

_____. 1991. "Government Officials React to Market Fire." FL1804190591. Port-au-Prince Tele-Haiti in French. 1230 GMT, 18 April.

_____. 1991. "Macoutes Arrested, Weapons Seized in Archaie." FL1904193591. Port-au-Prince Radio Antilles Internationales in French. 1145 GMT, 19 April.

_____. 1991. "Government Uncovers Plot; Urges Popular Vigilance." FL2404203391. Port-au-Prince Radio Haiti-Inter in French. 2100 GMT, 23 April.

_____. 1991. "Thousands Demonstrate Against High Cost of Living." FL2404215091. Port-au-Prince Radio Soleil Network in Creole. 1100 GMT, 24 April.

_____. 1991. "Peasant Congress Opens, Land Reforms Demanded." FL0105012691. Port-au-Prince Radio Soleil Network in Creole. 1100 GMT, 29 April/a.

_____. 1991. "Aristide Receives Peasants, Hears Demands." FL0105175491. Port-au-Prince Radio Metropole in French. 1600 GMT, 29 April/b.

_____. 1991. "Demonstration Reported in Grand Goave 4 May." FL0705001991. Port-au-Prince Radio Antilles Internationales in French. 1145 GMT, 6 May.

_____. 1991. "Aristide Donates Paycheck to Citizens Groups." FL1605012291. Port-au-Prince Radio Soleil Network in Creole. 1100 GMT, 15 May.

_____. 1991. "Minister of Justice Dismissed, Successor Named." FL2105144591. Port-au-Prince Radio Metropole in French. 1600 GMT, 20 May.

_____. 1991. "Popular Organizations Propose Economic Plan." FL2505002191. Port-au-Prince Radio Metropole in French. 1600 GMT, 23 May/a.

_____. 1991. "FNCD Call 'Legal Hat' Statement Betrayal." FL2405214991. Port-au-Prince Radio Soleil Network in Creole. 1100 GMT, 23 May/b.

_____. 1991. "Mesyeux Announces Operation Storm Wind." FL0306232591. Port-au-Prince Radio Antilles Internationales in French. 1145 GMT, 31 May.

_____. 1991. "Rights Honored; Aristide Donates Paycheck." FL1106002591. Port-au-Prince Radio Soleil Network in Creole. 1300 GMT, 10 June.

_____. 1991. "Government Implicated in Operation Storm Wind." FL1806011091. Port-au-Prince Radio Galaxie in French. 1130 GMT, 17 June.

_____. 1991. "Aristide Meets with Unemployed People 18 June." FL2006151691. Port-au-Prince Radio Soleil Network in Creole. 1100 GMT, 19 June.

_____. 1991. "Military-Peasant Conflict Reported in L'Estere." FL2106235391. Port-au-Prince Radio Soleil Network in Creole. 1100 GMT, 20 June.

_____. 1991. "Hundreds Demonstrate for Higher Minimum Wage." FL1207011291. Port-au-Prince Radio Soleil Network in Creole. 1100 GMT, 11 July.

_____. 1991. "President Aristide Addresses Youth Rally." FL0508222591. Port-au-Prince Radio Metropole in French. 1600 GMT, 5 August.

_____. 1991. "Bazin Comments on Aristide's First Six Months." FL0608215591. Port-au-Prince Radio Metropole in French. 1600 GMT, 6 August.

_____. 1991. "Aristide, Quayle Sign Two Aid Agreements." FL1308003891. Port-au-Prince Radio Metropole in French. 1600 GMT, 12 August.

_____. 1991. "Prime Minister, Deputies Trapped by Violent Mob." FL1408013791. Port-au-Prince Radio Metropole. 2200 GMT, 13 August.

_____. 1991. "Officials Condemn 13 August Attack on Deputies." FL1608180491. Port-au-Prince Radio Metropole in French. 1600 GMT, 14 August/a.

_____. 1991. "Police Use Tear Gas to End Demonstration 13 August." FL1408193291. Port-au-Prince Radio Galaxie in French. 1700 GMT, 14 August/b.

_____. 1991. "Tense, Quiet Climate Prevails." PA1408232391. Hamburg DPA in Spanish. 2002 GMT, 14 August/c.

_____. 1991. "Senate President Postpones Censuring Debate." FL1508120991. Bonaire Trans World Radio in English. 1130 GMT, 15 August.

_____. 1991. "Chamber of Deputies President Casseus Resigns." PA1708044091. Paris AFP in Spanish. 0358 GMT, 17 August.

_____. 1991. "Students Protest IMF, 'Imperialist Countries.'" FL2308200291. Port-au-Prince Radio Soleil Network in Creole. 1100 GMT, 23 August.

_____. 1991. "Private Sector Employers Condemn Wage Increase." FL3008190791. Port-au-Prince Radio Metropole in French. 1600 GMT, 29 August.

_____. 1991. "Trade Unions Protest Poor Living Conditions." FL1609183191. Port-au-Prince Radio Metropole in French. 1600 GMT, 13 September.

_____. 1991. "Aristide Comments on Negotiations with IMF." FL1709202491. Port-au-Prince Radio Metropole in French. 1600 GMT, 16 September.

Frank, Andre Gunder. 1969. *Capitalism and Underdevelopment in Latin America.* Rev. ed. New York: Monthly Review Press.

Freedman, Lawrence. 1992. "Order and Disorder in the New World Order." *Foreign Affairs* 17, no. 1:20–37.

French, Howard. 1990. "A Duvalier Ally and Foe Seeks Election in Haiti, Raising Fears of Violence." *New York Times,* 5 November.

_____. 1991a. "Haiti's Army Crushes Revolt by Duvalier Loyalist." *New York Times,* 8 January.

_____. 1991b. "Haiti's Victors Working to Soothe Fears." *New York Times,* 11 January.

_____. 1991c. "Haiti's Press Holds Its Critical Tongue." *New York Times,* 29 January.

_____. 1991d. "Haitian Victor's Backer Is Harsh Toward U.S." *New York Times,* 31 January.

_____. 1991e. "After 6 Months of Changes, Haiti Is Surprised by Its Leader's Moderation." *New York Times,* 4 August.

_____. 1991f. "Haiti's Parliament Shows Leader Its Backbone." *New York Times,* 11 September.

_____. 1991g. "Ex-Backers of Ousted Haitian Say He Alienated His Allies." *New York Times,* 22 October.

_____. 1992. "Premier-Designate Supports 'Modern Capitalism' and a True Reconstruction." *New York Times,* 12 January.

_____. 1993a. "Diplomats, and Aristide, See an End to Haiti Impasse." *New York Times,* 30 April.

_____. 1993b. "Observers See Haiti Police Force as Brutal Obstacle to Democracy." *New York Times,* 24 May.

_____. 1993c. "Leaders in Haiti Spurn Police Plan." *New York Times,* 25 May.

_____. 1993d. "Military Chief Signs Accord to End Haitian Crisis." *New York Times,* 4 July.

_____. 1993e. "Scores Disappear in Haitian Terror Campaign." *New York Times,* 5 September.

_____. 1994. "U.S. Tells Aristide to Bend on Plan." *New York Times,* February 23.

Friedman, Thomas L. 1993a. "Dole Plans Bill to Bar the Use of G.I.'s in Haiti." *New York Times,* 18 October.

_____. 1993b. "Clinton Vows to Fight Congress on His Powers to Use the Military." *New York Times,* 19 October.

Fukuyama, Francis. 1989. "The End of History?" *National Interest* (Summer):3–18.

Gaillard, Micha. 1991. "Gouvernement: Il faut redresser la barre!" in Suzy Castor, Micha Gaillard, Paul Laraque, and Gérard Pierre-Charles, *Haiti: À l'aube du changement.* Port-au-Prince: Centre de Recherche et de Formation Économique et Sociale pour le Développement.

Galeano, Eduardo. 1991. "A Child Lost in the Storm," in Robin Blackburn, ed., *After the Fall: The Failure of Communism and the Future of Socialism.* London: Verso.

Gellman, Barton, and Ruth Marcus. 1994. "U.S. Boosts Pressure on Haitians." *Washington Post*, 4 May.

George, Susan. 1990. *A Fate Worse Than Debt: The World Financial Crisis and the Poor.* New York: Grove Weidenfeld.

Gerth, H. H., and C. Wright Mills, eds. and trans. 1968. *From Max Weber: Essays in Sociology.* Oxford and New York: Oxford University Press.

Gilles, Alain. 1991. "Mouvement populaire et développement politique," in Cary Hector and Hérard Jadotte, eds., *Haiti et l'après-Duvalier: Continuités et ruptures.* Port-au-Prince: Henri Deschamps, and Montreal: CIDIHCA.

Girault, Christian A. 1981. *Le commerce du café en Haïti: Habitants, spéculateurs et exportateurs.* Paris: Editions du Centre National de la Recherche Scientifique.

Gordon, Michael R. 1993. "Military Plan Would Cut Forces but Have Them Ready for Two Wars." *New York Times*, 2 September.

Gorostiaga, Xabier. 1985. "Towards Alternative Policies for the Region," in George Irvin and Xabier Gorostiaga, eds., *Towards an Alternative for Central America and the Caribbean.* London: George Allen and Unwin.

Goshko, John M. 1991. "Aristide Seeks OAS Delegation to Confront Haiti Junta Leaders." *Washington Post*, 3 October.

_____. 1992. "Clinton Urged to Signal Strong Intentions on Haiti." *Washington Post*, 20 December.

_____. 1994a. "Aristide Renounces Treaty Allowing Return of Haitians." *Washington Post*, 7 April.

_____. 1994b. "Economic Recovery Program Given Top Priority." *Washington Post*, 18 September.

_____. 1994c. "Deposed Leader Visits Pentagon, Plans Transition." *Washington Post*, 22 September.

Goshko, John M., and Julia Preston. 1994. "Aristide Presses for Plan Opposed by U.S., U.N." *Washington Post*, 24 February.

Greenhouse, Steven. 1994a. "U.S. Aides Say They Still Back Aristide." *New York Times*, 7 January.

_____. 1994b. "U.S. Again Shifts Its Policy on Haiti." *New York Times*, 27 March.

_____. 1994c. "Haiti Policy in Stalemate." *New York Times*, 7 April.

_____. 1994d. "Aristide to End Accord That Allows U.S. to Seize Refugee Boats." *New York Times*, 8 April.

_____. 1994e. "Aristide Condemns Clinton's Haiti Policy as Racist." *New York Times*, 22 April.

Gutiérrez, Gustavo. 1990. "Expanding the View," in Marc H. Ellis and Otto Maduro, eds., *Expanding the View: Gustavo Gutiérrez and the Future of Liberation Theology.* Maryknoll, N.Y.: Orbis Books.

Haiti (République d'Haiti). 1991. Ministère de la Planification de la Coopération Externe et de la Fonction Publique and Ministère de l'Économie et des Finances. *Cadre de politique économique et programme d'investissement public.* Port-au-Prince: Republic of Haiti.

_____. 1994a. Cabinet Particulier du Président de la République. *Témoignages sur les performances économiques du Gouvernement Aristide/Préval.* Port-au-Prince: Republic of Haiti.

_____. 1994b. *Strategy of Social and Economic Reconstruction.* 22 August. Port-au-Prince: Republic of Haiti.

Haitian Information Bureau. 1994. "Events in Haiti, October 15, 1990–May 11, 1994," in James Ridgeway, ed. *The Haiti Files: Decoding the Crisis.* Washington, D.C.: Essential Books/Azul Editions.

Haiti Beat (no author given). 1988. "The Anatomy of a Coup." 3, no. 1.

Haiti en Marche (no author given). 1988. "Namphy abolit la Constitution." 13–19 July.

_____. 1988. "Les divisions au sein de l'Armée permettent le retour en force des Duvaliéristes." 24–30 August.

_____. 1988. "Haiti au lendemin du coup: Soulagement, déchoukaj, prudence." 21–27 September/a.

_____. 1988. "Qui est Prosper Avril?" 21–27 September/b.

_____. 1988. "Les élections d'Avril." 9–15 November.

_____. 1989. "Haiti: L'Occupation économique." 13–19 September.

_____. 1989. "Situation des droits de l'homme." 20–26 September.

_____. 1989. "Calendrier électoral." 27 September–3 October.

_____. 1989. "Pillage du budget public." 29 November–5 December.

_____. 1989. "Rebrassage des cartes politiques." 6–12 December.

_____. 1990. "Mgr. Romélus appelle au boycott du carnaval." 21–27 February.

_____. 1990. "Gouvernement de Consensus." 7–13 March.

_____. 1990. "Avril fut forcé de plier bagages." 14–20 March.

_____. 1990. "Le piège qui guette le Conseil d'État." 2–8 May.

_____. 1990. "Conseil d'État: Et Maintenant?" 15–22 August.

_____. 1990. "Rebrassage des Cartes: Confrontation evitée in extrémis devant le BED." 24–30 October.

_____. 1990. "Aristide: Le Danger d'une candidature unitaire." 31 October–6 November/a.

_____. 1990. "Le Peuple est incontournable: Interview avec Aristide." 31 October–6 November/b.

_____. 1990. "L'Opération Lavalas enflamme Miami et New York." 7–13 November/a.

_____. 1990. "Remise des carnets." 7–13 November/b.

_____. 1991. "Coup d'État: Le Mystère reste entier." 15–21 January.

_____. 1991. "Les Ministres." 27 February–1 March.

_____. 1991. "Le Gouvernement attaque: Mesures contre la vie chère et la fraude fiscale; la police sous le contrôle de la Justice." 27 March–2 April.

_____. 1991. "Les Riches ont peur de la démocratie." 8–14 May.

_____. 1991. "Aristide-FNCD: Ça barde!." 29 May–4 June.

_____. 1991. "Armée: Abraham a-t-il été 'démissionné'?" 10–16 July.

_____. 1991. "L'Atmosphère autour du procès." 31 July–6 August/a.

_____. 1991. "'Procès du siècle' ou 'procès baclé'?" 31 July–6 August/b.

_____. 1991. "Révocations en masse." 7–13 August.

_____. 1991. "La Politique économique du gouvernement: Rencontre avec le Ministre des Finances Marie-Michèle Rey." 14–20 August.

_____. 1991. "FNCD-Gouvernement: Le Rapport des forces." 21–27 August.

_____. 1991. "Les Négociations entre le gouvernement et le FMI se poursuivent: Note de presse du Ministère des Finances." 18–24 September.

_____. 1993. "Robert Malval Premier Ministre 'désigné.'" 28 July–3 August.

_____. 1995. "Claudette Werleigh: Premier Ministre." 25–31 October.

Haiti Observateur (no author given). 1987. "La Constitution de la République d'Haiti." 20–27 March.

_____. 1988. "Ouvert au dialogue, le Général Namphy aspire à durer le plus longtemps possible au pouvoir." 15–22 July.

_____. 1989. "Le Congrès du MIDH." 1–8 November.

_____. 1989. "Avril pour cinq ans?" 15–22 November.

_____. 1989. "Le Gouvernement Avril met en place une répression modulée." 29 November–6 December.

_____. 1991. "Aristide préfère une presse domestiquée." 16–23 January.

_____. 1991. "Le Premier Ministre Préval expose les grandes lignes de sa politique générale." 20–27 February.

_____. 1991. "Le Conflit Aristide-Armée demeure." 17–24 July.

_____. 1991. "Another Coup d'État?" 24–31 July.

_____. 1991. "Mobilisation contre Aristide et la bourgeoisie." 11–18 September.

_____. 1991. "Réalites économiques obligent: L'Accord avec le FMI signé à la cloche de bois." 18–25 September.

_____. 1991. "Vitriolic Speech of Aristide." 2–9 October.

_____. 1991. "President Aristide's September 27 Speech." 9–16 October.

Haiti Progrès (no author given). 1991. "Les 100 jours d'Aristide: Une Interview exclusive sur des questions brûlantes." 15–21 May.

_____. 1991. "Qui veut piéger le gouvernement Aristide/Préval?." 12–18 June.

_____. 1991. "'Vent Tempête': Une Provocation." 19–25 June.

Halperin, Morton H. 1993. "Guaranteeing Democracy." *Foreign Policy*, no. 91 (Summer):105–122.

Harris, John F., and Douglas Farrah. 1994. "Carter Team Wins Promise After Two Days of Talks." *Washington Post*, 19 September.

Hartlyn, Jonathan, Lars Schoultz, and Augusto Varas, eds. *The United States and Latin America in the 1990's: Beyond the Cold War.* Chapel Hill: University of North Carolina Press.

Hector, Cary, and Hérard Jadotte, eds. *Haiti et l'après-Duvalier: Continuités et ruptures.* Port-au-Prince: Henri Deschamps, and Montreal: CIDIHCA.

Henwood, Doug. 1993. "Impeccable Logic: Trade, Development and Free Markets in the Clinton Era." *NACLA Report on the Americas* 24, no. 5 (May):23–28.

Hérard, Jean-Robert. 1990. "Pour questionner la candidature d'Aristide." *Haiti en Marche*, 24–30 October.

Hitchens, Christopher. 1991. "Realpolitik in the Gulf." *New Left Review*, no. 186 (March-April):89–101.

Hockstader, Lee. 1991a "Haitian Army Crushes Coup by Duvalierist; 37 Are Killed." *Washington Post*, 8 January.

_____. 1991b. "Haiti to Inaugurate Leftist Priest Today." *Washington Post*, 7 February.

_____. 1991c. "Haiti's New President Purges Army." *Washington Post*, 8 February.

Holmes, Steven A. 1993. "U.S. Orders Ship Back to Sea—Asks Ban." *New York Times*, 13 October.

Hooper, Michael S. 1987. "The Monkey's Tail Still Strong." *NACLA Report on the Americas* 21, no. 3 (May-June):24–31.

_____. 1995. "Model Underdevelopment," in NACLA, ed., *Haiti: Dangerous Crossroads.* Boston: South End Press.

Huntington, Samuel P. 1993. "The Clash of Civilizations?" *Foreign Affairs* 72, no. 3 (Summer):22–49.

Hurbon, Laennec. 1987. *Comprendre Haiti: Essay sur l'Etat, la nation, la culture.* Port-au-Prince: Henri Deschamps.

———. 1994. "The Hope for Democracy." *New York Review of Books* (3 November):38–39.

Ifill, Gwen. 1994. "President Names Black Democrat as Haitian Envoy." *New York Times,* 9 May.

Inter-American Development Bank. 1994. *Report of the Joint Assessment Mission.* Washington, D.C.: Inter-American Development Bank.

Irvin, George, and Xabier Gorostiaga, eds. 1985. *Towards an Alternative for Central America and the Caribbean.* London: George Allen and Unwin.

Ives, Kim. 1991. "Flood of Hope Marks Haiti's 200th Year." *Guardian,* 28 August.

———. 1995a. "The Unmaking of a President," in NACLA, ed., *Haiti: Dangerous Crossroads.* Boston: South End Press.

———. 1995b. "Haiti's Second Occupation," in NACLA, ed., *Haiti: Dangerous Crossroads.* Boston: South End Press.

Jackson, Robert H., and Carl G. Rosberg. 1982. *Personal Rule in Black Africa: Prince, Autocrat, Prophet, Tyrant.* Berkeley: University of California Press.

James, C.L.R. 1963. *The Black Jacobins: Toussaint L'Ouverture and the San Domingo Revolution.* New York: Random House.

Jehl, Douglas. 1994a. "Right-Wing Lawmakers in Haiti Swear In a Provisional President." *New York Times,* 12 May.

———. 1994b. "Troops to Land." *New York Times,* 19 September.

———. 1994c. "Haiti Generals Regain Access to $79 Million." *New York Times,* 14 October.

Joseph, Leo. 1990. "Business in Shock as Haiti Adjusts to New President." *Wall Street Journal,* 21 December.

Judis, John B. 1994. "World Bunk," in Kevin Danaher, ed., *50 Years Is Enough: The Case Against the World Bank and the International Monetary Fund.* Boston: South End Press.

Kaufman, Michael. 1985. *Jamaica Under Michael Manley: Dilemmas of Socialism and Democracy.* London: Zed Books.

Kelley, Jack, and Tom Squitieri. 1994. "Unkind Farewell to Cedras." *USA Today,* 11 October.

Klare, Michael T. 1990. "Policing the Gulf and the World." *The Nation,* 15 October.

———. 1993. "The Two-War Strategy." *The Nation,* 4 October:347–350.

Krauss, Clifford. 1991a. "Military's Role Raises U.S. Hopes for Better Ties." *New York Times,* 8 January.

———. 1991b. "In Policy Shift, U.S. Pressures Haitian on Rights Abuses." *New York Times,* 7 October.

Laguerre, Michel S. 1987. "Electoral Politics in Haiti: A Public Opinion Poll." Working Papers Series. Berkeley: Institute for the Study of Social Change, University of California.

Laraque, Franck. 1982. "Prologue de la révolution: Un Comité de libération et de reconstruction du pays." *Haiti Observateur,* 19–26 March.

———. 1995. "Transition démocratique et Haiti." Paper presented at the Colloque International sur les Transitions Démocratiques, Port-au-Prince, Haiti, 6–8 July. Also published in *Haiti en Marche,* 16–22 August.

Latin America Newsletter (no author given). 1988. "Haiti: Budget Cut Due to Aid Suspension." RC-88-04. 12 May.

Layne, Christopher, and Benjamin Schwartz. 1993. "American Hegemony—Without an Enemy." *Foreign Policy*, no. 92 (Fall):5–23.

Lee, Jessica. 1994. "Aristide Ends Silence with Offer of Thanks." *USA Today*, 22 September.

Lewis, Gordon K. 1987. *Grenada: The Jewel Despoiled*. Baltimore: Johns Hopkins University Press.

Lewis, Paul. 1994. "U.N. Council Votes Tougher Embargo on Haiti Trade." *New York Times*, 7 May.

Lipietz, Alain. 1987. *Mirages and Miracles: The Crises of Global Fordism*. London: Verso.

Lipset, Seymour Martin. 1994. "The Social Requisites of Democracy Revisited." *American Sociological Review* 59, no. 1:1–22.

Louverture, Jean-Jacques. 1987. "Terreur sur commande: Un Long sillage de sang." *Libération Magazine*, no. 8 (December).

Lowenthal, Abraham F. 1993. "Changing U.S. Interests and Policies in a New World," in Jonathan Hartlyn, Lars Schoultz, and Augusto Varas, eds., *The United States and Latin America in the 1990's: Beyond the Cold War*. Chapel Hill: University of North Carolina Press.

Löwy, Michael. 1993. "Marxism and Christianity in Latin America." *Latin American Perspectives* 20, no. 4 (Fall):28–42.

MacEwan, Arthur. 1992. "Why the Emperor Can't Afford New Clothes: International Change and Fiscal Disorder in the United States," in Cynthia Peters, ed., *Collateral Damage: The New World Order at Home and Abroad*. Boston: South End Press.

Maguire, Robert E. 1991. "The Peasantry and Political Change in Haiti." *Caribbean Affairs* 4, no. 2:1–18.

Maingot, Anthony. 1994. "Grasping the Nettle: A 'National Liberation' Option for Haiti." *North-South Agenda Papers*, no. 6 (March).

Mandle, Jay R. 1989. "British Caribbean Economic History: An Interpretation," in Franklin W. Knight and Colin A. Palmer, eds., *The Modern Caribbean*. Chapel Hill: University of North Carolina Press.

Manley, Michael. 1991. *Poverty of Nations: Reflections on Underdevelopment and the World Economy*. London: Pluto Press.

Mann, Jim. 1993. "CIA's Aid Plan Would Have Undercut Aristide in '87–'88." *Los Angeles Times*, 31 October.

Marquis, Christopher. 1993a. "Clinton: Peacekeepers May Be Needed in Haiti After a Settlement." *Miami Herald*, 24 April.

_____. 1993b. "U.S. Freezes Assets of Coup Backers in Haiti." *Miami Herald*, 5 June.

_____. 1993c. "U.N. Slaps Sweeping Sanctions on Haiti." *Miami Herald*, 17 June.

_____. 1993d. "Aristide Balks at Haiti Plan." *Miami Herald*, 3 July.

_____. 1993e. "Aristide Signs Haiti Agreement." *Miami Herald*, 4 July.

_____. 1993f. "Haitian Killings Linked to Brash Police Chief." *Miami Herald*, 14 September.

_____. 1993g. "Aristide Ouster Surprised CIA, Officials Say." *Miami Herald*, 15 December.

_____. 1993h. "CIA Analyst Discounted Haiti Terror." *Miami Herald*, 18 December.

_____. 1993i. "U.S. Fears Haiti Tactics Backfiring." *Miami Herald*, 22 December.

_____. 1993j. "Bitterness Growing Between Aristide and U.S. Officials." *Miami Herald*, 23 December.

_____. 1994. "Legislators Prod U.S. on Haiti." *Miami Herald*, 16 January.

Martin, Atherton, with Steve Hellinger and Daniel Solomon. 1985. *Prospects and Reality: The CBI Revisited.* Washington, D.C.: Development Group for Alternative Policies.

Martin, Ian. 1994. "Haiti: Mangled Multilateralism." *Foreign Policy*, no. 95 (Summer):72–89.

Marx, Karl, and Friedrich Engels. 1978. "Manifesto of the Communist Party," in Robert C. Tucker, ed., *The Marx-Engels Reader.* 2d ed. New York: W. W. Norton.

McAfee, Kathy. 1991. *Storm Signals: Structural Adjustment and Development Alternatives in the Caribbean.* Boston: South End Press.

McGuire, James W. 1995. "Development Policy and Its Determinants in East Asia and Latin America." *Journal of Public Policy* 14, no. 2:205–242.

Mead, Walter Russel. 1991. "The Bush Administration and the New World Order." *World Policy Journal* 3, no. 3 (Summer):375–420.

Mearsheimer, John J. 1992. "Disorder Restored," in Graham Allison and Gregory F. Treverton, eds., *Rethinking America's Security.* New York: W. W. Norton.

Meiksins Wood, Ellen. 1986. *The Retreat from Class: A New "True" Socialism.* London: Verso.

_____. 1995. *Democracy Against Capitalism.* Cambridge: Cambridge University Press.

Meisler, Stanley. 1994. "Haiti Orders Out Rights Monitors." *Los Angeles Times*, 12 July.

Merida, Kevin. 1994a. "Clinton Allies Denounce Haiti Policy." *Washington Post*, 20 March.

_____. 1994b. "Hill's Black Caucus Faults U.S. Policy on Haiti, Presses for Aristide's Return." *Washington Post*, 24 March.

_____. 1994c. "TransAfrica Leader to Fast in Protest." *Washington Post*, 12 April.

Miami Herald (no author given). 1991. "12 Haitians Die After Rumor of Plot to Free Coup Leader." 28 January.

_____. 1991. "Haiti President Ousts Two Cabinet Ministers." 15 June.

Midy, Franklin. 1988. "Qui êtes-vous, père Aristide?" *Haiti en Marche*, 26 October–2 November.

_____. 1990–1991. "Aristide: Entre le prophète et le prince." *Haiti en Marche*, 26 December–1 January.

_____. 1991. "Il faut que ça change: L'Imaginaire en liberté," in Cary Hector and Hérard Jadotte, eds., *Haiti et l'après Duvalier: Continuités et ruptures.* Vol. 1. Port-au-Prince: Henri Deschamps, and Montreal: CIDIHCA.

Moïse, Claude. 1980. "Jean-Claudisme: Le Plein est fait." *Collectif Paroles*, no. 8 (September-October):5–7.

_____. 1990. *Constitutions et luttes de pouvoir en Haiti: 1915–1987.* Vol. 2. Montreal: Les Éditions du CIDIHCA.

Moïse, Claude, and Émile Olivier. 1992. *Repenser Haiti: Grandeur et misères d'un mouvement démocratique.* Montreal: Les Éditions du CIDIHCA.

Mouvement pour l'Instauration de la démocratie en Haiti. 1986. *Un Programme d'action pour l'avenir.* Port-au-Prince: MIDH.

NACLA. 1993. "A Market Solution for the Americas?" *NACLA Report on the Americas* 26, no. 4 (February):16–17.

NACLA, ed. 1995. *Haiti: Dangerous Crossroads*. Boston: South End Press.

Nairn, Allan. 1994a. "The Eagle Is Landing." *The Nation*, 3 October.

_____. 1994b. "Our Man in FRAPH: Behind Haiti's Paramilitaries." *The Nation*, 24 October.

_____. 1994c. "He's Our S.O.B." *The Nation*, 31 October.

_____. 1996. "Haiti Under the Gun." *The Nation*, 8–15 January.

National Labor Committee. 1994. "Sweatshop Development," in James Ridgeway, ed., *The Haiti Files: Decoding the Crisis*. Washington, D.C.: Essential Books/Azul Editions.

New York Times (no author given). 1994. "U.N. Resolution for Invasion of Haiti." 1 August.

Nicholls, David. 1979. From Dessalines to Duvalier: Race, Color and National Independence in Haiti. Cambridge: Cambridge University Press.

_____. 1986. "Haiti: The Rise and Fall of Duvalierism." *Third World Quarterly* 8, no. 4 (October):1239–1252.

Nusser, Nancy, and Harold Maass. 1994. "U.S. Understating Abuses in Haiti, U.N. Observer Says." *Palm Beach (Fla.) Post*, 16 February.

Nye, Joseph S., Jr. 1992. "What New World Order?" *Foreign Affairs* 17, no. 2 (Spring):83–96.

O'Neill, William. 1993. "The Roots of Human Rights Violations in Haiti." *Georgetown Immigration Law Journal* 7, no. 1:87–117.

Opération Lavalas. 1990a. *La Chance qui passe*. Port-au-Prince: Opération Lavalas.

_____. 1990b. *La Chance à prendre*. Port-au-Prince: Opération Lavalas.

Oreste, Nader. 1992. "Réponse à Manno Charlemagne." *Haiti en Marche*, 26 August–1 September.

Organisation Politique Lavalas. 1992. "Pour convertir nos rêves en victoires." Mimeograph.

Peters, Cynthia, ed. 1992. *Collateral Damage: The "New World Order" at Home and Abroad*. Boston: South End Press.

Petras, James F. 1991. "The Meaning of the New World Order: A Critique." *America*, 11 May:512–515.

Pierre-Charles, Gérard. 1988. "The Democratic Revolution in Haiti." *Latin American Perspectives* 15, no. 3 (Summer):64–76.

_____. 1991. "Fondements sociologiques de la victoire électorale de Jean-Bertrand Aristide," in Suzy Castor, Micha Gaillard, Paul Laraque, and Gérard Pierre-Charles, *Haiti: À l'aube du changement*. Port-au-Prince: Centre de Recherche et de Formation Économique et Sociale pour le Développement.

_____. 1993. "Fondements sociologiques de la victoire électorale de Jean-Bertrand Aristide," in Gérard Barthélemy and Christian Girault, eds., *La République haitienne: État des lieux et perspectives*. Paris: Éditions KARTHALA.

Polanyi-Levitt, Kari. 1991. "Haiti's National Income: Another View." *Sunday Express*, 30 June.

Preeg, Ernest H. 1985. *Haiti and the CBI: A Time of Change and Opportunity*. Miami, Fla.: Institute of Interamerican Studies, Graduate School of International Studies, University of Miami.

Preston, Julia. 1994. "U.N. Widens Sanctions Against Haiti." *Washington Post*, 7 May.

Przeworski, Adam. 1985. *Capitalism and Social Democracy*. Cambridge: Cambridge University Press.

_____. 1991. *Democracy and the Market: Political and Economic Reforms in Eastern Europe and Latin America*. Cambridge and New York: Cambridge University Press.

Reiss, Spencer. 1993. "Malval Says Aristide 'Has Grown Up a Lot.'" *Washington Times*, 4 October.

Rey, Marie-Michèle. 1994. "A Framework for a Sustainable Economic Recovery." Republic of Haiti: Ministère de l'Économie et des Finances, 13 November.

Ridgeway, James. 1994a. "Haiti's Family Affairs," in James Ridgeway, ed., *The Haiti Files: Decoding the Crisis*. Washington, D.C.: Essential Books/Azul Editions.

Ridgeway, James, ed. 1994b. *The Haiti Files: Decoding the Crisis*. Washington, D.C.: Essential Books/Azul Editions.

Robberson, Tod. 1994. "Compensation of Ousted Gen. Cedras Provokes Outburst in Port-au-Prince." *Washington Post*, 15 October.

Robinson, Randall. 1994. "Haiti's Agony, Clinton's Shame." *New York Times*, 17 April.

Rohter, Larry. 1994. "Haiti's Military Power Structure Is Showing Signs of Falling Apart." *New York Times*, 5 October.

Rubenstein, Richard E., and Farle Crocker. 1994. "Challenging Huntington." *Foreign Policy*, no. 96 (Fall):113–128.

Ruccio, David. 1993. "The Hidden Successes of Failed Economic Policies." *NACLA Report on the Americas* 26, no. 4 (February):38–43.

Rueschemeyer, Dietrich, Evelyne Huber Stephens, and John D. Stephens. 1992. *Capitalist Development and Democracy*. Chicago: University of Chicago Press.

Rupert, James. 1994. "U.S. Rebuffs Defiance by Haiti Rulers." *Washington Post*, 23 September.

Saint-Gérard, Yves. 1988. *Haiti: Sortir du cauchemar*. Paris: L'Harmattan.

Sanchez Otero, German. 1993. "Neoliberalism and Its Discontents." *NACLA Report on the Americas* 26, no. 4 (February):18–21.

Sanders, Jerry W. 1991. "Retreat from World Order: The Perils of Triumphalism." *World Policy Journal* 8, no. 2 (Spring):227–250.

Schlesinger, James. 1991–1992. "New Instabilities, New Priorities." *Foreign Policy*, no. 85 (Winter):3–24.

Sciolino, Elaine. 1993. "Pentagon and State Department at Odds over Sending of Soldiers to Haiti." *New York Times*, 8 October.

_____. 1994. "Embassy in Haiti Doubts Aristide's Rights Reports." *New York Times*, 9 May.

Sims, Calvin. 1994. "Panama Grants Asylum to Leaders of Haiti Junta." *New York Times*, 13 October.

Singham, A. W. 1968. *The Hero and the Crowd in a Colonial Polity*. New Haven: Yale University Press.

Sklar, Holly. 1992. "Brave New World Order," in Cynthia Peters, ed., *Collateral Damage: The New World Order at Home and Abroad*. Boston: South End Press.

Slavin, J. P. 1991. "Purge of Army Officers Continues in Haiti." *Miami Herald*, 4 July.

Sontag, Debbie. 1990. "Populist Priest Captures Hearts of Haitians." *Miami Herald*, 26 November.

Soukar, Michel. 1987. *Seize ans de lutte pour un pays normal*. Port-au-Prince: Éditions SCIHLA.

Spiegelman, Arthur. 1994. "Aristide Aide Fears U.S.-Sponsored U.N. Resolution." *Reuters*, 25 February.

Sweezy, Paul M. 1991. "What's New in the New World Order?" *Monthly Review* 43, no. 2 (June):1–4.

Tarr, Michael. 1991a. "Haiti Wins Regard for Economic Moves Under Aristide." *Miami Herald*, August 22.

_____. 1991b. "Haitian President Gets Respite in Feud with Parliament." *Miami Herald*, September 27.

_____. 1993. "Haiti Observers Find 'Grave' Rights Abuses by Armed Forces." *Miami Herald*, May 6.

Thomas, Clive Y. 1984. *The Rise of the Authoritarian State in Peripheral Societies.* New York: Monthly Review Press.

_____. 1988. *The Poor and the Powerless: Economic Policy and Change in the Caribbean.* New York: Monthly Review Press.

Thomas, Teddy. 1988. "L'Armée dans la lutte populaire." *Haiti en Marche*, 28 September–4 October.

Thrupp, Lori Ann. 1994. "New Harvests, Old Problems: Feeding the Global Supermarket." *NACLA Report on the Americas* 28, no. 3 (November-December):22–27.

Trouillot, Michel-Rolph. 1990. *Haiti: State Against Nation.* New York: Monthly Review Press.

Tucker, Robert C., ed. 1978. *The Marx-Engels Reader.* 2d ed. New York: W. W. Norton.

United Nations Department of Humanitarian Affairs. 1994. *Haiti: Emergency Programme Towards the Alleviation of Poverty—Bridging Humanitarian Assistance and Reconstruction Programmes.* Section I: Sectors. New York: United Nations Department of Humanitarian Affairs.

United Nations Development Program. 1992. *Human Development Report.* New York and London: Oxford University Press.

_____. 1993a. *Emergency Economic Recovery Program: Haiti: Preliminary Report of the Joint Mission.* New York: United Nations, July.

_____. 1993b. *Emergency Economic Recovery Program: Haiti: Report of the Joint Mission.* New York: United Nations, October.

United States Agency for International Development. 1993. *USAID/Haiti: Briefing Book.* Washington, D.C.: Agency for International Development, July.

United States Department of Labor. 1990. *Worker Rights in Export Processing Zones: Haiti.* Report Submitted to Congress Under the Omnibus Trade and Competitiveness Act of 1988. Vol. 2. Washington, D.C.: U.S. Department of Labor, Bureau of International Labor Affairs.

Vilas, Carlos M. 1992. "What Future for Socialism?" *NACLA Report on the Americas* 25, no. 5 (May):13–16.

Walker, James L., and Giovanni Caprio. 1991. "Haiti Macroeconomic Assessment." Staff Working Paper No. 3. Washington, D.C.: Bureau for Latin America and the Caribbean, Agency for International Development.

Wallerstein, Immanuel. 1985. *The Politics of the World-Economy: The States, the Movements and the Civilizations.* New York: Cambridge University Press.

_____. 1993. "Foes as Friends?" *Foreign Policy*, no. 90 (Spring):145–157.

Watson, Hilbourne A., ed. 1994. *Human Resources and Institutional Requirements for Global Adjustments: Strategies for the Caribbean.* Special issue of *21st Century Policy Review* 2 (Spring):1–2.

Weber, Max. 1968. *From Max Weber: Essays in Sociology.* Edited and Translated by H. H. Gerth and C. Wright Mills. Oxford and New York: Oxford University Press.

_____. 1978. *Economy and Society: An Outline of Interpretive Sociology.* Edited by Gwenther Roth and Claus Wittich. 2 vols. Los Angeles and Berkeley: University of California Press.

Weiner, Tim. 1993. "CIA Formed Haitian Unit Later Tied to Narcotics Trade." *New York Times,* 14 November.

Weymouth, Lally. 1992. "Haiti vs. Aristide." *Washington Post,* 18 December.

Wilentz, Amy. 1989. *The Rainy Season: Haiti Since Duvalier.* New York: Simon and Schuster.

_____. 1990. "Preface," in Jean-Bertrand Aristide, *In the Parish of the Poor: Writings from Haiti.* Translated and edited by Amy Wilentz. Maryknoll, N.Y.: Orbis Books.

_____. 1991. "The Oppositionists." *New Republic,* 28 October.

_____. 1994. "Aristide, the Comeback Kid." *Washington Post,* 2 October.

_____. 1994–1995. "Lives in the Balance." *New Yorker,* 26 December–2 January.

Williams, Daniel. 1993. "Aristide Rejects New U.S. Effort to Jump-Start Talks." *Washington Post,* 22 December.

_____. 1994. "Aristide Beats Clinton to Moral High Ground." *Washington Post,* 6 May.

Wilson, Michael. 1991. "Will Aid Reap Bitter Fruit?" *Washington Times,* 18 February.

World Bank. 1990a. *Le Redressement de l'économie haitienne: Résultats, problèmes et perspectives.* Washington, D.C.: Banque Mondiale.

_____. 1990b. *World Development Report 1990: Poverty.* Oxford and New York: Oxford University Press.

_____. 1991a. *Haiti: Agricultural Sector Review,* Report no. 9357-HA. March.

_____. 1991b. *World Development Report: 1991—The Challenge of Development.* Oxford and New York: Oxford University Press.

About the Book and Author

ABOUT THE BOOK AND AUTHOR

This book, a critical study of Haiti's place in the "New World Order," examines the limits of its "democratic revolution" and the prospects for social change. Exploring why the successive military governments in power between 1986 and 1990 were unable to implement the neoliberal economic reforms sanctioned by the World Bank and USAID, Dupuy also analyzes the emergence, composition, and objectives of the popular democratic movement that challenged the military and led to the electoral victory of Jean-Bertrand Aristide.

The book provides a comprehensive evaluation of Aristide's religious, social, and political thought and practice; the nature of the opposition to Aristide from the Catholic Church, the Haitian bourgeoisie, and the military; and the causes of the military coup d'état in 1991. Dupuy explains why, in a clear policy shift, the United States opposed a coup against the radical populist president, enumerates the concessions it won from Aristide as a condition of his return, and discusses the implications for the democratic process of military intervention and the adoption of the neoliberal model.

Alex Dupuy is professor of sociology and dean of the Social Sciences and Interdisciplinary Programs at Wesleyan University. He is the author of *Haiti in the World Economy: Class, Race, and Underdevelopment Since 1700* (Westview, 1989).

INDEX